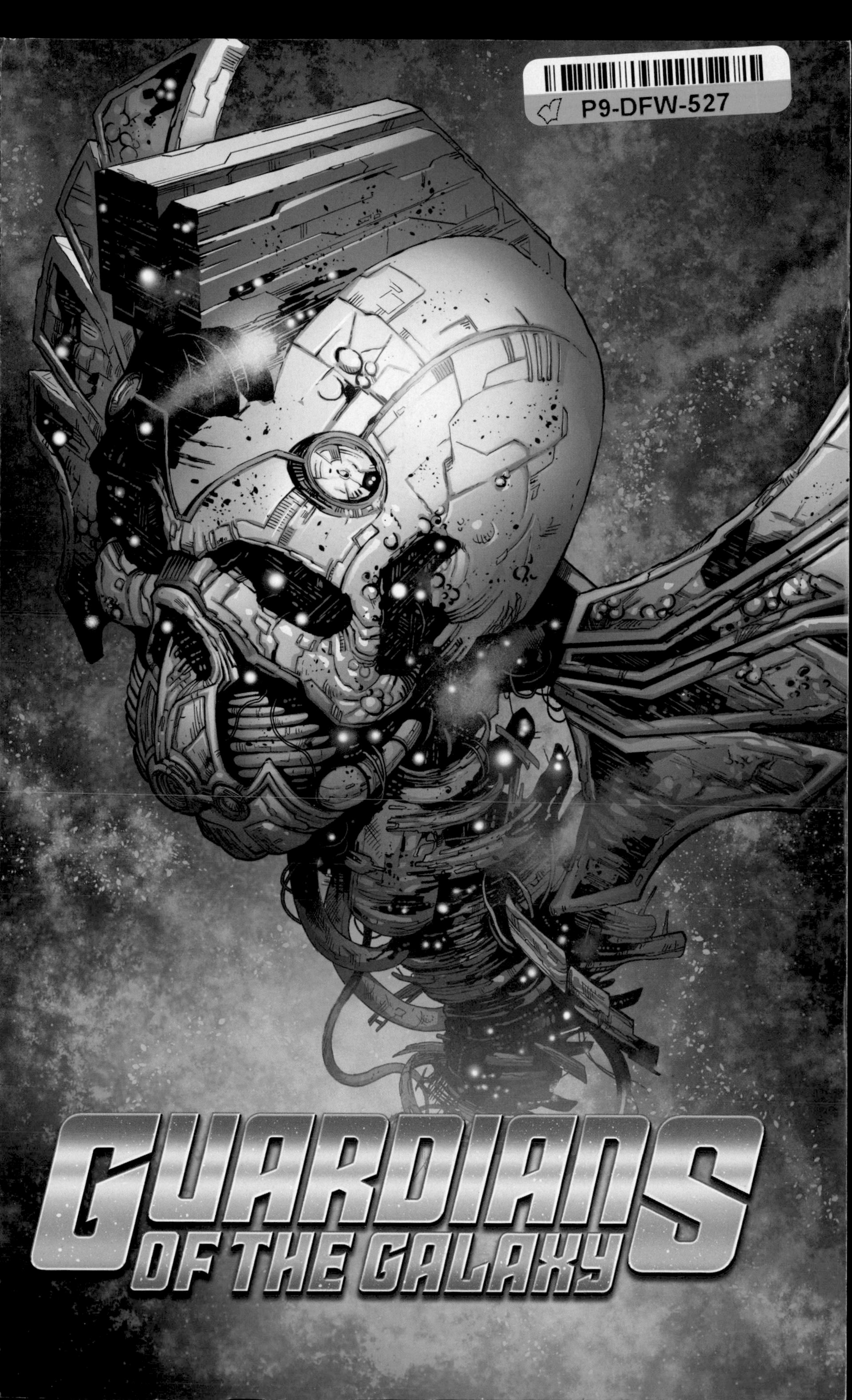
GUARDIANS
OF THE GALAXY

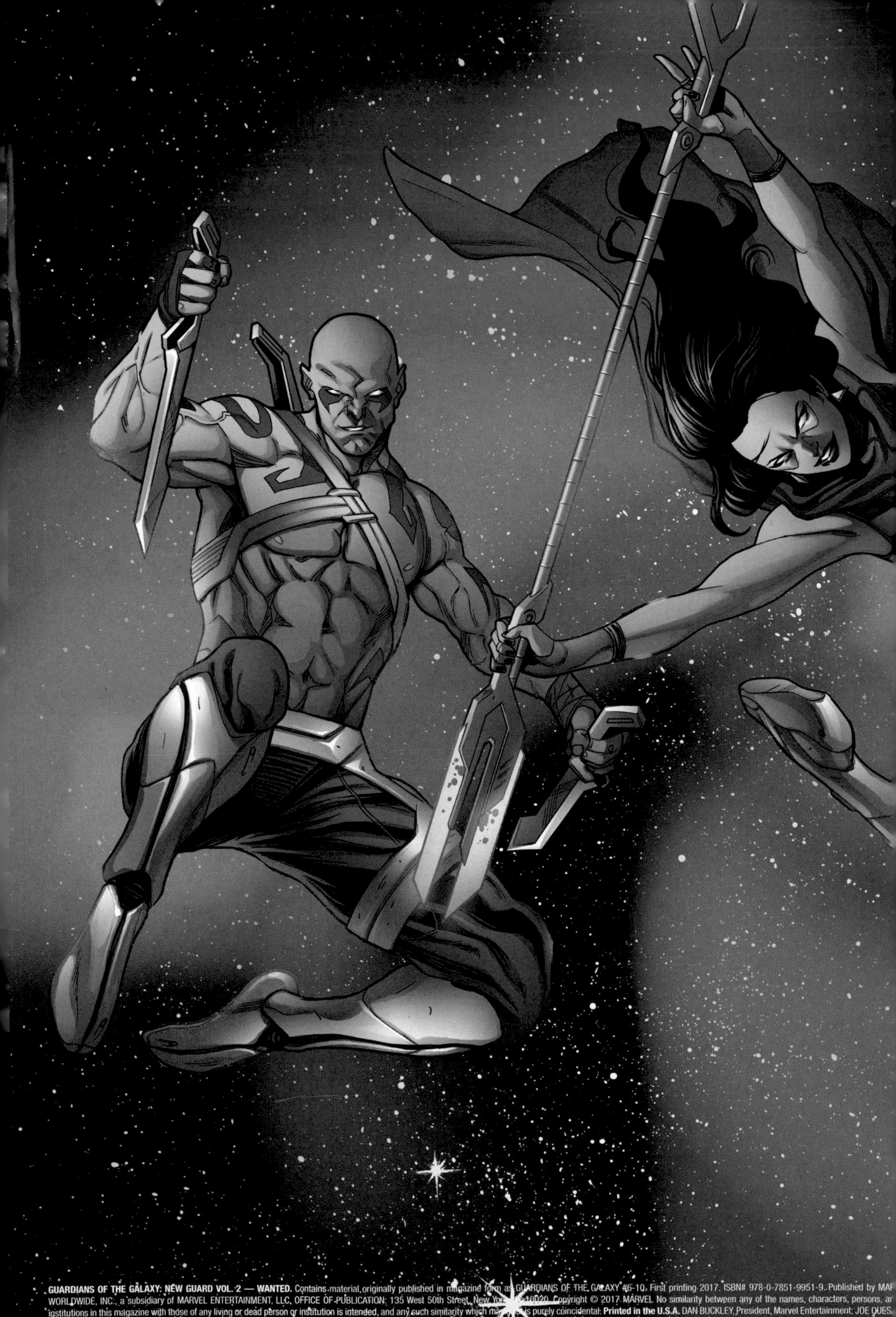

**GUARDIANS OF THE GALAXY: NEW GUARD VOL. 2 — WANTED.** Contains material originally published in magazine form as GUARDIANS OF THE GALAXY #6-10. First printing 2017. ISBN# 978-0-7851-9951-9. Published by MAR WORLDWIDE, INC., a subsidiary of MARVEL ENTERTAINMENT, LLC. OFFICE OF PUBLICATION: 135 West 50th Street, New York, [illegible] 10020.  **Printed in the U.S.A.** 
**Manufactured between 5/19/2017 and 6/20/2017 by LSC COMMUNICATIONS INC., SALEM, VA, USA.**

10 9 8 7 6 5 4 3 2 1

# GUARDIANS OF THE GALAXY

## WANTED

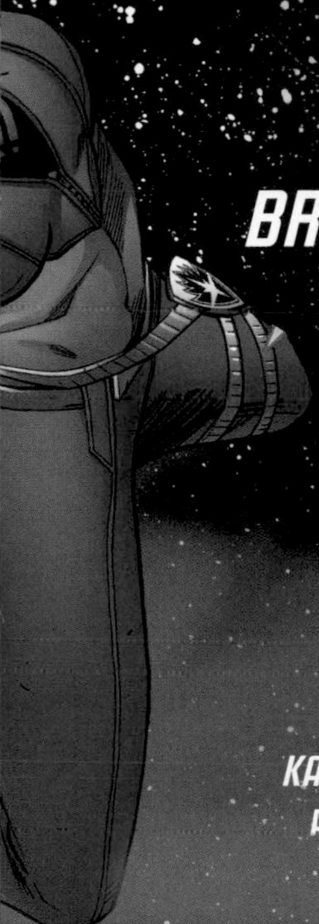

**BRIAN MICHAEL BENDIS**
WRITER

**VALERIO SCHITI**
ARTIST

**RICHARD ISANOVE**
COLOR ARTIST

**VC'S CORY PETIT**
LETTERER

**ARTHUR ADAMS & JASON KEITH**
COVER ART

**KATHLEEN WISNESKI**
ASSISTANT EDITOR

**JAKE THOMAS**
ASSOCIATE EDITOR

**NICK LOWE**
EXECUTIVE EDITOR


COLLECTION EDITOR: *JENNIFER GRÜNWALD*
ASSISTANT EDITOR: *CAITLIN O'CONNELL*
ASSOCIATE MANAGING EDITOR: *KATERI WOODY*
EDITOR, SPECIAL PROJECTS: *MARK D. BEAZLEY*
VP PRODUCTION & SPECIAL PROJECTS: *JEFF YOUNGQUIST*
SVP PRINT, SALES & MARKETING: *DAVID GABRIEL*

EDITOR IN CHIEF: *AXEL ALONSO*
CHIEF CREATIVE OFFICER: *JOE QUESADA*
PRESIDENT: *DAN BUCKLEY*
EXECUTIVE PRODUCER: *ALAN FINE*

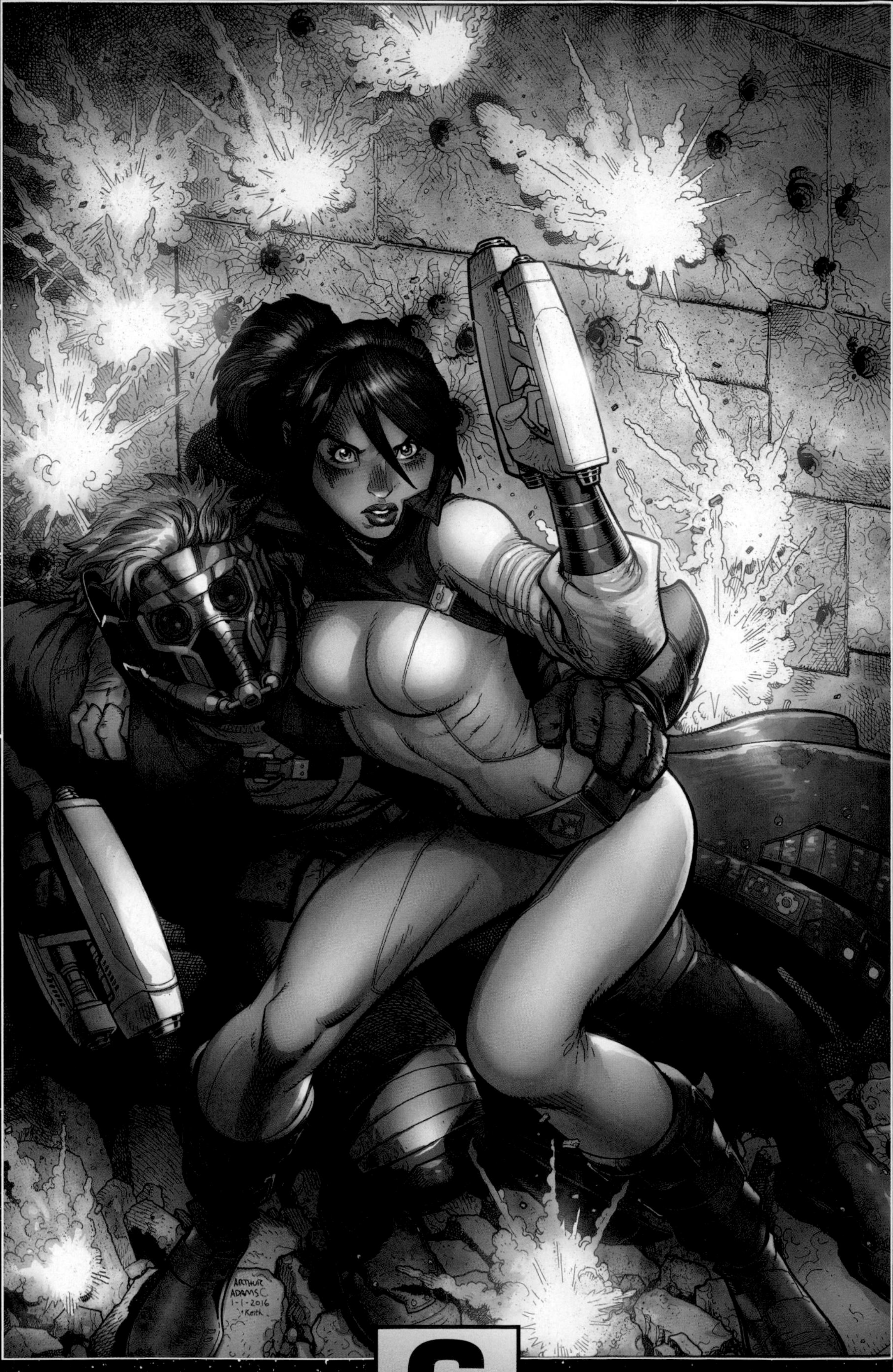
ARTHUR ADAMS
1-1-2016
Keith

# 6

The entire galaxy is a mess. Warring empires and cosmic terrorists plague every corner. Someone has to rise above it all and fight for those who have no one to fight for them. A group of misfits--***Drax the Destroyer***, ***Gamora***, ***Rocket Raccoon***, ***Groot***, and ***Flash Thompson***, a.k.a. ***Venom***--joined together under the leadership of ***Peter Quill, Star-Lord.*** With new members ***Kitty Pryde*** and ***Ben Grimm***, a.k.a. ***The Thing***, they serve a higher cause as the…

# GUARDIANS OF THE GALAXY

Hala, the last Kree Accuser, held Peter Quill responsible for the destruction of her home planet, and ransacked Spartax as revenge. Working together, all nine Guardians of the Galaxy managed to bring her down, but not before she demolished the capital. In their crumbling offices, Spartax government administrators were all too eager to blame Star-Lord for the disaster.

He's now *former* president, and current fugitive, of Spartax. So the Guardians are on the run, and all together again…mostly.

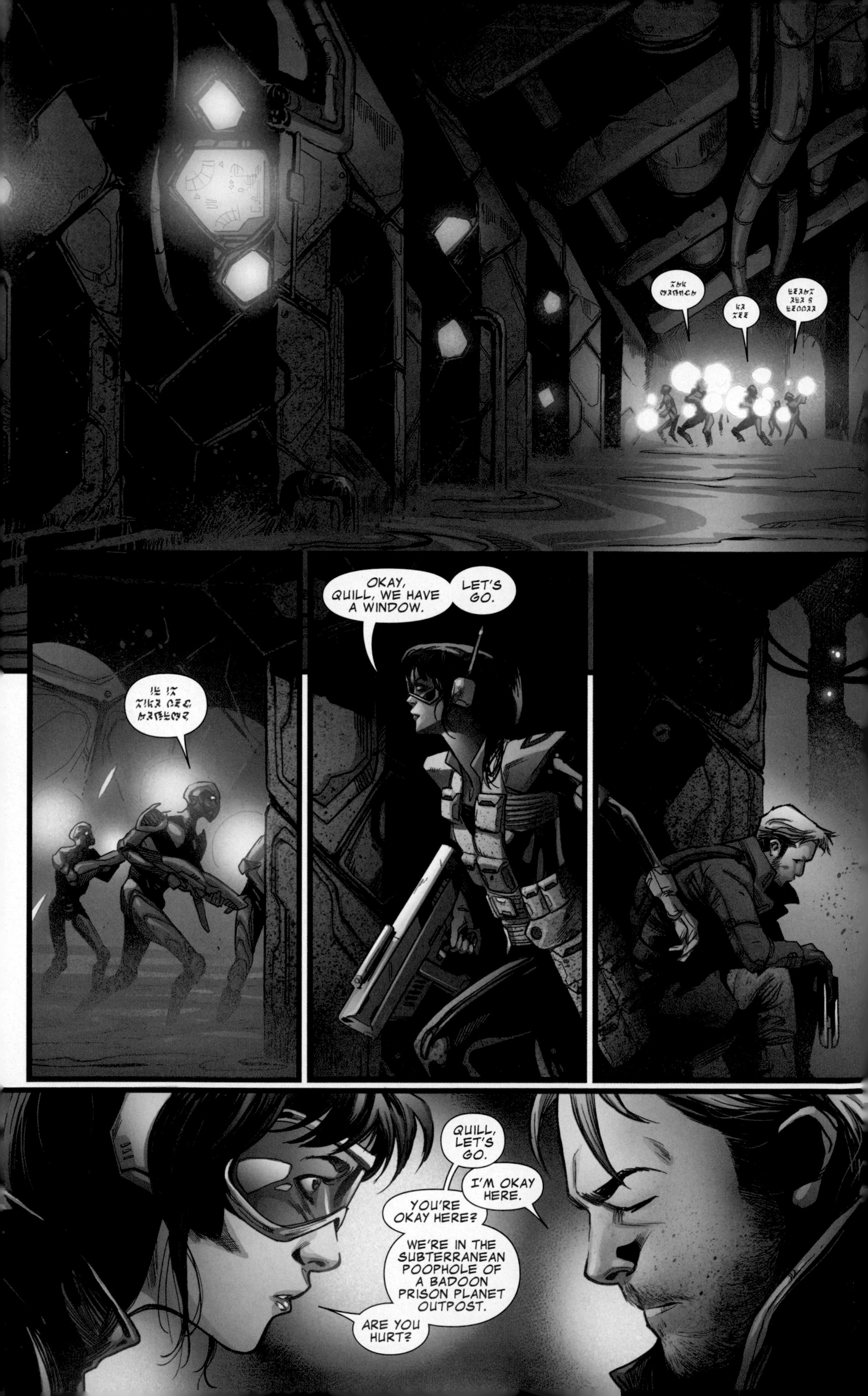
OKAY, QUILL, WE HAVE A WINDOW.
LET'S GO.
QUILL, LET'S GO.
I'M OKAY HERE.
YOU'RE OKAY HERE?
WE'RE IN THE SUBTERRANEAN POOPHOLE OF A BADOON PRISON PLANET OUTPOST.
ARE YOU HURT?

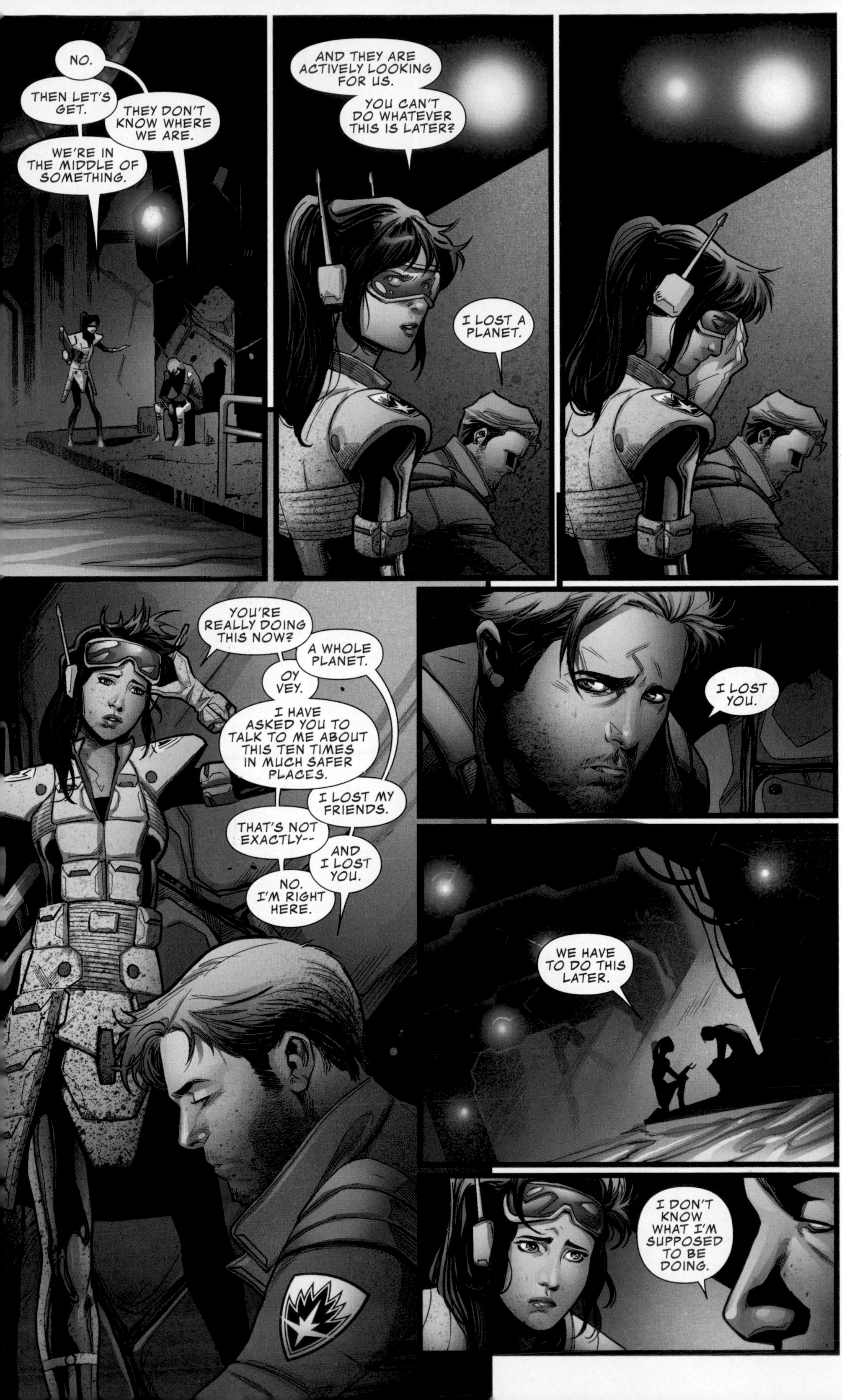
NO.
THEN LET'S GET.
THEY DON'T KNOW WHERE WE ARE.
WE'RE IN THE MIDDLE OF SOMETHING.
AND THEY ARE ACTIVELY LOOKING FOR US.
YOU CAN'T DO WHATEVER THIS IS LATER?
I LOST A PLANET.
YOU'RE REALLY DOING THIS NOW?
A WHOLE PLANET.
OY VEY.
I HAVE ASKED YOU TO TALK TO ME ABOUT THIS TEN TIMES IN MUCH SAFER PLACES.
I LOST MY FRIENDS.
THAT'S NOT EXACTLY--
AND I LOST YOU.
NO. I'M RIGHT HERE.
I LOST YOU.
WE HAVE TO DO THIS LATER.
I DON'T KNOW WHAT I'M SUPPOSED TO BE DOING.

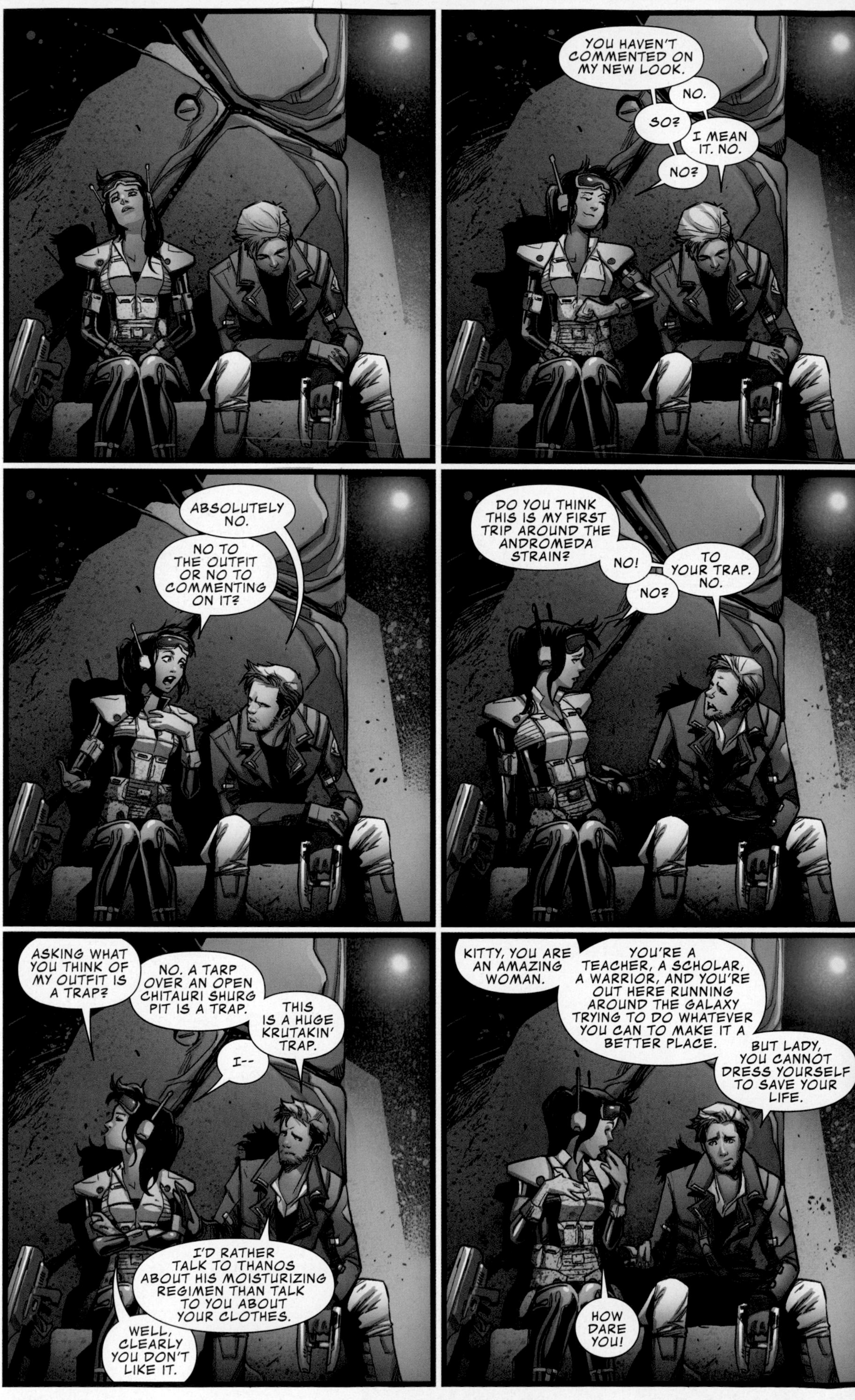
YOU HAVEN'T COMMENTED ON MY NEW LOOK.
NO.
SO?
I MEAN IT. NO.
NO?
ABSOLUTELY NO.
NO TO THE OUTFIT OR NO TO COMMENTING ON IT?
DO YOU THINK THIS IS MY FIRST TRIP AROUND THE ANDROMEDA STRAIN?
NO!
NO?
TO YOUR TRAP. NO.
ASKING WHAT YOU THINK OF MY OUTFIT IS A TRAP?
NO. A TARP OVER AN OPEN CHITAURI SHURG PIT IS A TRAP.
THIS IS A HUGE KRUTAKIN' TRAP.
I--
I'D RATHER TALK TO THANOS ABOUT HIS MOISTURIZING REGIMEN THAN TALK TO YOU ABOUT YOUR CLOTHES.
WELL, CLEARLY YOU DON'T LIKE IT.
KITTY, YOU ARE AN AMAZING WOMAN.
YOU'RE A TEACHER, A SCHOLAR, A WARRIOR, AND YOU'RE OUT HERE RUNNING AROUND THE GALAXY TRYING TO DO WHATEVER YOU CAN TO MAKE IT A BETTER PLACE.
BUT LADY, YOU CANNOT DRESS YOURSELF TO SAVE YOUR LIFE.
HOW DARE YOU!

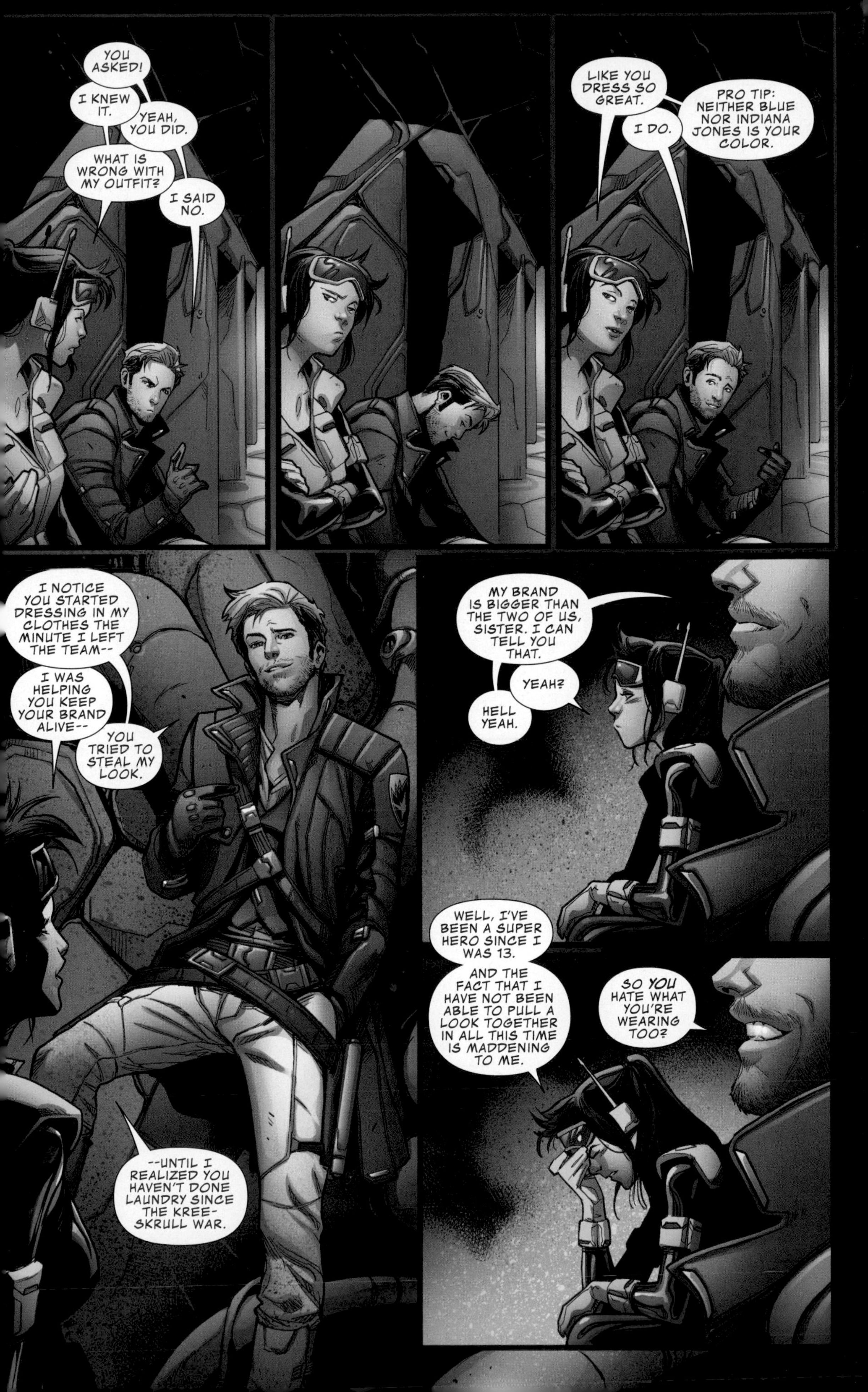
YOU ASKED!
I KNEW IT.
YEAH, YOU DID.
WHAT IS WRONG WITH MY OUTFIT?
I SAID NO.
LIKE YOU DRESS SO GREAT.
I DO.
PRO TIP: NEITHER BLUE NOR INDIANA JONES IS YOUR COLOR.
I NOTICE YOU STARTED DRESSING IN MY CLOTHES THE MINUTE I LEFT THE TEAM--
I WAS HELPING YOU KEEP YOUR BRAND ALIVE--
YOU TRIED TO STEAL MY LOOK.
--UNTIL I REALIZED YOU HAVEN'T DONE LAUNDRY SINCE THE KREE-SKRULL WAR.
MY BRAND IS BIGGER THAN THE TWO OF US, SISTER. I CAN TELL YOU THAT.
YEAH?
HELL YEAH.
WELL, I'VE BEEN A SUPER HERO SINCE I WAS 13.
AND THE FACT THAT I HAVE NOT BEEN ABLE TO PULL A LOOK TOGETHER IN ALL THIS TIME IS MADDENING TO ME.
SO YOU HATE WHAT YOU'RE WEARING TOO?

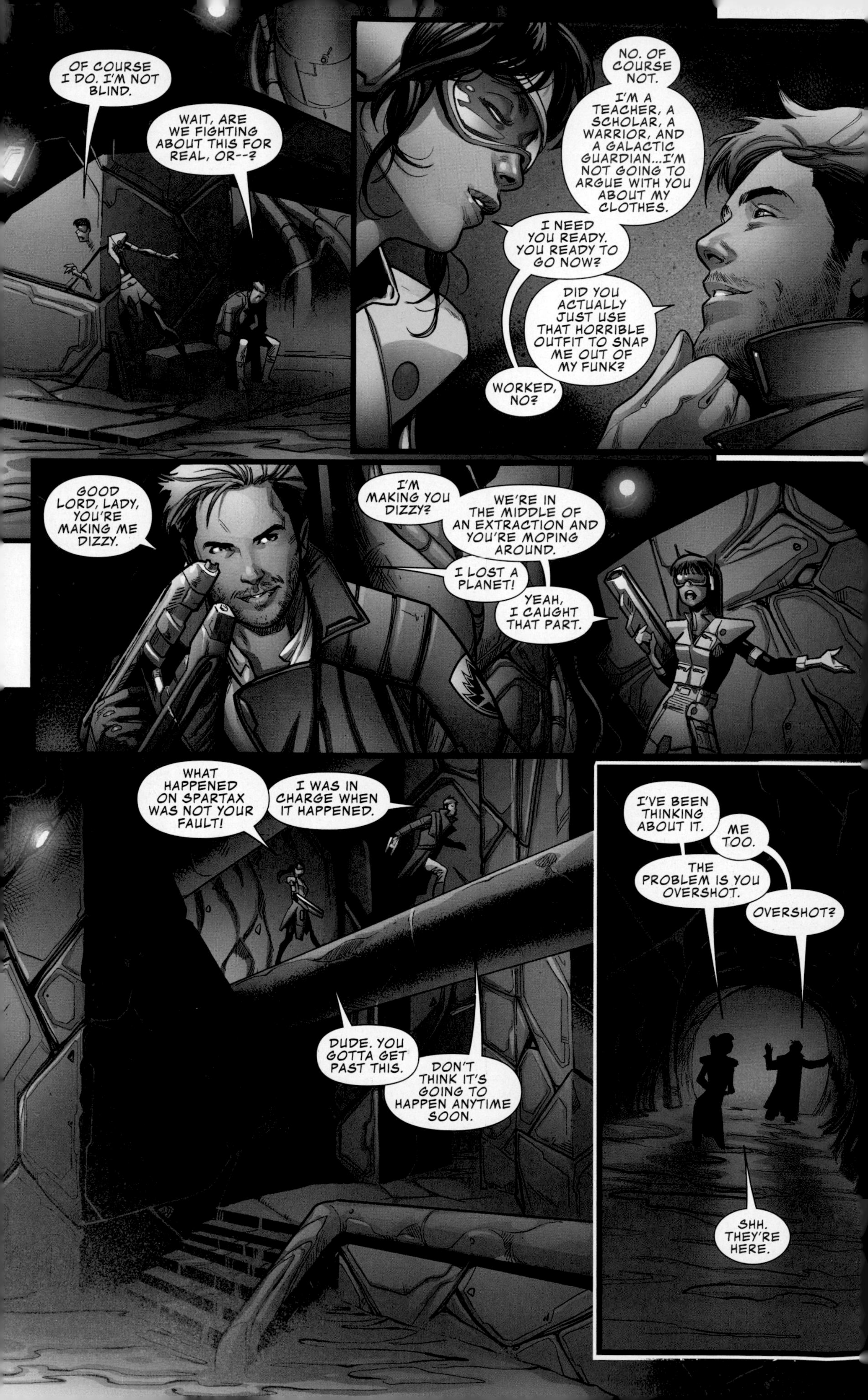

OF COURSE I DO. I'M NOT BLIND.
WAIT, ARE WE FIGHTING ABOUT THIS FOR REAL, OR--?
NO. OF COURSE NOT.
I'M A TEACHER, A SCHOLAR, A WARRIOR, AND A GALACTIC GUARDIAN...I'M NOT GOING TO ARGUE WITH YOU ABOUT MY CLOTHES.
I NEED YOU READY. YOU READY TO GO NOW?
DID YOU ACTUALLY JUST USE THAT HORRIBLE OUTFIT TO SNAP ME OUT OF MY FUNK?
WORKED, NO?
GOOD LORD, LADY, YOU'RE MAKING ME DIZZY.
I'M MAKING YOU DIZZY?
WE'RE IN THE MIDDLE OF AN EXTRACTION AND YOU'RE MOPING AROUND.
I LOST A PLANET!
YEAH, I CAUGHT THAT PART.
WHAT HAPPENED ON SPARTAX WAS NOT YOUR FAULT!
I WAS IN CHARGE WHEN IT HAPPENED.
DUDE. YOU GOTTA GET PAST THIS.
DON'T THINK IT'S GOING TO HAPPEN ANYTIME SOON.
I'VE BEEN THINKING ABOUT IT.
ME TOO.
THE PROBLEM IS YOU OVERSHOT.
OVERSHOT?
SHH. THEY'RE HERE.

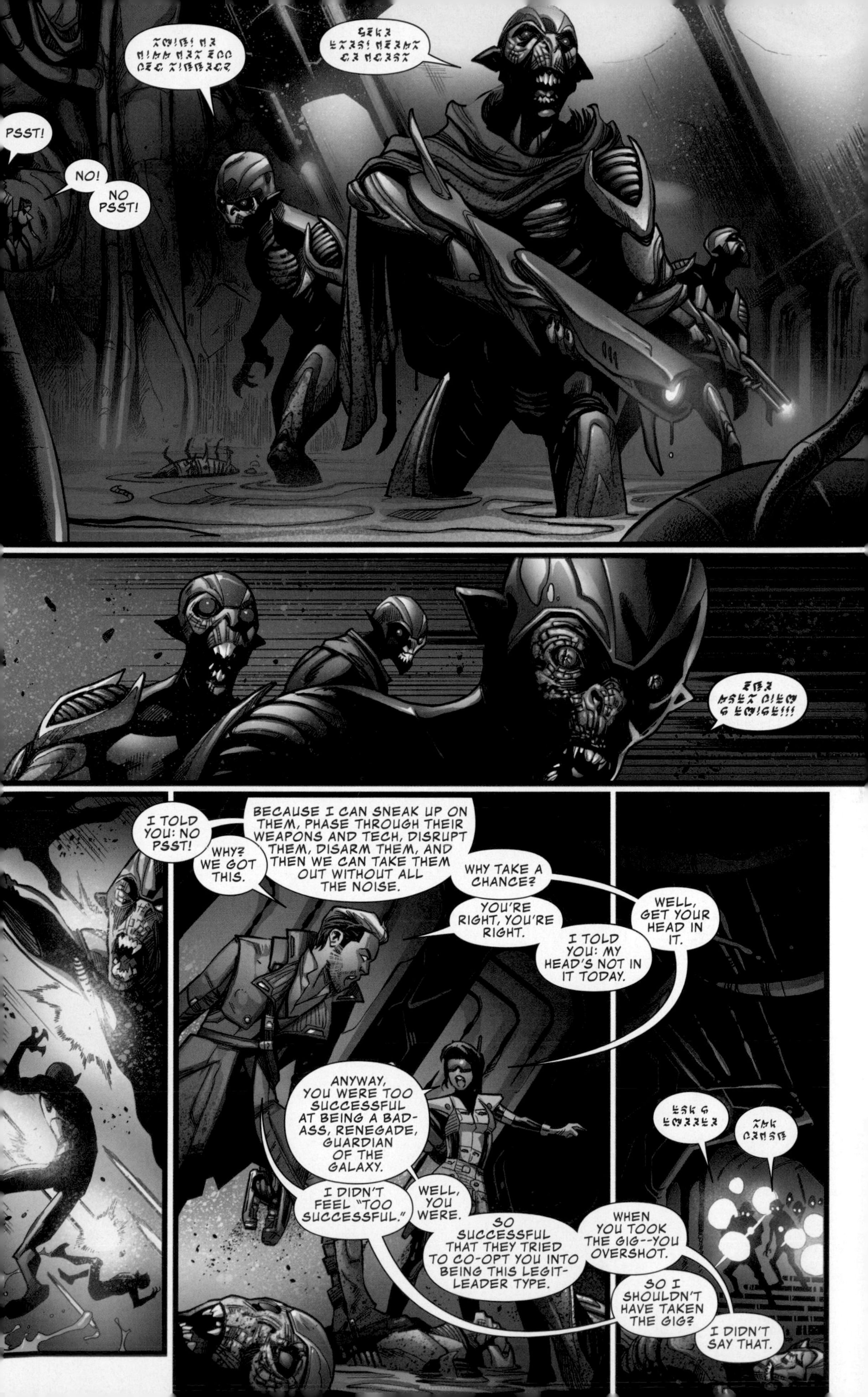
PSST!
NO!
NO PSST!
I TOLD YOU: NO PSST!
WHY? WE GOT THIS.
BECAUSE I CAN SNEAK UP ON THEM, PHASE THROUGH THEIR WEAPONS AND TECH, DISRUPT THEM, DISARM THEM, AND THEN WE CAN TAKE THEM OUT WITHOUT ALL THE NOISE.
WHY TAKE A CHANCE?
YOU'RE RIGHT, YOU'RE RIGHT.
WELL, GET YOUR HEAD IN IT.
I TOLD YOU: MY HEAD'S NOT IN IT TODAY.
ANYWAY, YOU WERE TOO SUCCESSFUL AT BEING A BAD-ASS, RENEGADE, GUARDIAN OF THE GALAXY.
I DIDN'T FEEL "TOO SUCCESSFUL."
WELL, YOU WERE.
SO SUCCESSFUL THAT THEY TRIED TO CO-OPT YOU INTO BEING THIS LEGIT-LEADER TYPE.
WHEN YOU TOOK THE GIG--YOU OVERSHOT.
SO I SHOULDN'T HAVE TAKEN THE GIG?
I DIDN'T SAY THAT.

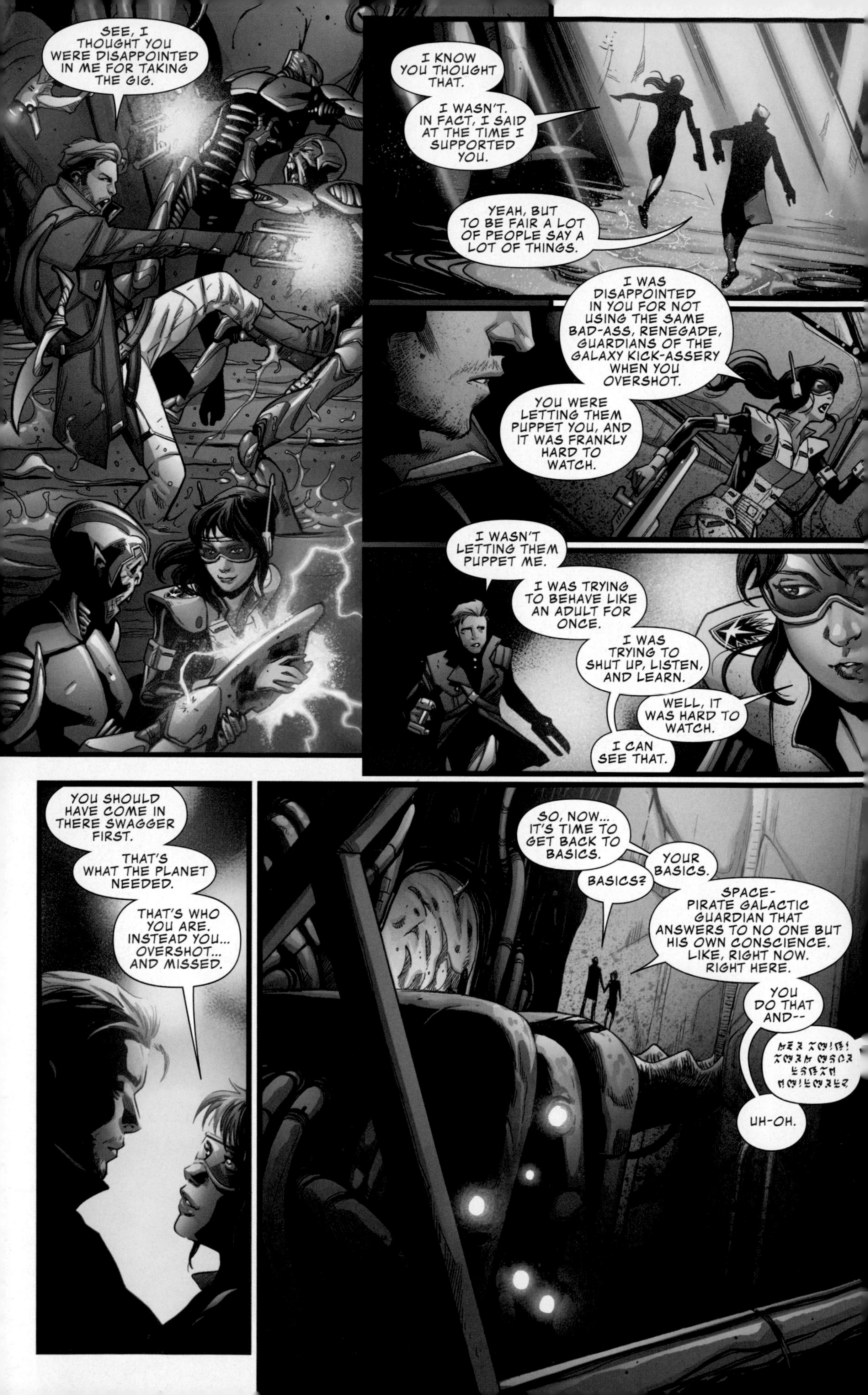
SEE, I THOUGHT YOU WERE DISAPPOINTED IN ME FOR TAKING THE GIG.
I KNOW YOU THOUGHT THAT.
I WASN'T. IN FACT, I SAID AT THE TIME I SUPPORTED YOU.
YEAH, BUT TO BE FAIR A LOT OF PEOPLE SAY A LOT OF THINGS.
I WAS DISAPPOINTED IN YOU FOR NOT USING THE SAME BAD-ASS, RENEGADE, GUARDIANS OF THE GALAXY KICK-ASSERY WHEN YOU OVERSHOT.
YOU WERE LETTING THEM PUPPET YOU, AND IT WAS FRANKLY HARD TO WATCH.
I WASN'T LETTING THEM PUPPET ME.
I WAS TRYING TO BEHAVE LIKE AN ADULT FOR ONCE.
I WAS TRYING TO SHUT UP, LISTEN, AND LEARN.
WELL, IT WAS HARD TO WATCH.
I CAN SEE THAT.
YOU SHOULD HAVE COME IN THERE SWAGGER FIRST.
THAT'S WHAT THE PLANET NEEDED.
THAT'S WHO YOU ARE. INSTEAD YOU... OVERSHOT... AND MISSED.
SO, NOW... IT'S TIME TO GET BACK TO BASICS.
BASICS?
YOUR BASICS.
SPACE-PIRATE GALACTIC GUARDIAN THAT ANSWERS TO NO ONE BUT HIS OWN CONSCIENCE. LIKE, RIGHT NOW. RIGHT HERE.
YOU DO THAT AND--
UH-OH.

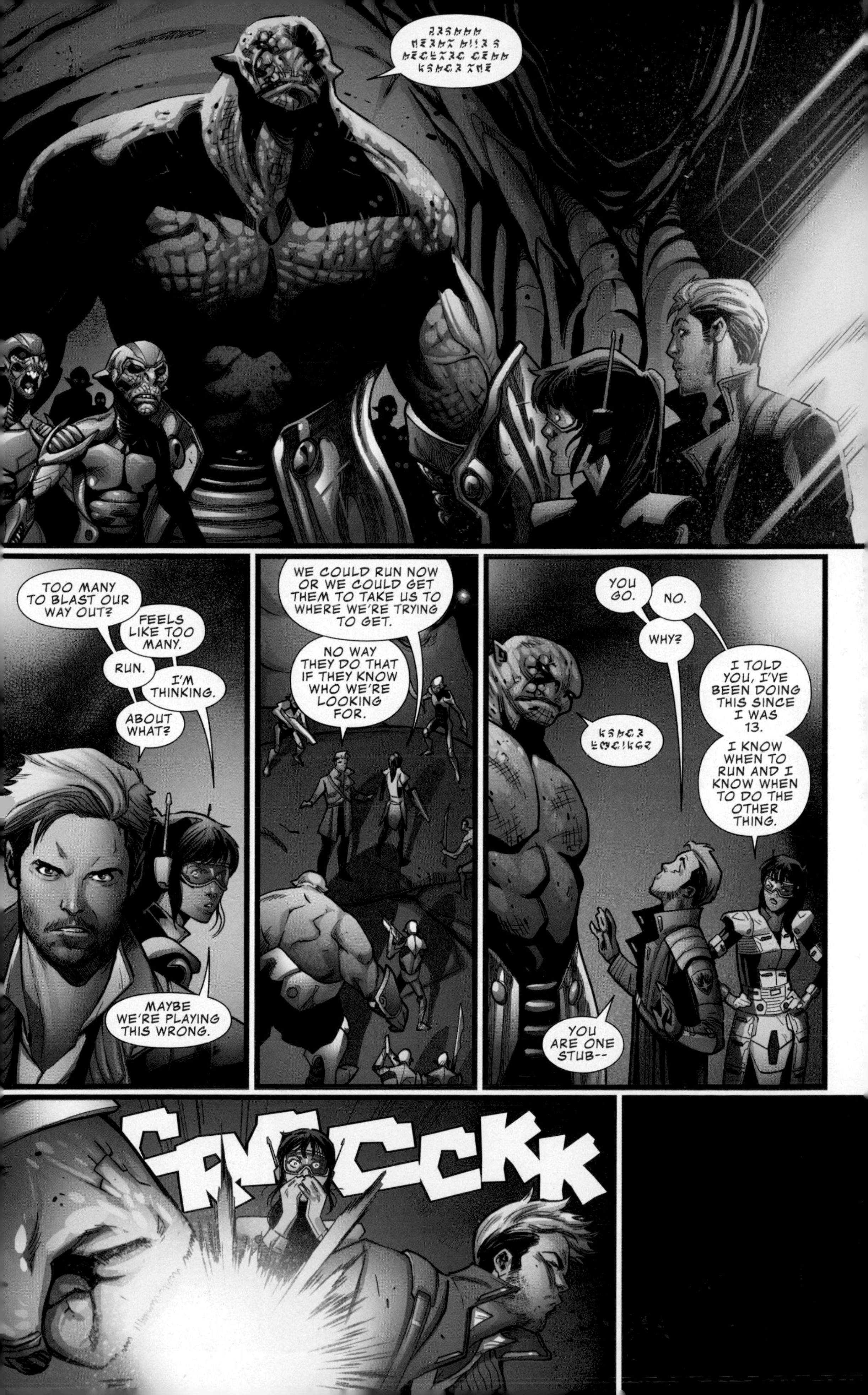
TOO MANY TO BLAST OUR WAY OUT?
FEELS LIKE TOO MANY.
RUN.
I'M THINKING.
ABOUT WHAT?
MAYBE WE'RE PLAYING THIS WRONG.
WE COULD RUN NOW OR WE COULD GET THEM TO TAKE US TO WHERE WE'RE TRYING TO GET.
NO WAY THEY DO THAT IF THEY KNOW WHO WE'RE LOOKING FOR.
YOU GO.
NO.
WHY?
I TOLD YOU, I'VE BEEN DOING THIS SINCE I WAS 13.
I KNOW WHEN TO RUN AND I KNOW WHEN TO DO THE OTHER THING.
YOU ARE ONE STUB--

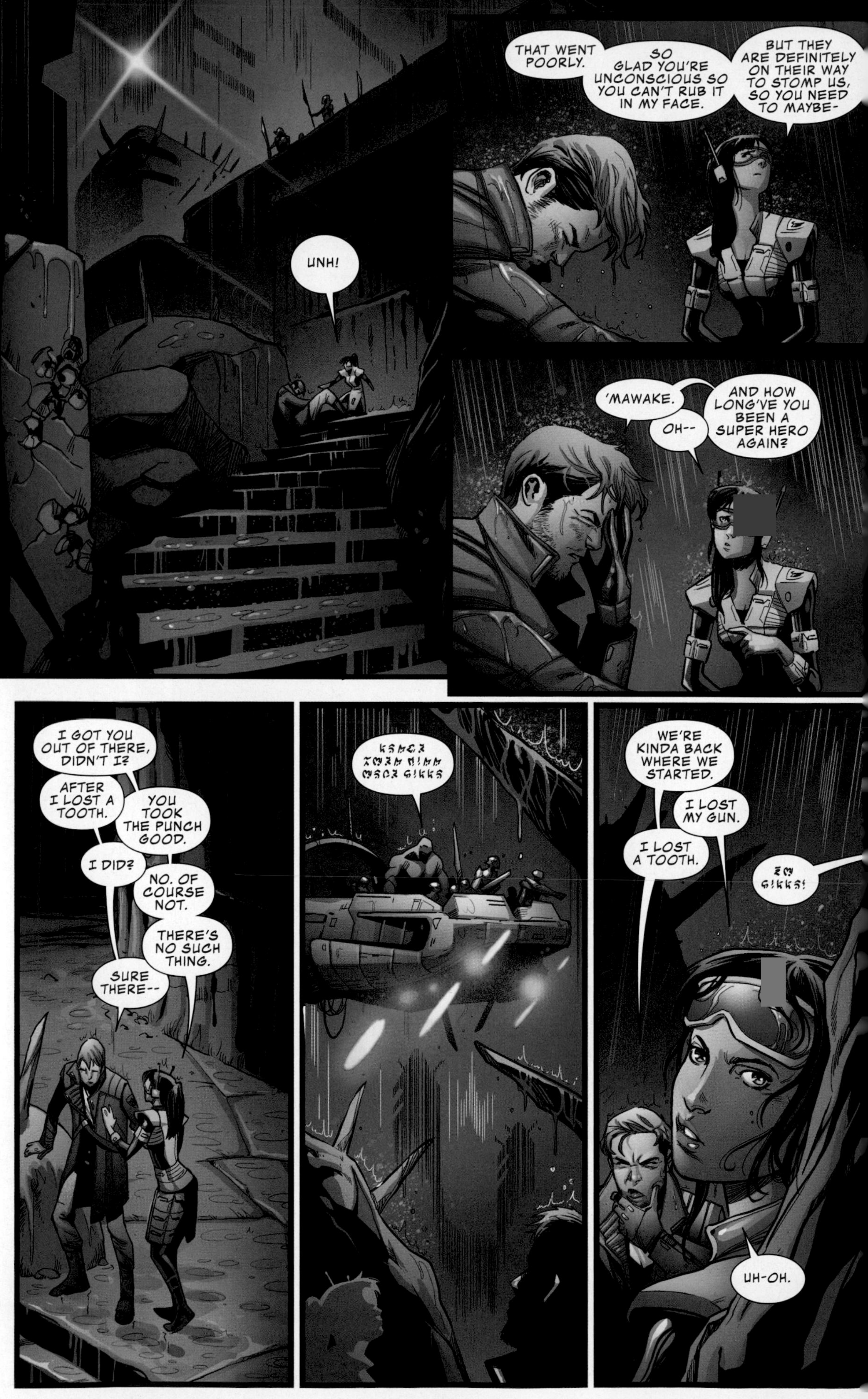
UNH!
THAT WENT POORLY.
SO GLAD YOU'RE UNCONSCIOUS SO YOU CAN'T RUB IT IN MY FACE.
BUT THEY ARE DEFINITELY ON THEIR WAY TO STOMP US, SO YOU NEED TO MAYBE-
'MAWAKE.
OH--
AND HOW LONG'VE YOU BEEN A SUPER HERO AGAIN?
I GOT YOU OUT OF THERE, DIDN'T I?
AFTER I LOST A TOOTH.
YOU TOOK THE PUNCH GOOD.
I DID?
NO. OF COURSE NOT.
THERE'S NO SUCH THING.
SURE THERE--
WE'RE KINDA BACK WHERE WE STARTED.
I LOST MY GUN.
I LOST A TOOTH.
UH-OH.

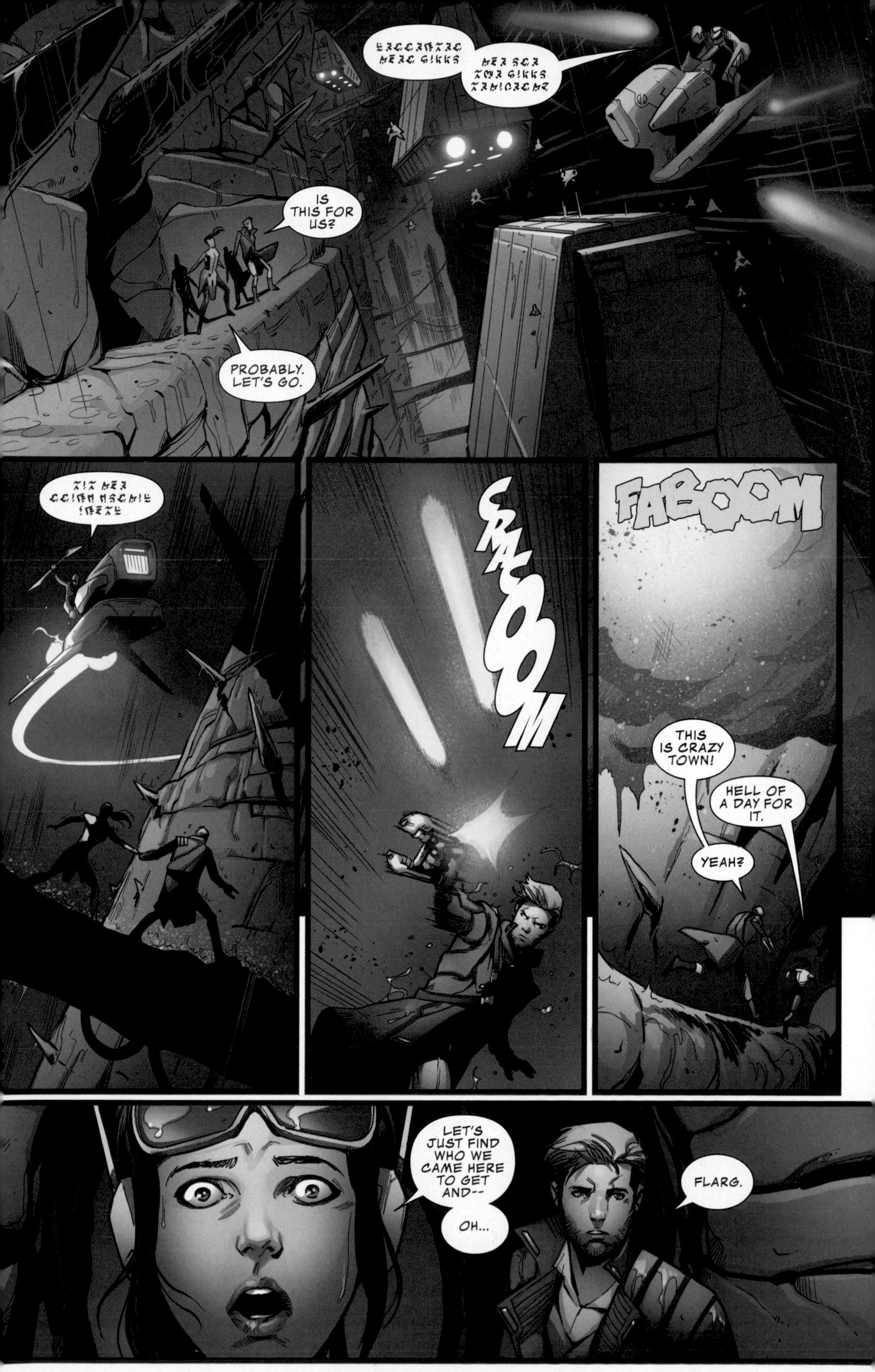
IS THIS FOR US?
PROBABLY. LET'S GO.
CRACOOM
FABOOM
THIS IS CRAZY TOWN!
YEAH?
HELL OF A DAY FOR IT.
LET'S JUST FIND WHO WE CAME HERE TO GET AND--
OH...
FLARG.

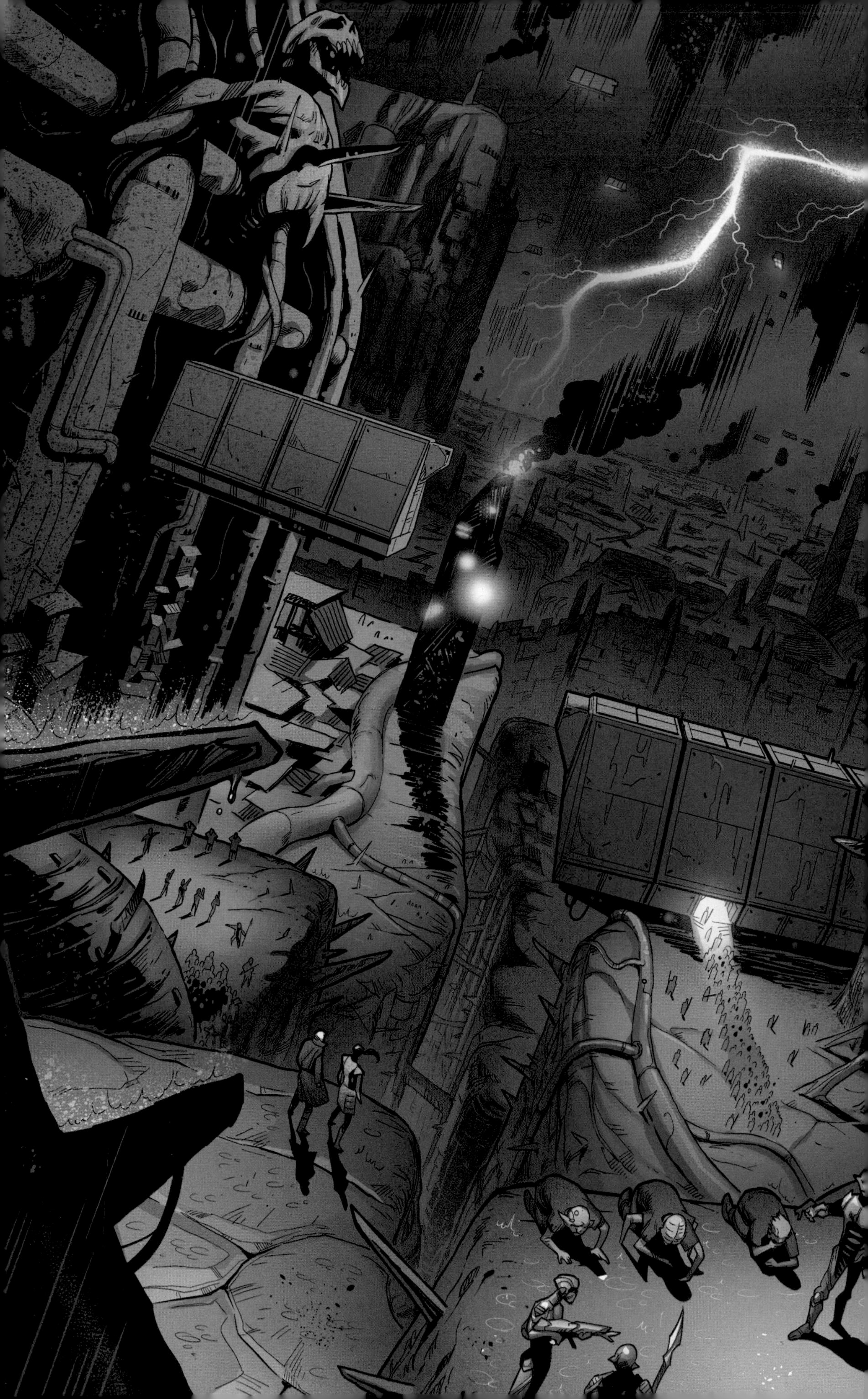

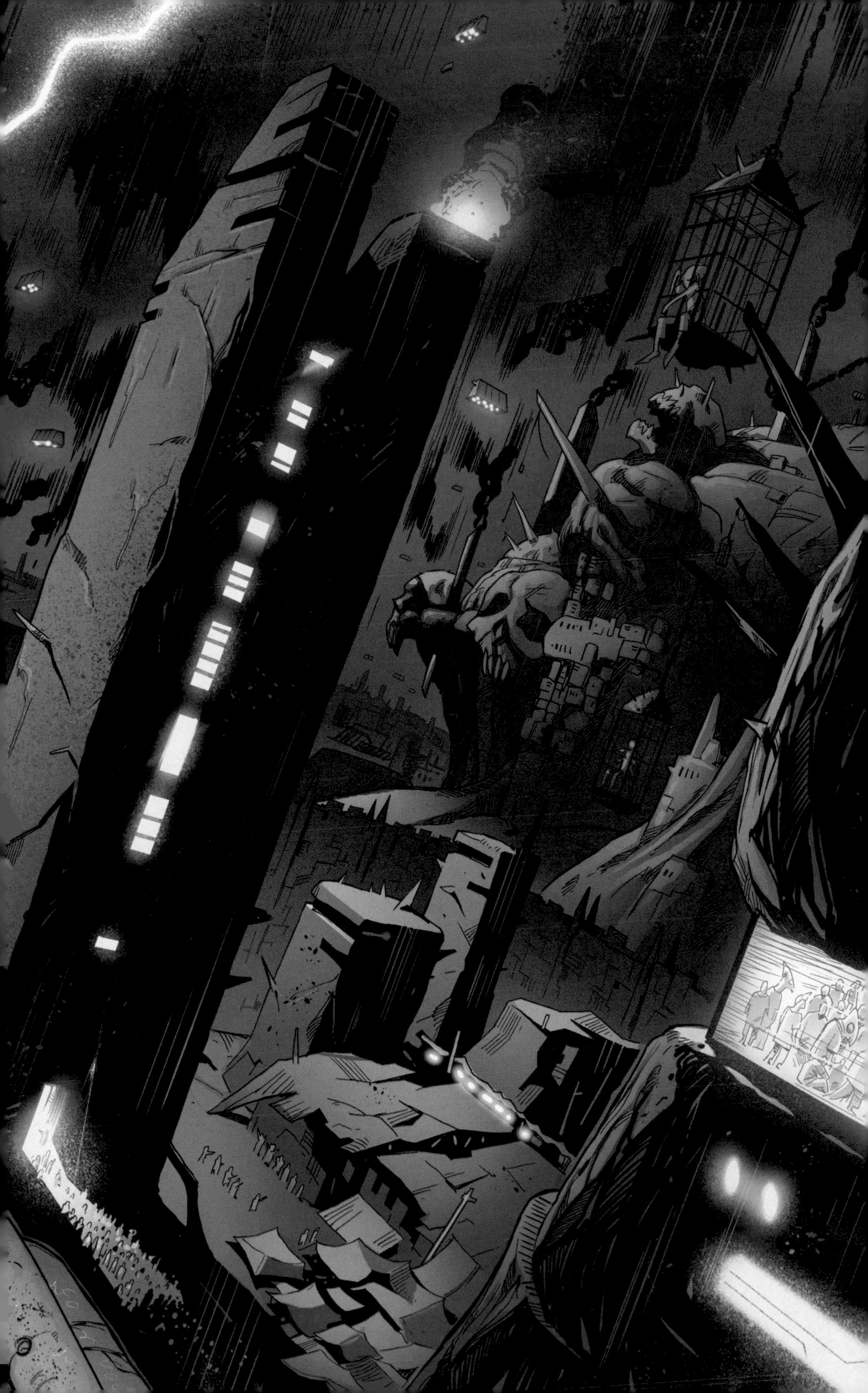

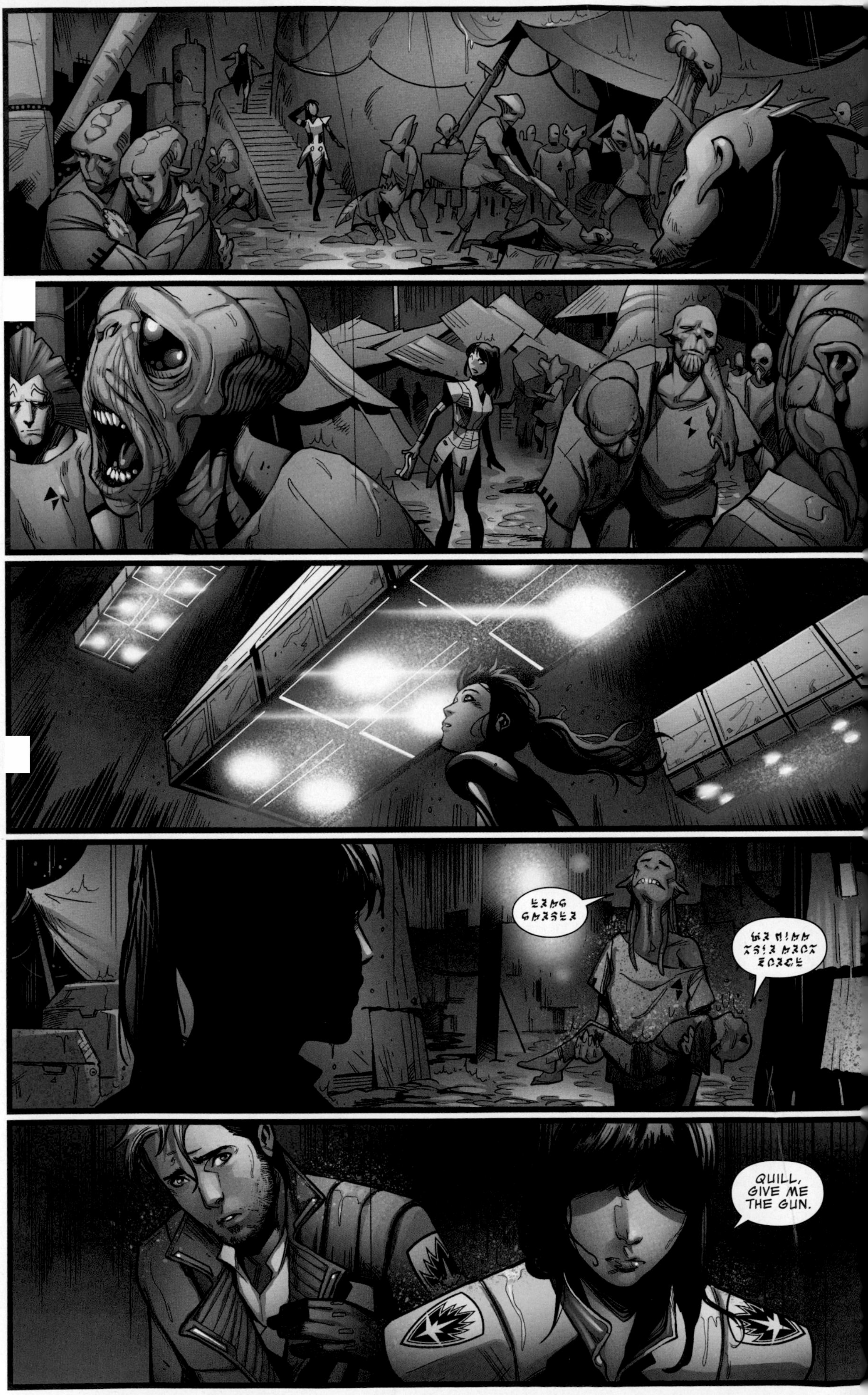
QUILL, GIVE ME THE GUN.

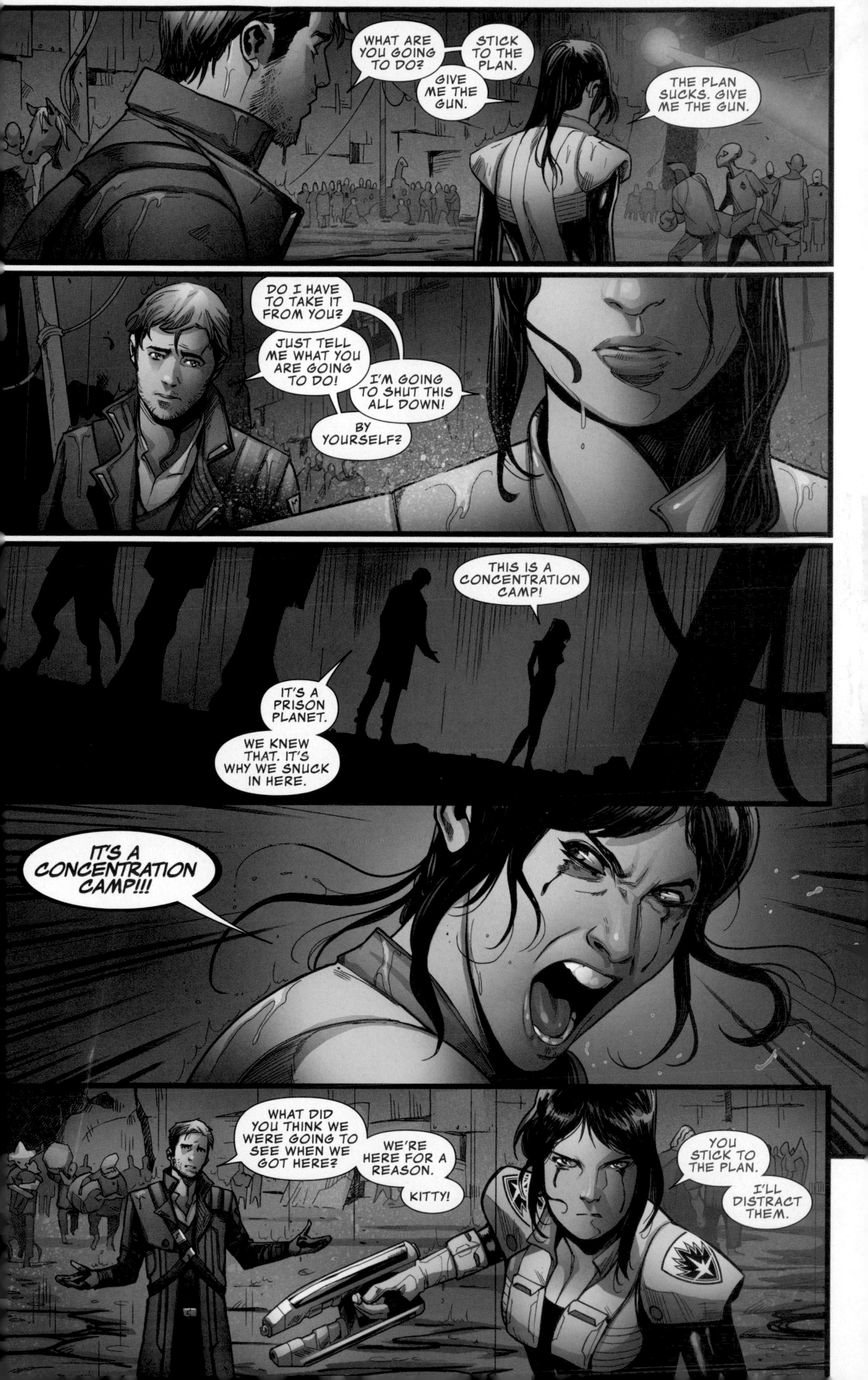
WHAT ARE YOU GOING TO DO?
STICK TO THE PLAN.
GIVE ME THE GUN.
THE PLAN SUCKS. GIVE ME THE GUN.
DO I HAVE TO TAKE IT FROM YOU?
JUST TELL ME WHAT YOU ARE GOING TO DO!
I'M GOING TO SHUT THIS ALL DOWN!
BY YOURSELF?
THIS IS A CONCENTRATION CAMP!
IT'S A PRISON PLANET.
WE KNEW THAT. IT'S WHY WE SNUCK IN HERE.
IT'S A CONCENTRATION CAMP!!!
WHAT DID YOU THINK WE WERE GOING TO SEE WHEN WE GOT HERE?
WE'RE HERE FOR A REASON.
KITTY!
YOU STICK TO THE PLAN.
I'LL DISTRACT THEM.

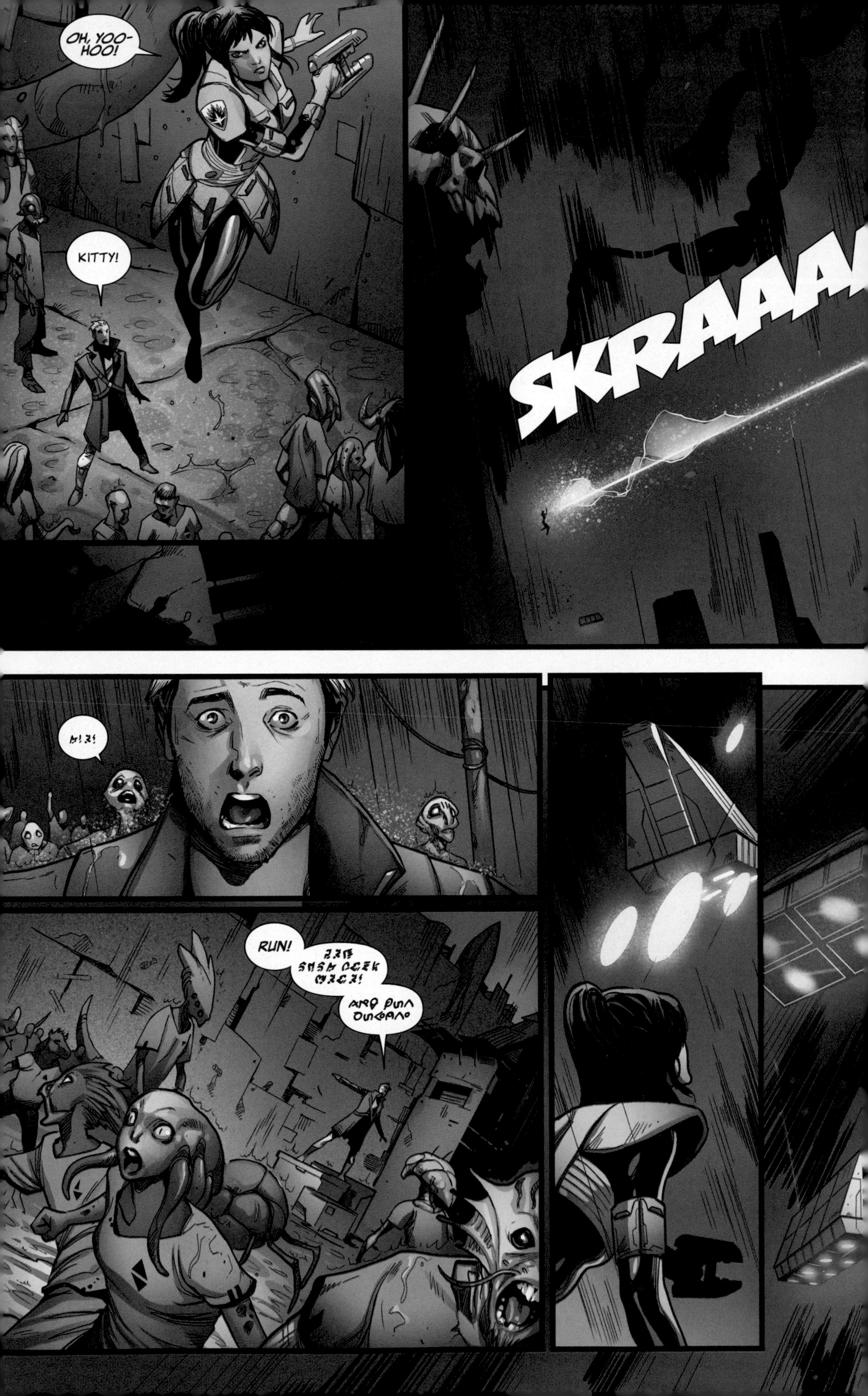
OH, YOO-HOO!
KITTY!
SKRAAAA
RUN!

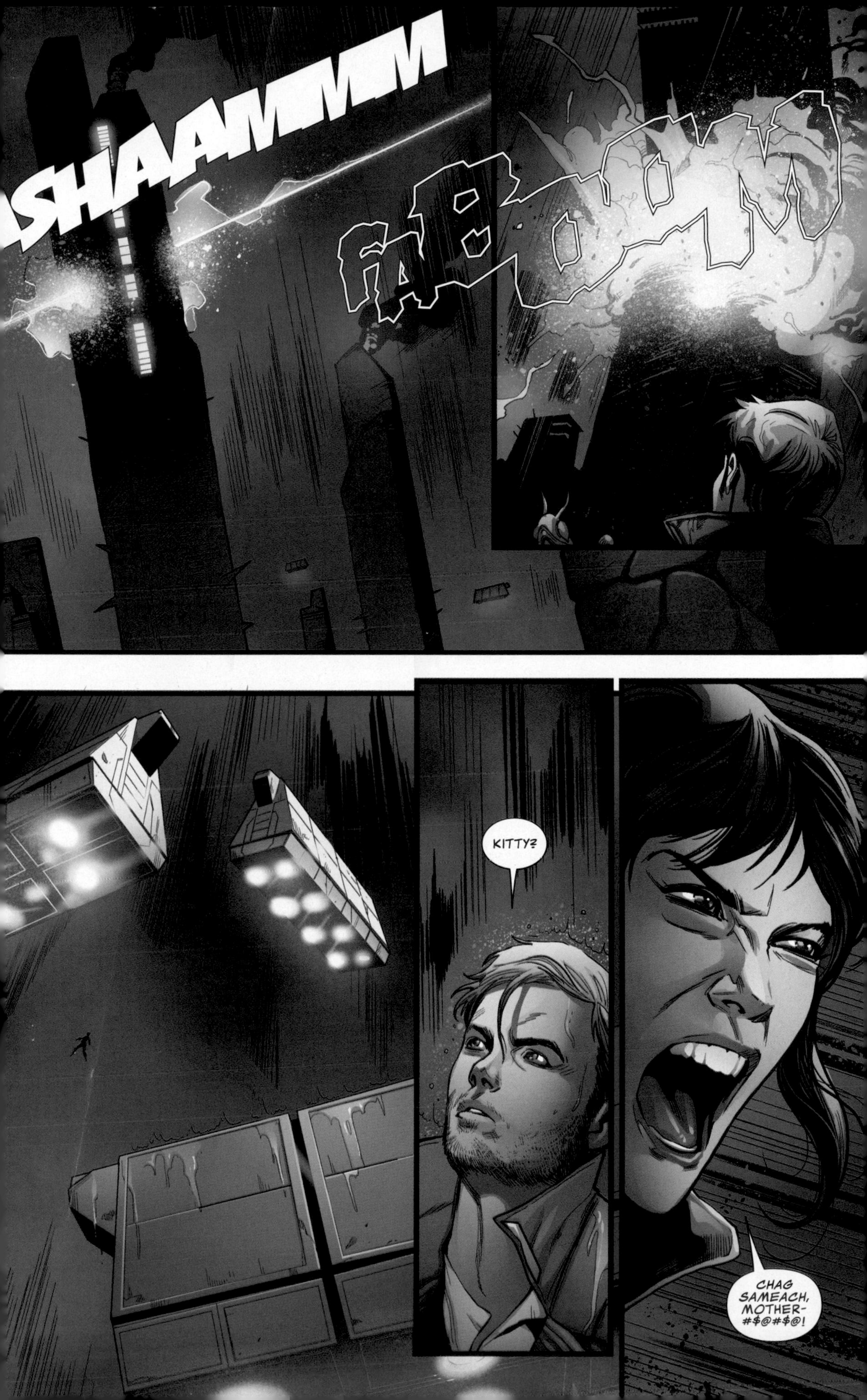
SHAAMMMM
FABOOOM
KITTY?
CHAG SAMEACH, MOTHER-#$@#$@!

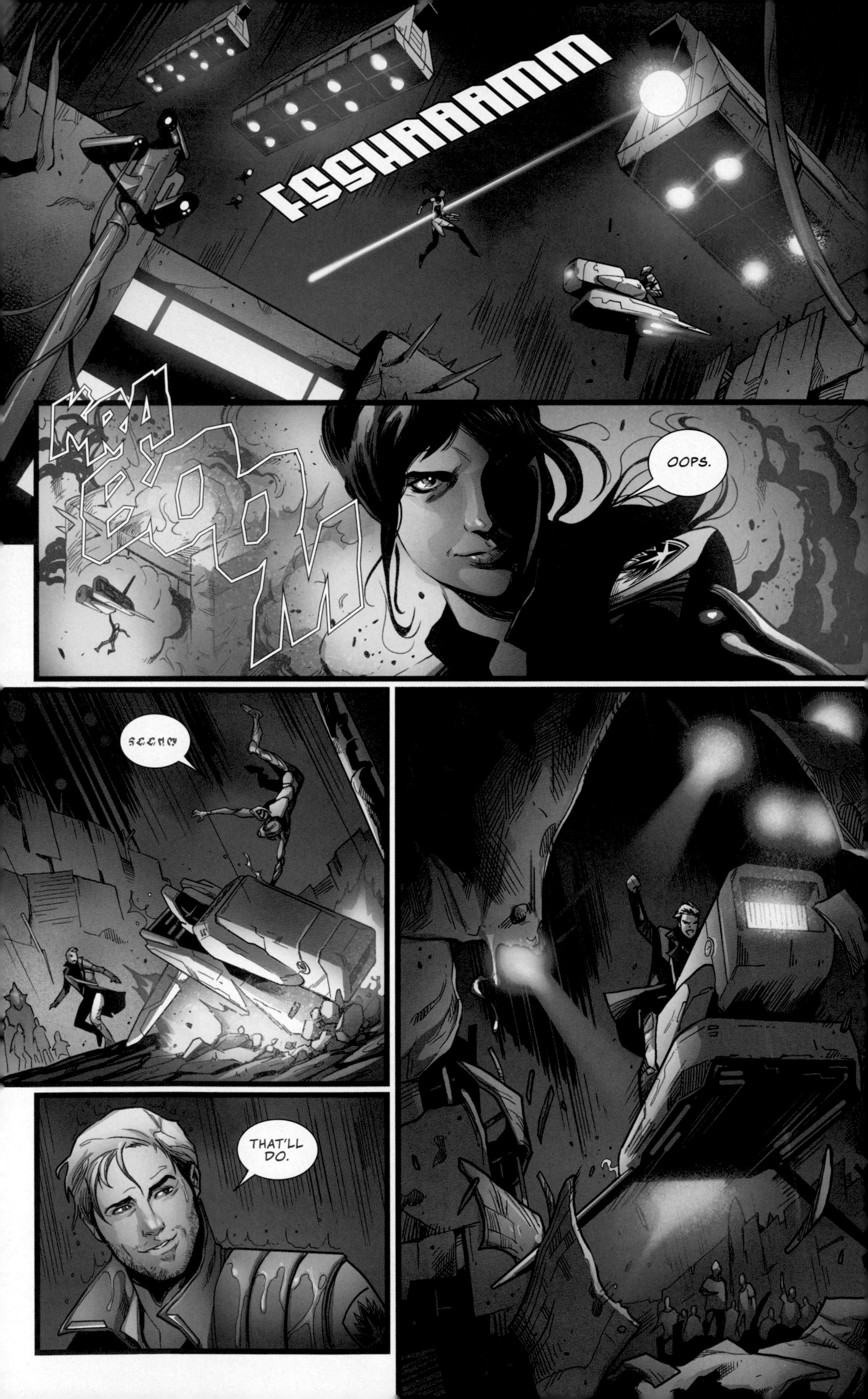
FSSHAAAMM
KA-BOOM
OOPS.
THAT'LL DO.

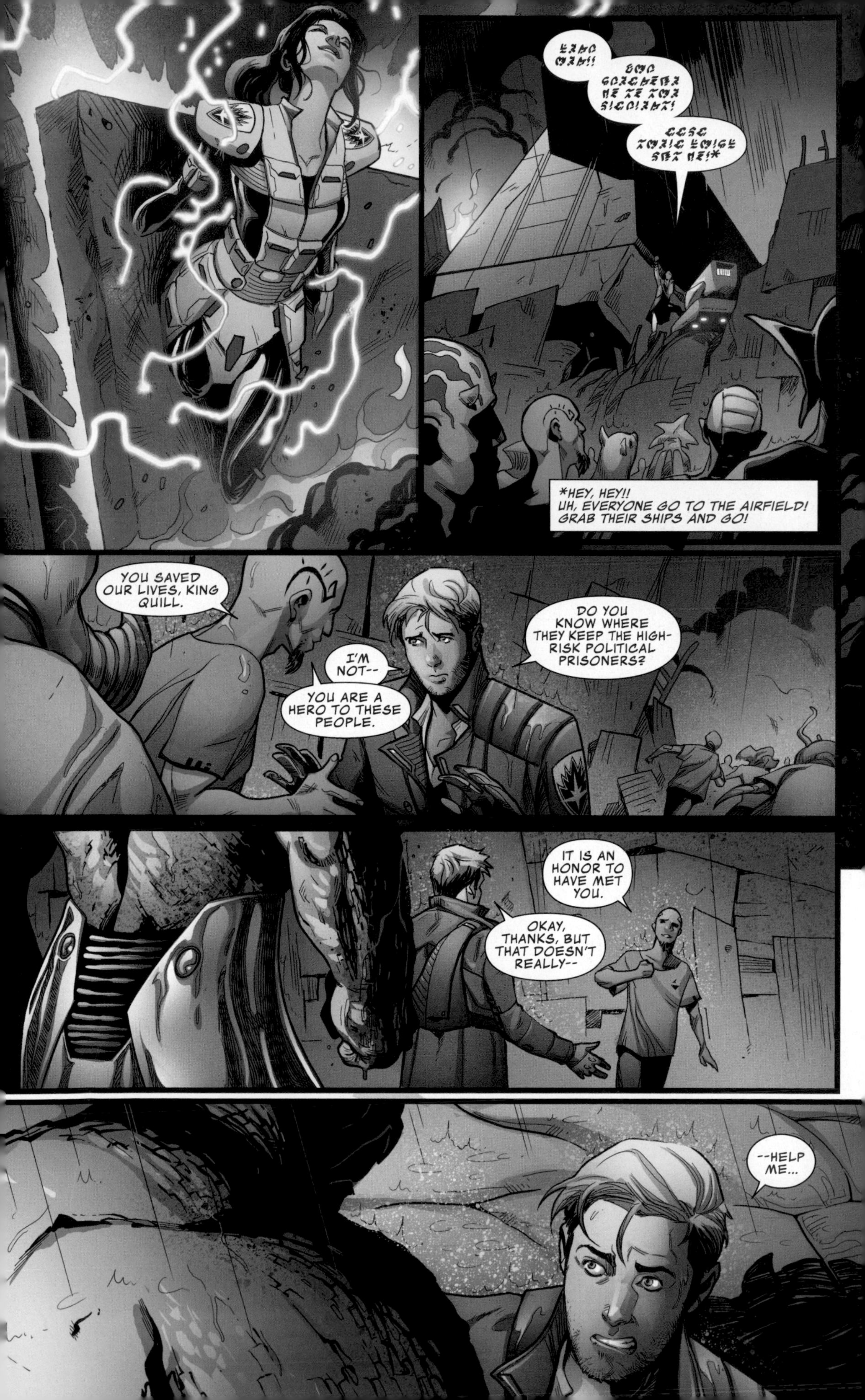
*HEY, HEY!! UH, EVERYONE GO TO THE AIRFIELD! GRAB THEIR SHIPS AND GO!
YOU SAVED OUR LIVES, KING QUILL.
I'M NOT--
YOU ARE A HERO TO THESE PEOPLE.
DO YOU KNOW WHERE THEY KEEP THE HIGH-RISK POLITICAL PRISONERS?
IT IS AN HONOR TO HAVE MET YOU.
OKAY, THANKS, BUT THAT DOESN'T REALLY--
--HELP ME...

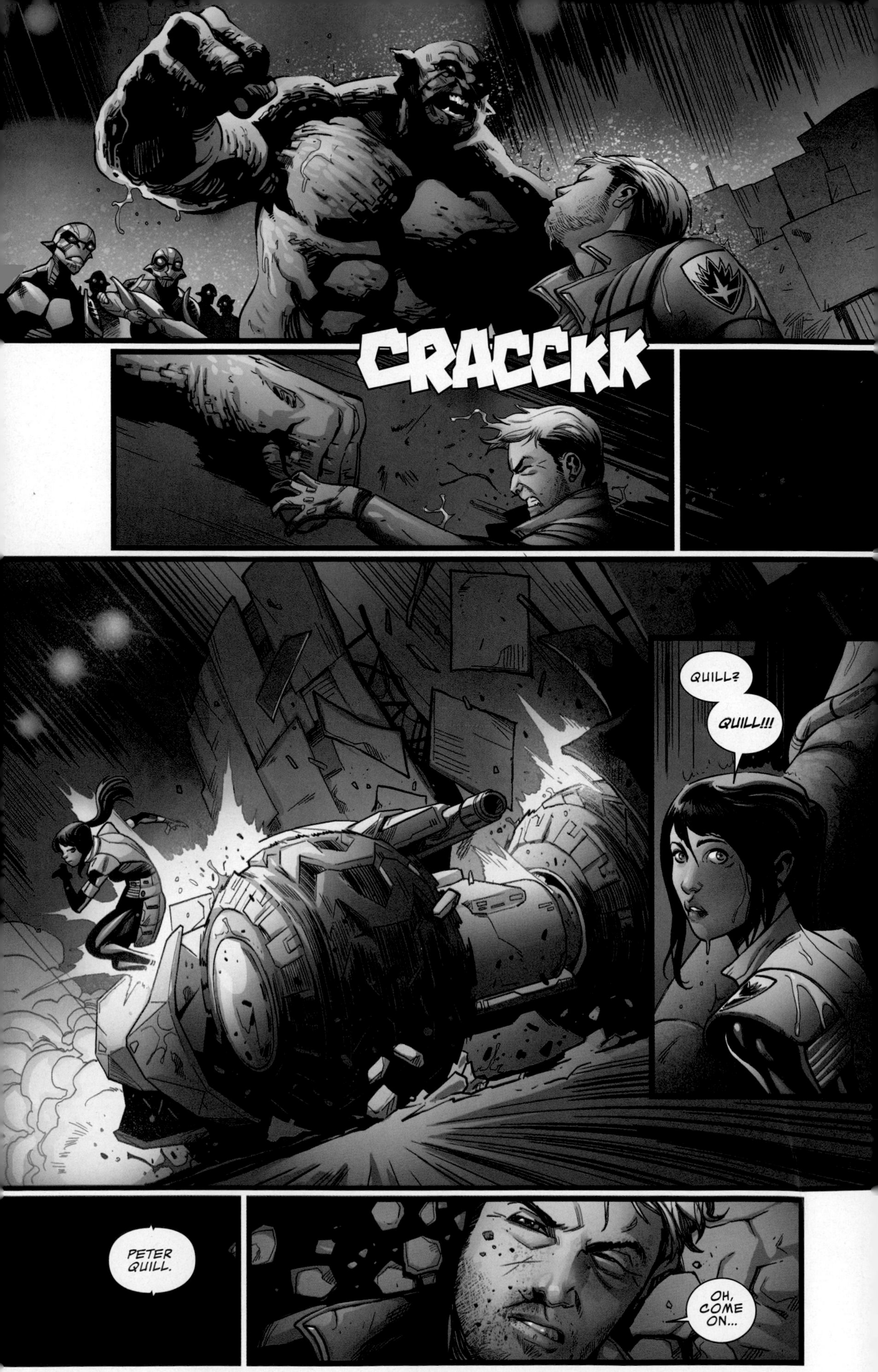
CRACCKK
QUILL?
QUILL!!!
PETER QUILL.
OH, COME ON...

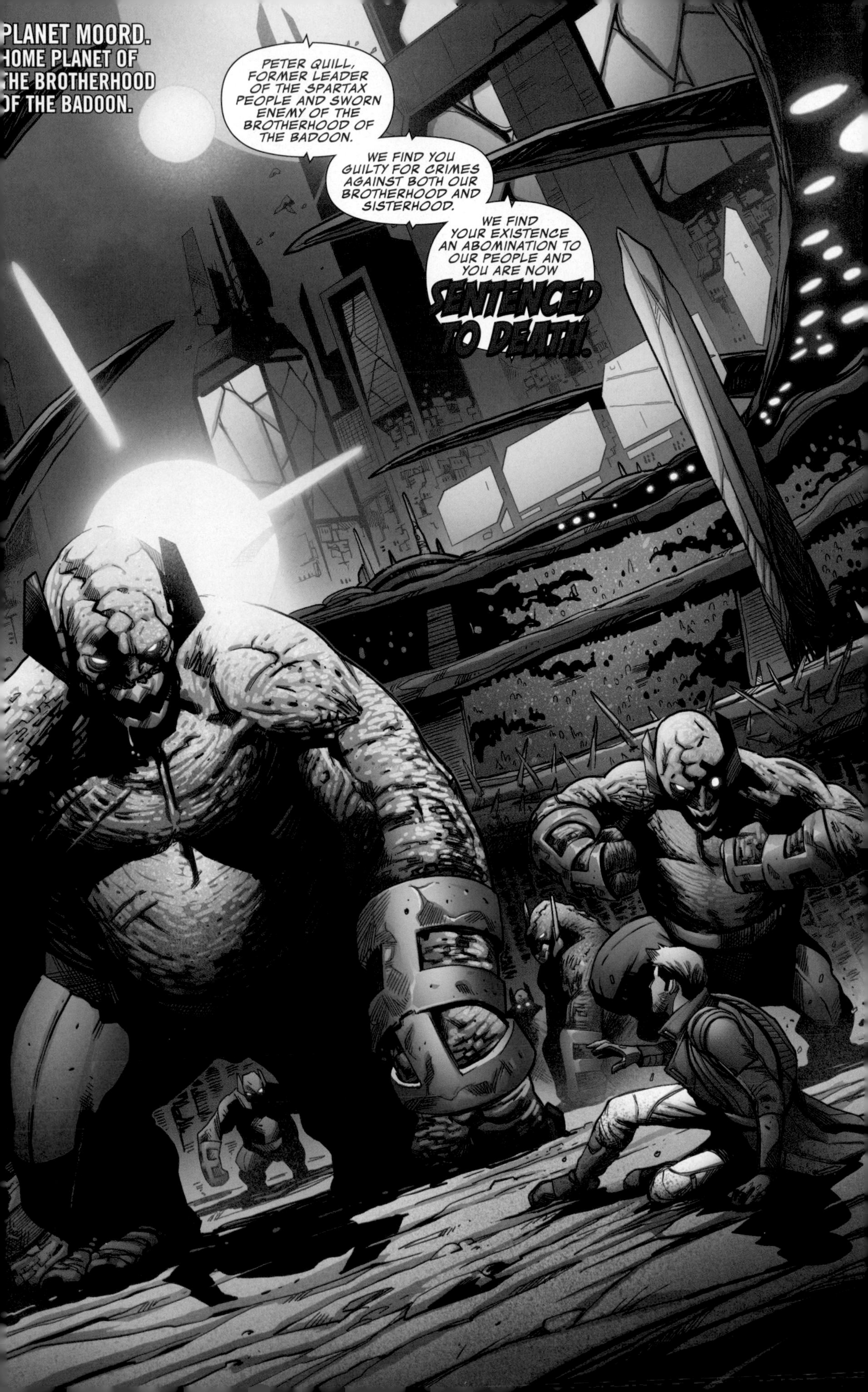
PLANET MOORD. HOME PLANET OF THE BROTHERHOOD OF THE BADOON.
PETER QUILL, FORMER LEADER OF THE SPARTAX PEOPLE AND SWORN ENEMY OF THE BROTHERHOOD OF THE BADOON.
WE FIND YOU GUILTY FOR CRIMES AGAINST BOTH OUR BROTHERHOOD AND SISTERHOOD.
WE FIND YOUR EXISTENCE AN ABOMINATION TO OUR PEOPLE AND YOU ARE NOW SENTENCED TO DEATH.

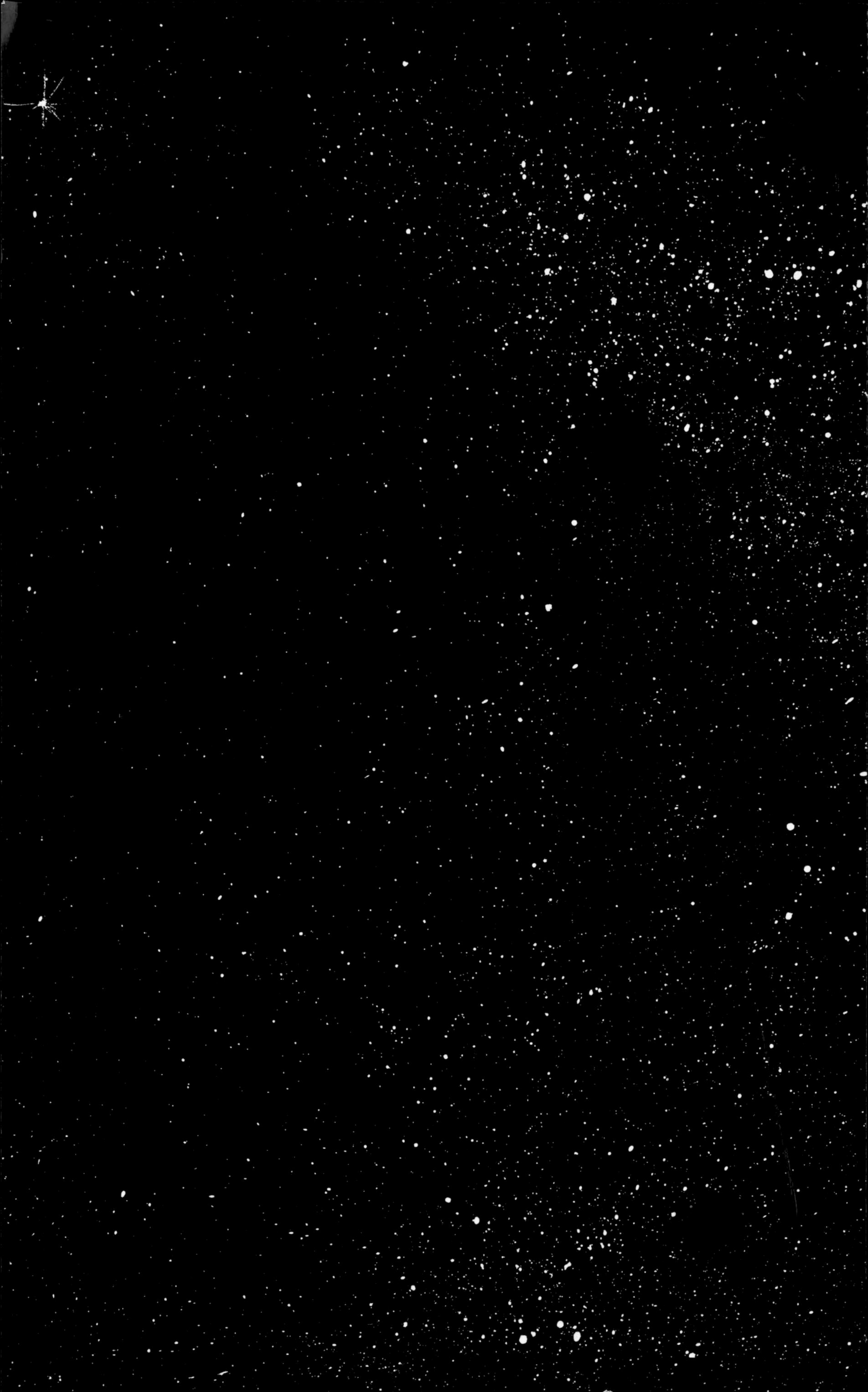

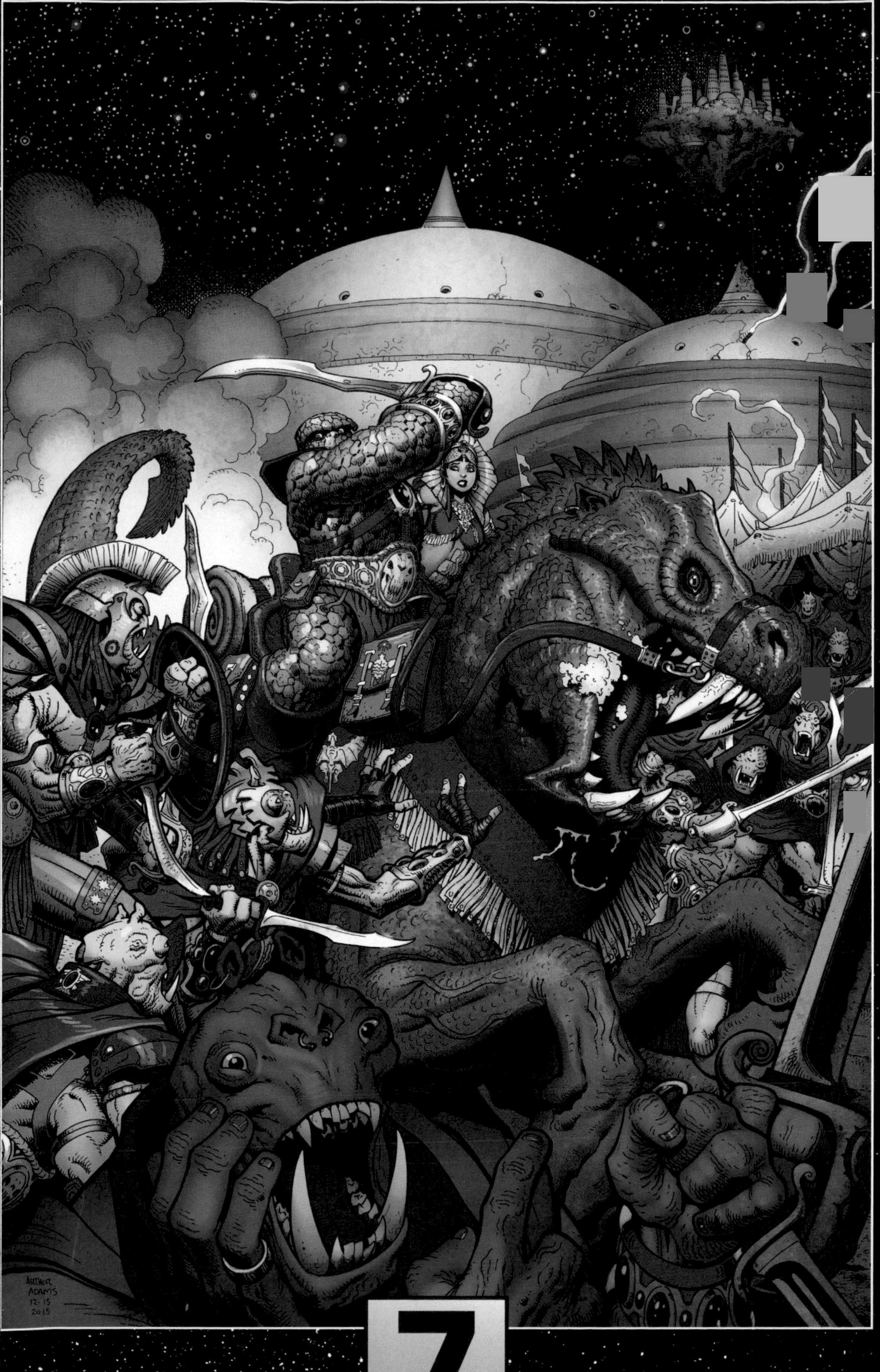
ARTHUR ADAMS
12-15
2015

# 7

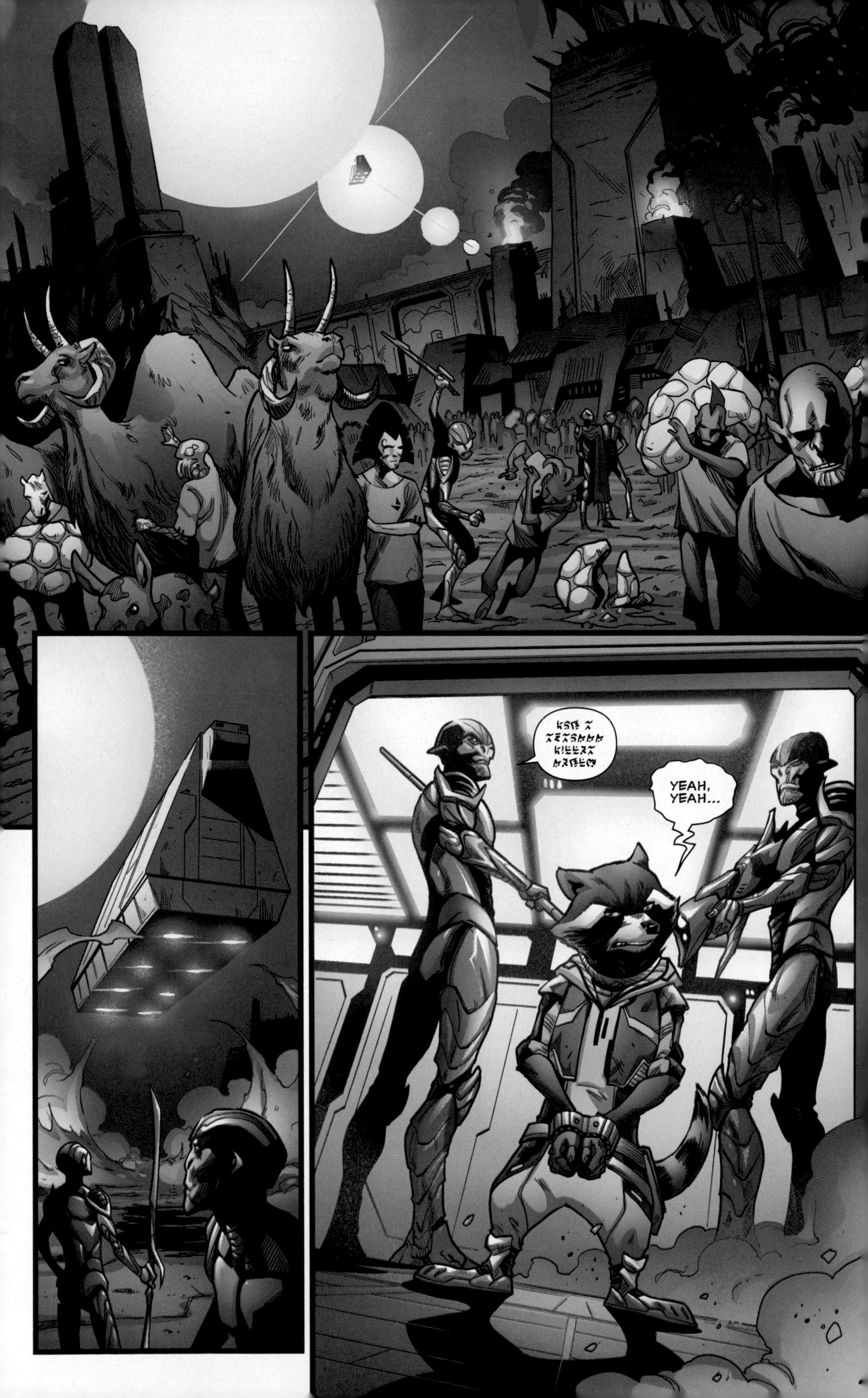
YEAH, YEAH...

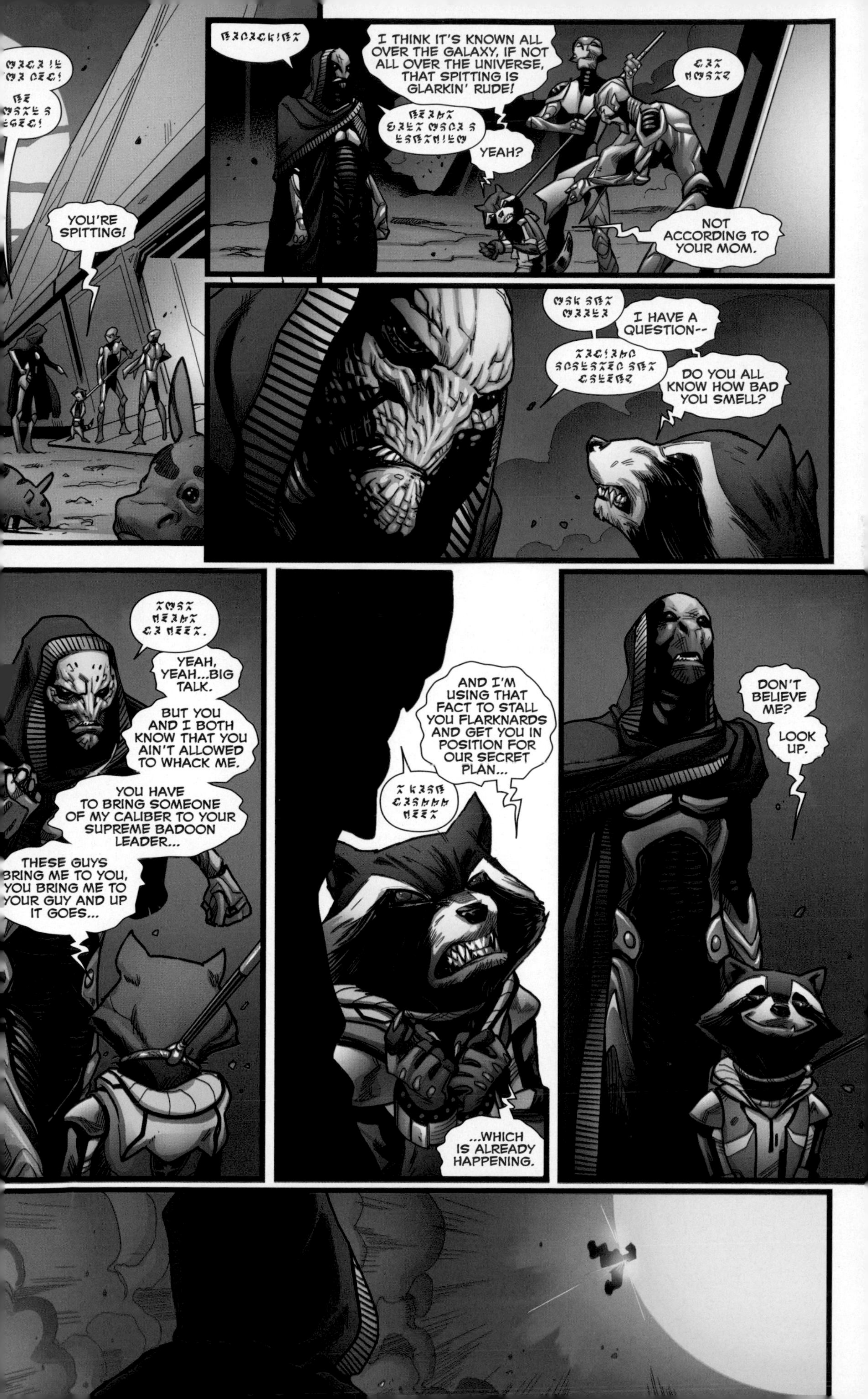
YOU'RE SPITTING!
I THINK IT'S KNOWN ALL OVER THE GALAXY, IF NOT ALL OVER THE UNIVERSE, THAT SPITTING IS GLARKIN' RUDE!
YEAH?
NOT ACCORDING TO YOUR MOM.
I HAVE A QUESTION--
DO YOU ALL KNOW HOW BAD YOU SMELL?
YEAH, YEAH...BIG TALK.
BUT YOU AND I BOTH KNOW THAT YOU AIN'T ALLOWED TO WHACK ME.
YOU HAVE TO BRING SOMEONE OF MY CALIBER TO YOUR SUPREME BADOON LEADER...
THESE GUYS BRING ME TO YOU, YOU BRING ME TO YOUR GUY AND UP IT GOES...
AND I'M USING THAT FACT TO STALL YOU FLARKNARDS AND GET YOU IN POSITION FOR OUR SECRET PLAN...
...WHICH IS ALREADY HAPPENING.
DON'T BELIEVE ME?
LOOK UP.

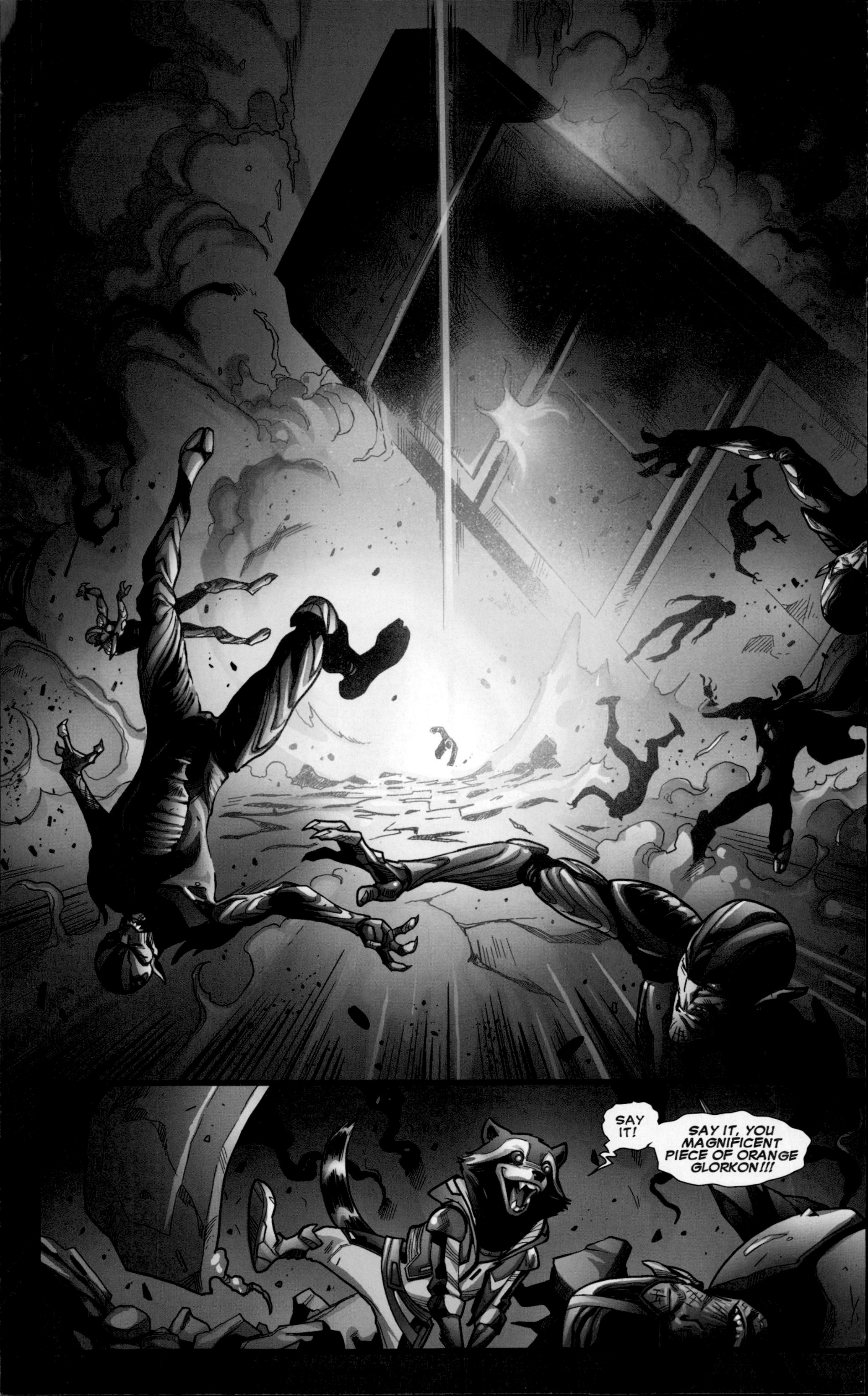
SAY IT!
SAY IT, YOU MAGNIFICENT PIECE OF ORANGE GLORKON!!!

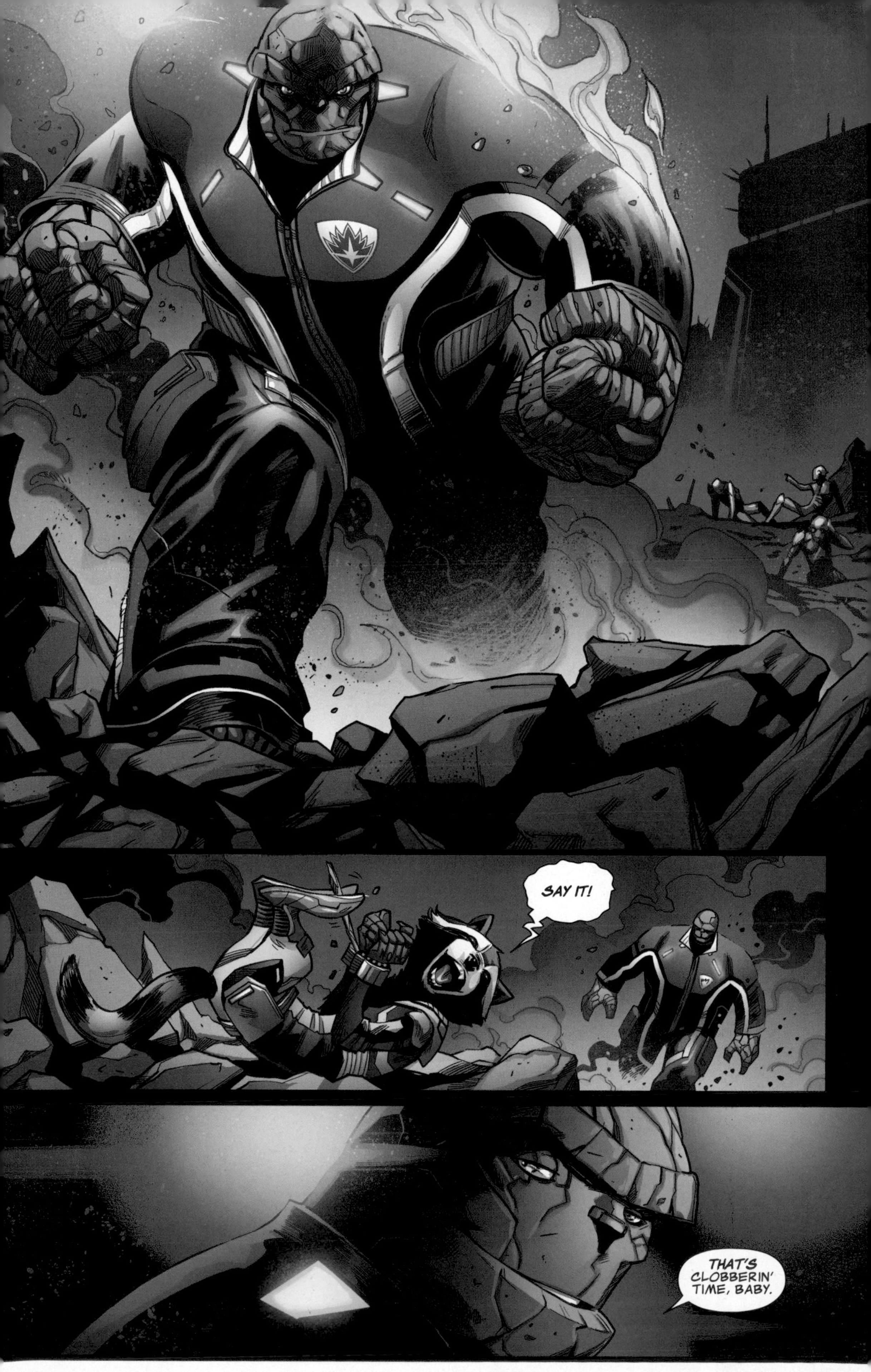
SAY IT!
THAT'S CLOBBERIN' TIME, BABY.

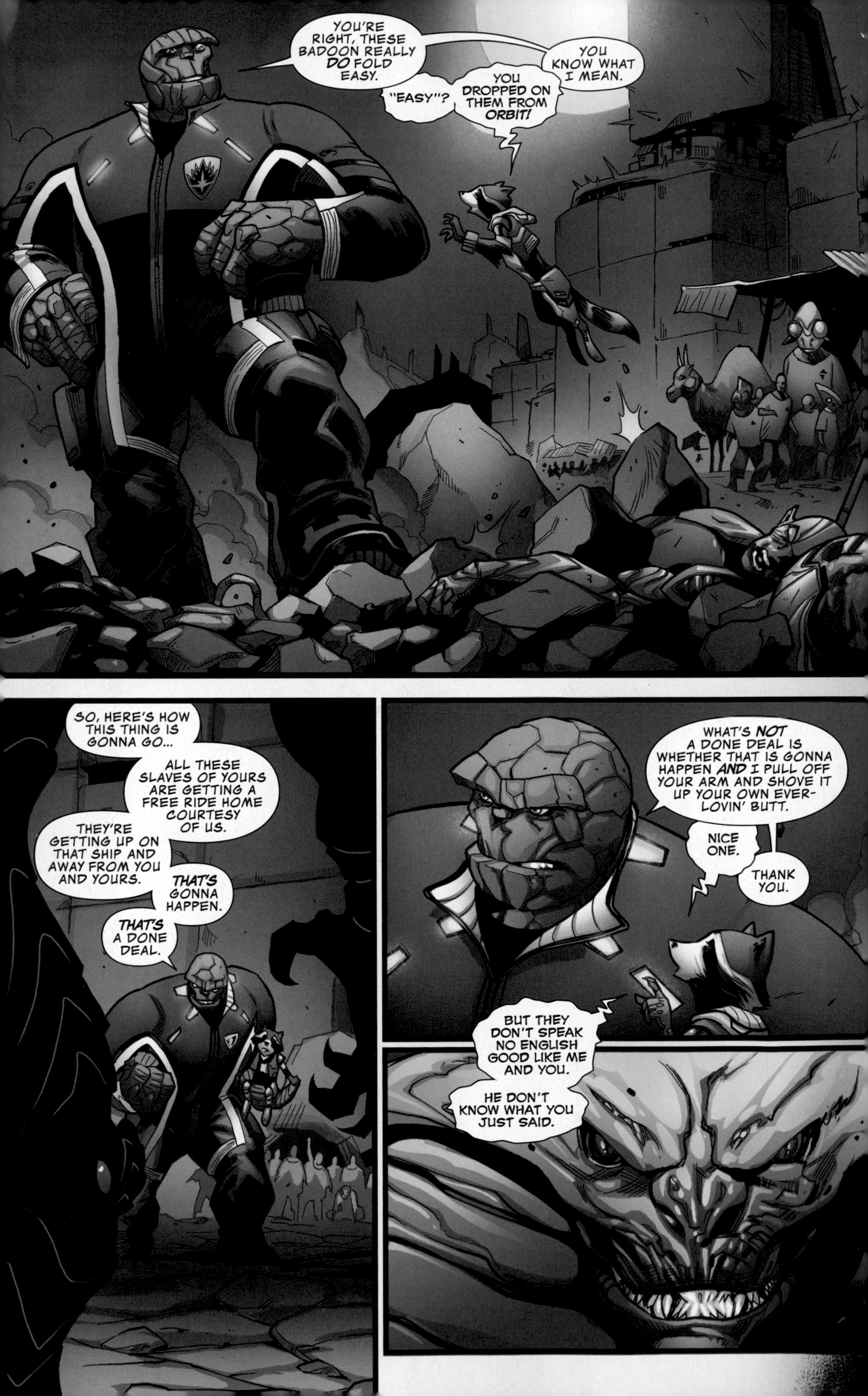
YOU'RE RIGHT, THESE BADOON REALLY DO FOLD EASY.
"EASY"?
YOU DROPPED ON THEM FROM ORBIT!
YOU KNOW WHAT I MEAN.
SO, HERE'S HOW THIS THING IS GONNA GO...
ALL THESE SLAVES OF YOURS ARE GETTING A FREE RIDE HOME COURTESY OF US.
THEY'RE GETTING UP ON THAT SHIP AND AWAY FROM YOU AND YOURS.
THAT'S GONNA HAPPEN.
THAT'S A DONE DEAL.
WHAT'S NOT A DONE DEAL IS WHETHER THAT IS GONNA HAPPEN AND I PULL OFF YOUR ARM AND SHOVE IT UP YOUR OWN EVER-LOVIN' BUTT.
NICE ONE.
THANK YOU.
BUT THEY DON'T SPEAK NO ENGLISH GOOD LIKE ME AND YOU.
HE DON'T KNOW WHAT YOU JUST SAID.

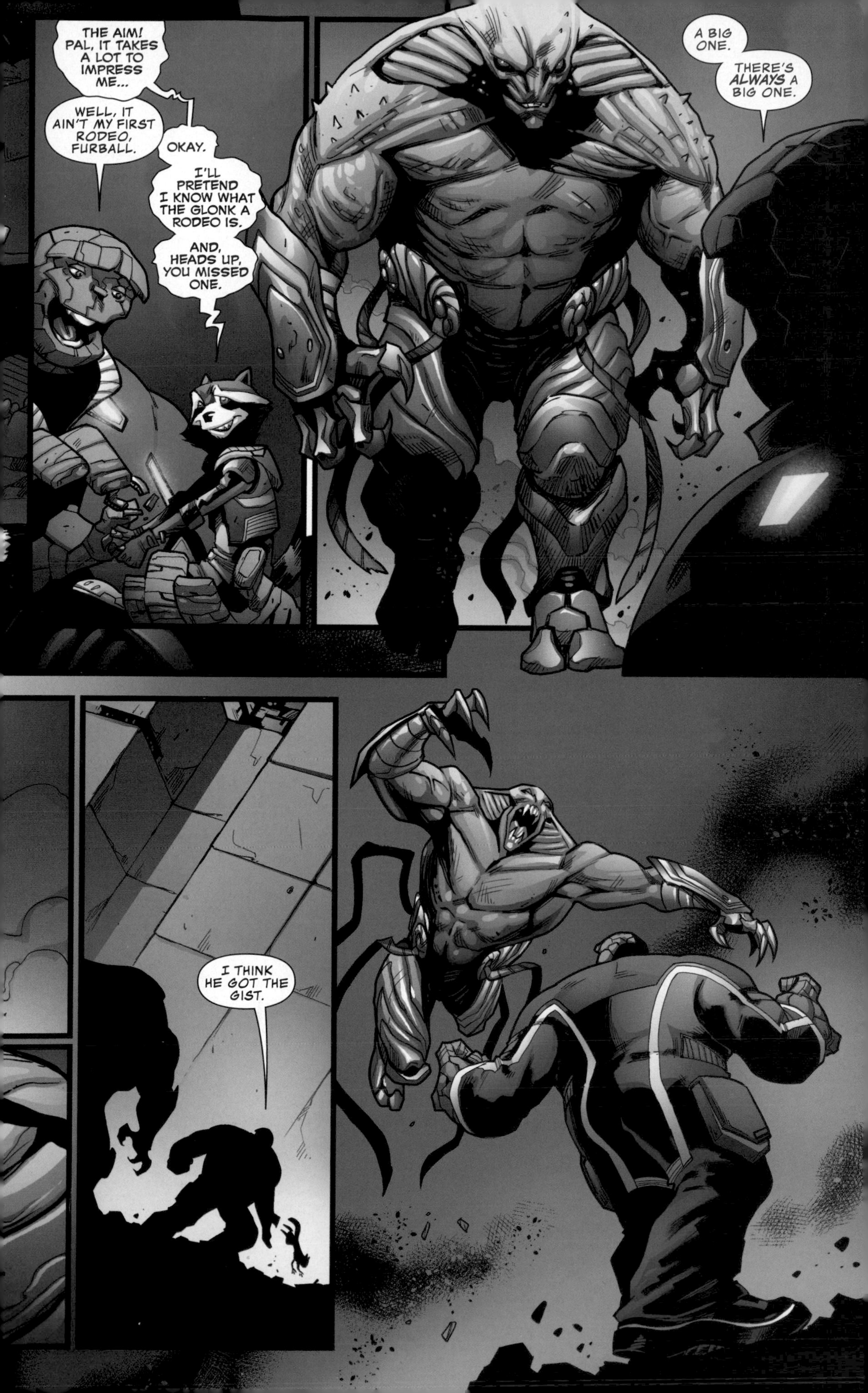
THE AIM! PAL, IT TAKES A LOT TO IMPRESS ME...
WELL, IT AIN'T MY FIRST RODEO, FURBALL.
OKAY.
I'LL PRETEND I KNOW WHAT THE GLONK A RODEO IS.
AND, HEADS UP, YOU MISSED ONE.
A BIG ONE.
THERE'S *ALWAYS* A BIG ONE.
I THINK HE GOT THE GIST.

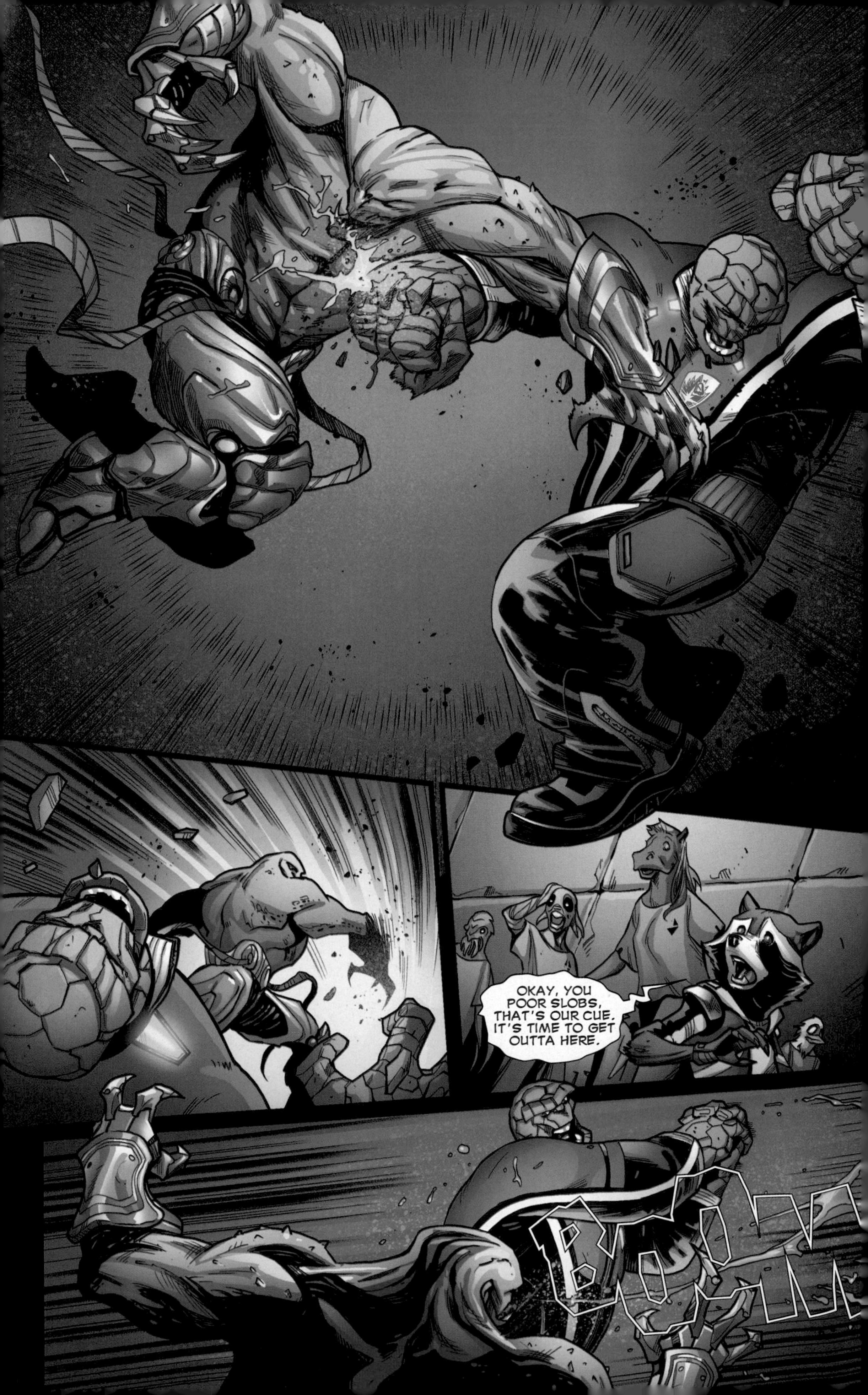
OKAY, YOU POOR SLOBS, THAT'S OUR CUE. IT'S TIME TO GET OUTTA HERE.
BOOM

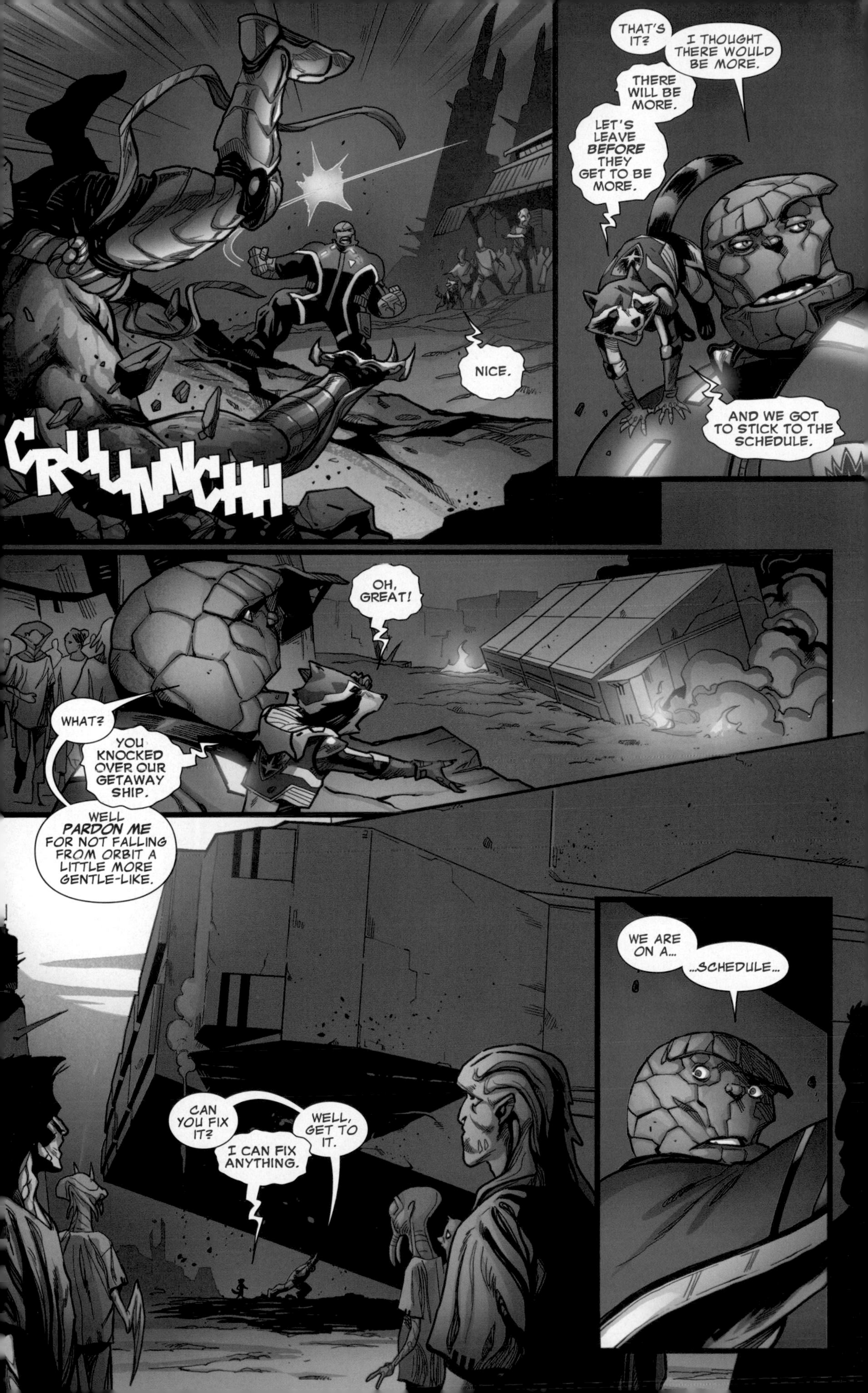
NICE.
CRUUNNCHH
THAT'S IT?
I THOUGHT THERE WOULD BE MORE.
THERE WILL BE MORE.
LET'S LEAVE BEFORE THEY GET TO BE MORE.
AND WE GOT TO STICK TO THE SCHEDULE.
OH, GREAT!
WHAT?
YOU KNOCKED OVER OUR GETAWAY SHIP.
WELL PARDON ME FOR NOT FALLING FROM ORBIT A LITTLE MORE GENTLE-LIKE.
WE ARE ON A...
...SCHEDULE...
CAN YOU FIX IT?
I CAN FIX ANYTHING.
WELL, GET TO IT.

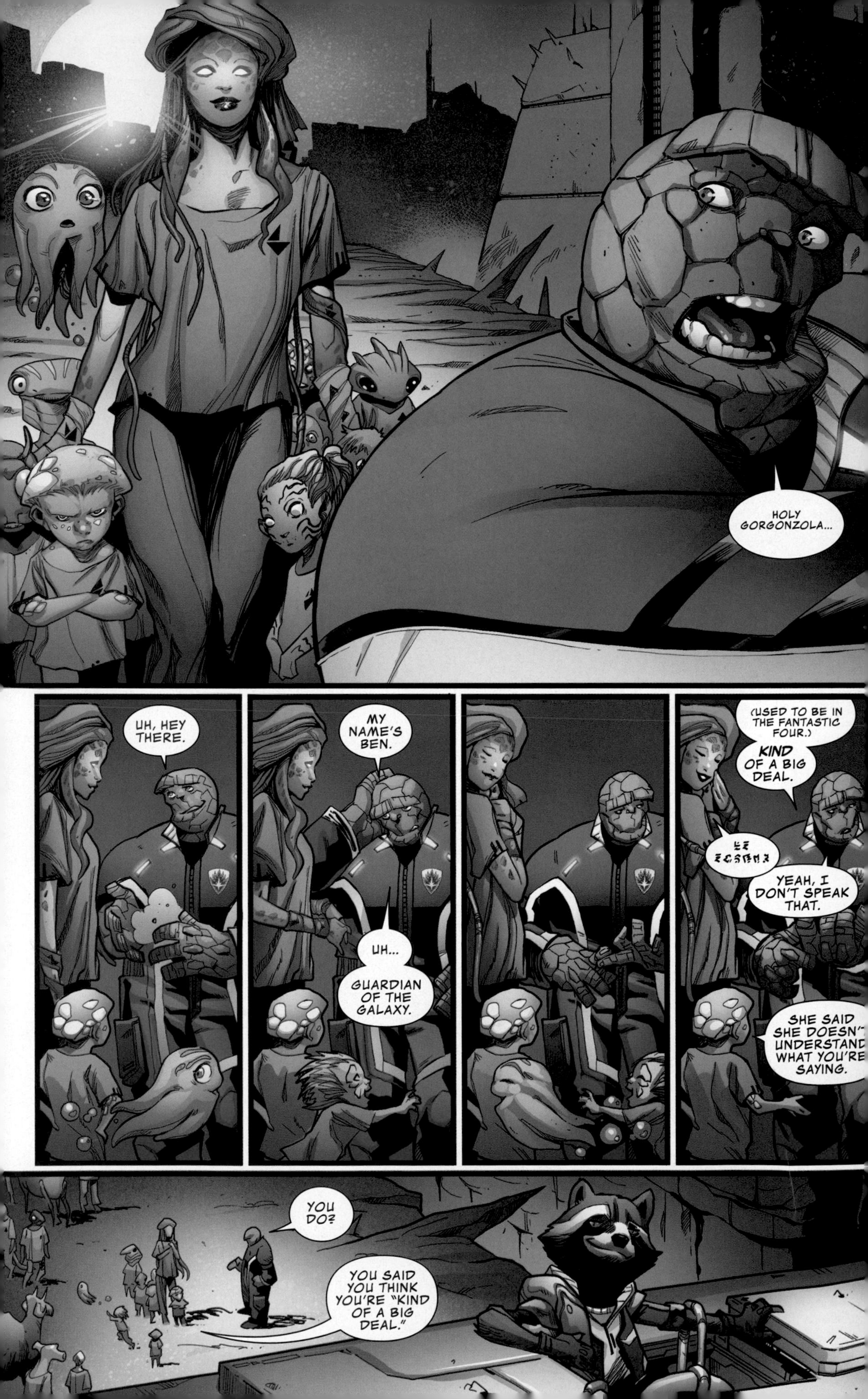
HOLY GORGONZOLA...
UH, HEY THERE.
MY NAME'S BEN.
UH... GUARDIAN OF THE GALAXY.
(USED TO BE IN THE FANTASTIC FOUR.)
*KIND* OF A BIG DEAL.
YEAH, I DON'T SPEAK THAT.
SHE SAID SHE DOESN'T UNDERSTAND WHAT YOU'RE SAYING.
YOU DO?
YOU SAID YOU THINK YOU'RE "KIND OF A BIG DEAL."

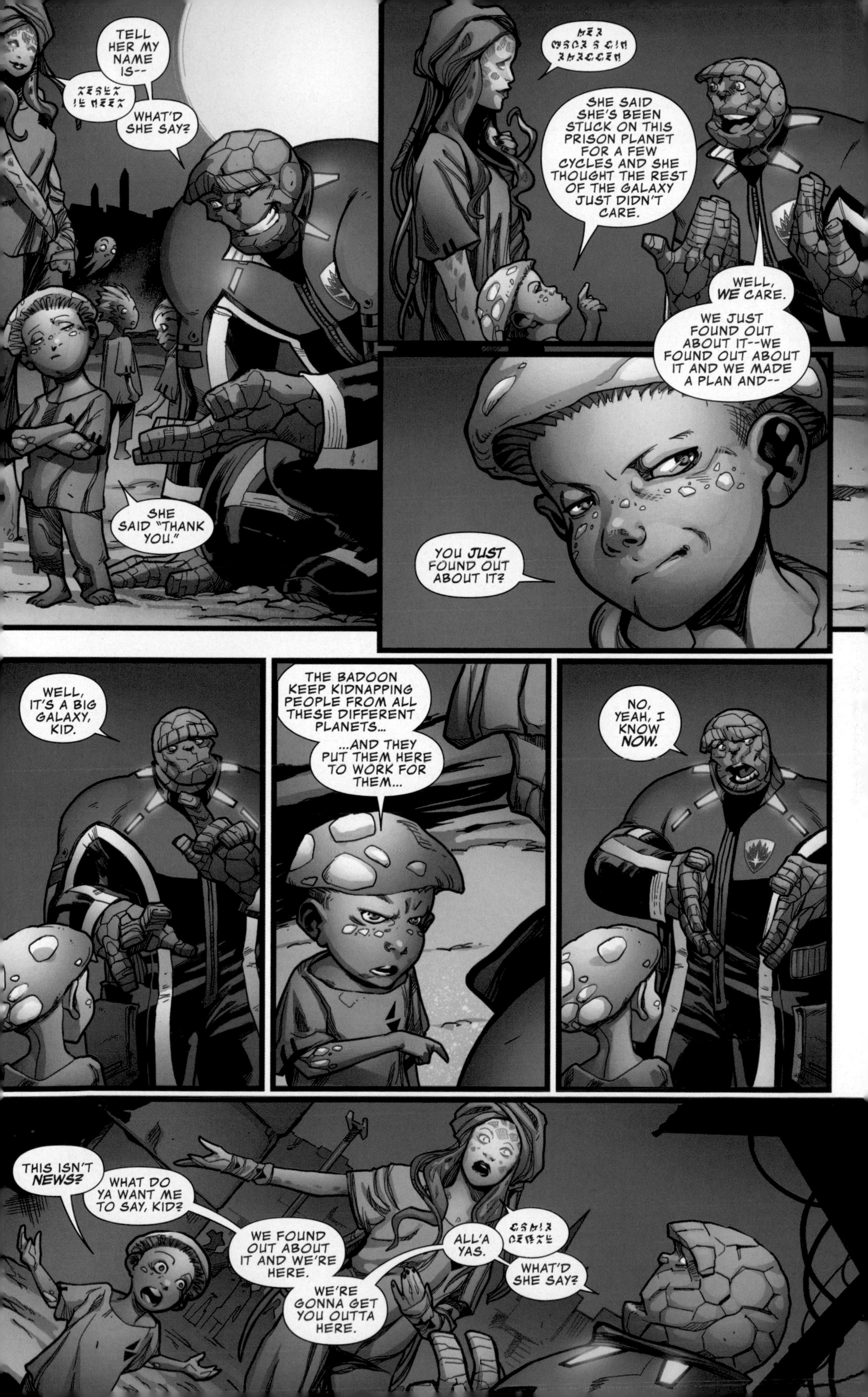

TELL HER MY NAME IS--
WHAT'D SHE SAY?
SHE SAID "THANK YOU."
SHE SAID SHE'S BEEN STUCK ON THIS PRISON PLANET FOR A FEW CYCLES AND SHE THOUGHT THE REST OF THE GALAXY JUST DIDN'T CARE.
WELL, WE CARE.
WE JUST FOUND OUT ABOUT IT--WE FOUND OUT ABOUT IT AND WE MADE A PLAN AND--
YOU JUST FOUND OUT ABOUT IT?
WELL, IT'S A BIG GALAXY, KID.
THE BADOON KEEP KIDNAPPING PEOPLE FROM ALL THESE DIFFERENT PLANETS...
...AND THEY PUT THEM HERE TO WORK FOR THEM...
NO, YEAH, I KNOW NOW.
THIS ISN'T NEWS?
WHAT DO YA WANT ME TO SAY, KID?
WE FOUND OUT ABOUT IT AND WE'RE HERE.
WE'RE GONNA GET YOU OUTTA HERE.
ALL'A YAS.
WHAT'D SHE SAY?

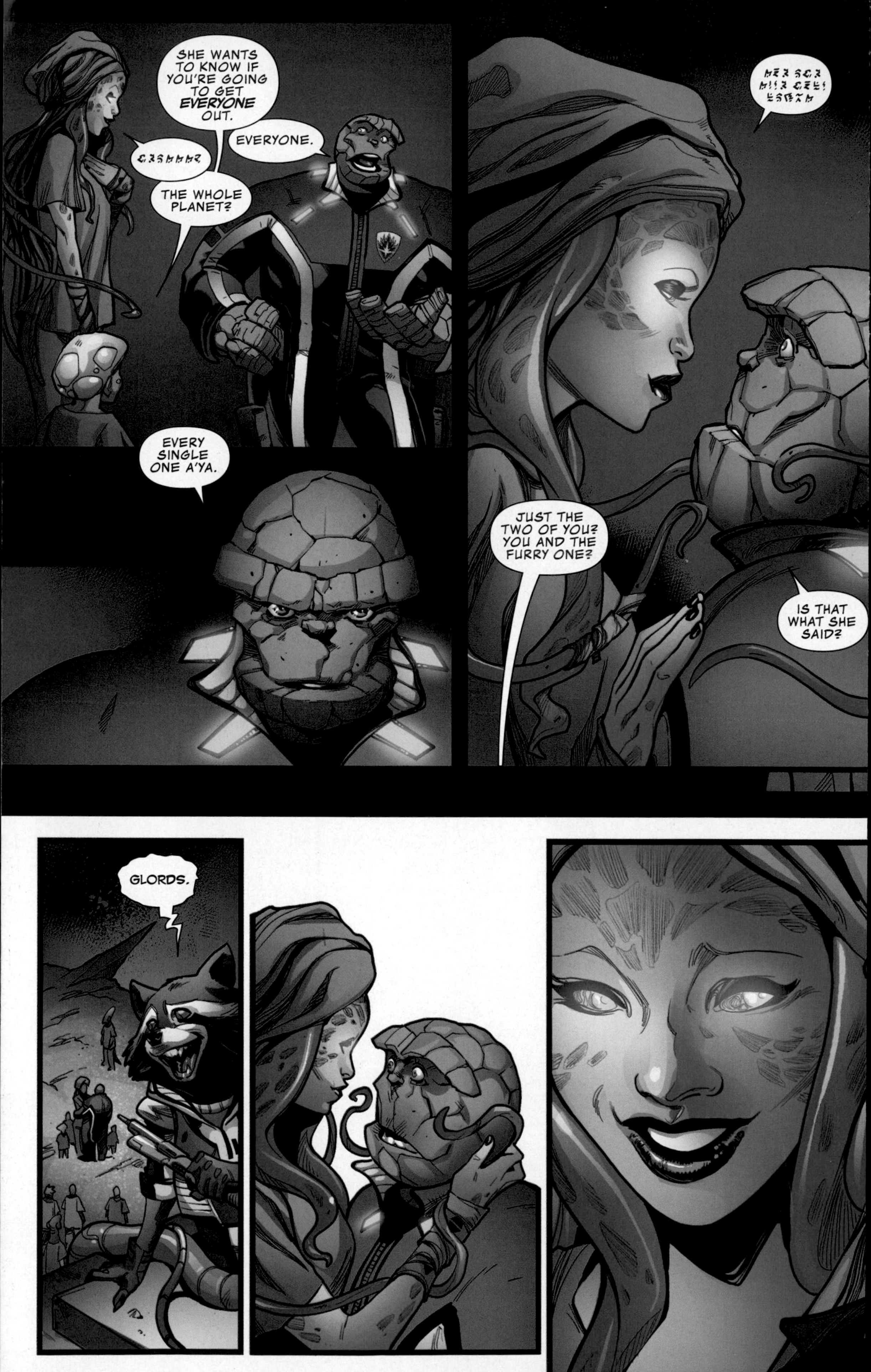
SHE WANTS TO KNOW IF YOU'RE GOING TO GET EVERYONE OUT.
EVERYONE.
THE WHOLE PLANET?
EVERY SINGLE ONE A'YA.
JUST THE TWO OF YOU? YOU AND THE FURRY ONE?
IS THAT WHAT SHE SAID?
GLORDS.

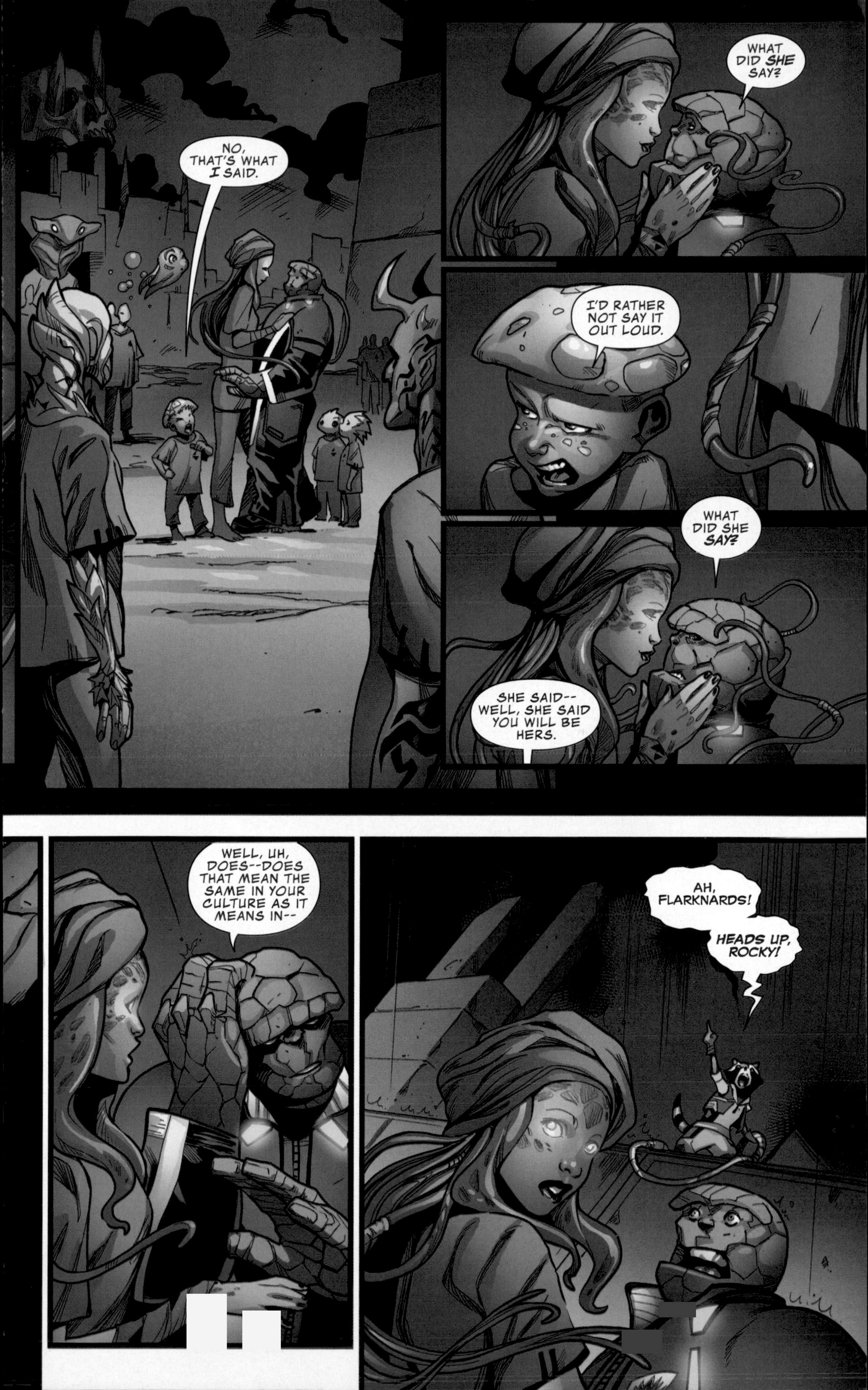
NO, THAT'S WHAT I SAID.
WHAT DID SHE SAY?
I'D RATHER NOT SAY IT OUT LOUD.
WHAT DID SHE SAY?
SHE SAID-- WELL, SHE SAID YOU WILL BE HERS.
WELL, UH, DOES--DOES THAT MEAN THE SAME IN YOUR CULTURE AS IT MEANS IN--
AH, FLARKNARDS!
HEADS UP, ROCKY!

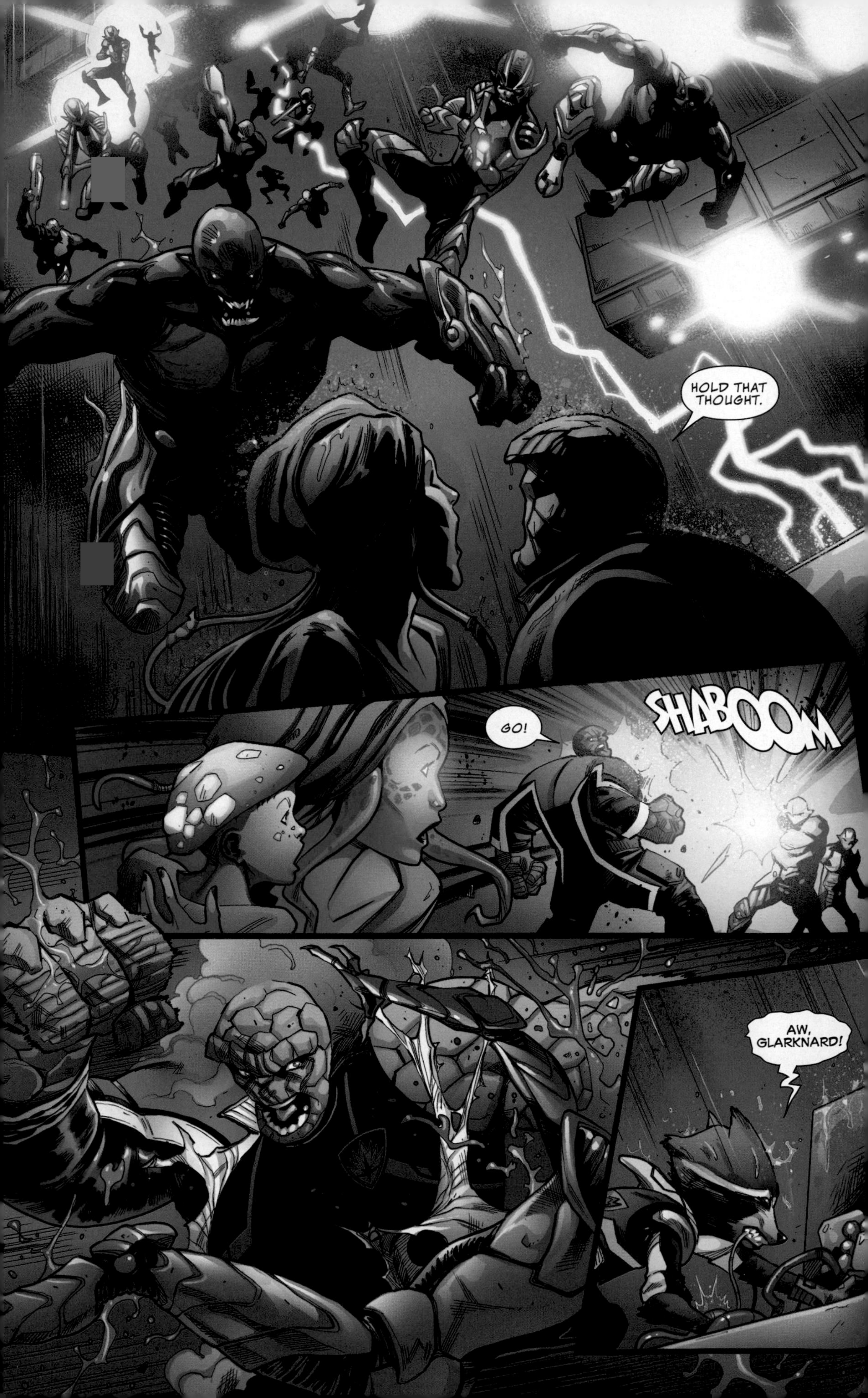
HOLD THAT THOUGHT.
GO!
SHABOOM
AW, GLARKNARD!

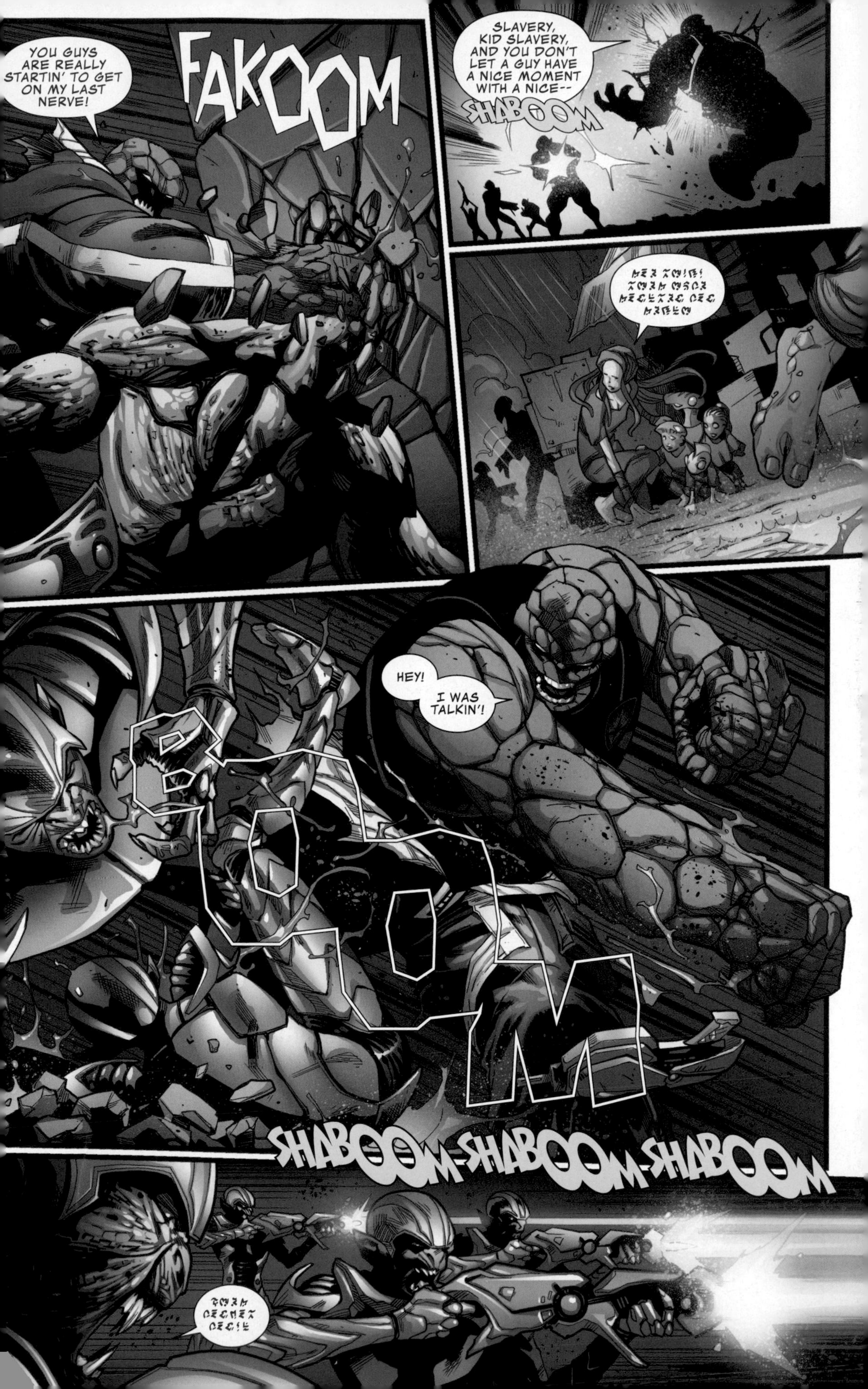
YOU GUYS ARE REALLY STARTIN' TO GET ON MY LAST NERVE!
FAKOOM
SLAVERY, KID SLAVERY, AND YOU DON'T LET A GUY HAVE A NICE MOMENT WITH A NICE--
SHABOOM
HEY! I WAS TALKIN'!
BOOM
SHABOOM-SHABOOM-SHABOOM

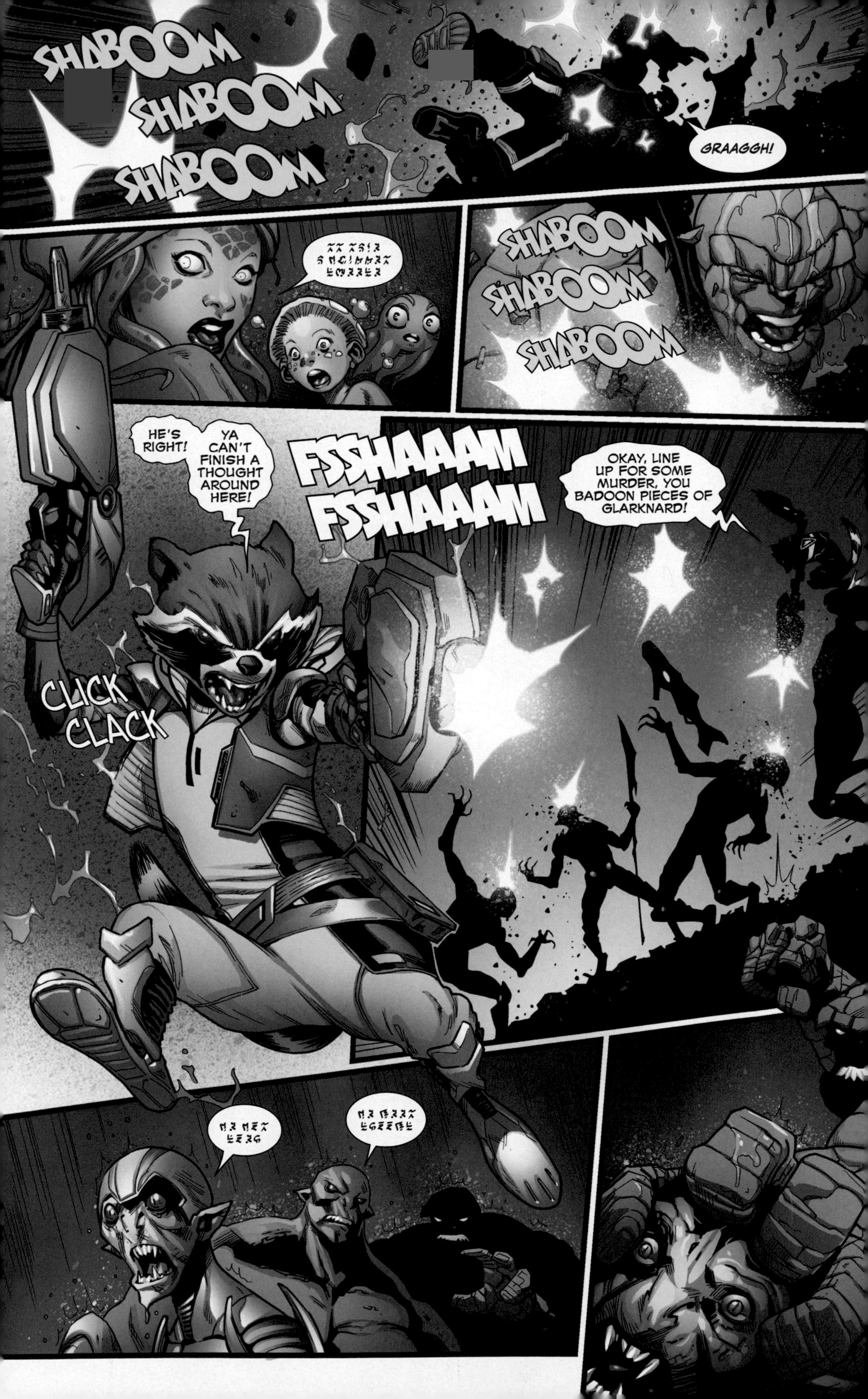
SHABOOM
SHABOOM
SHABOOM
GRAAGGH!
SHABOOM
SHABOOM
SHABOOM
HE'S RIGHT!
YA CAN'T FINISH A THOUGHT AROUND HERE!
CLICK CLACK
FSSHAAAM
FSSHAAAM
OKAY, LINE UP FOR SOME MURDER, YOU BADOON PIECES OF GLARKNARD!

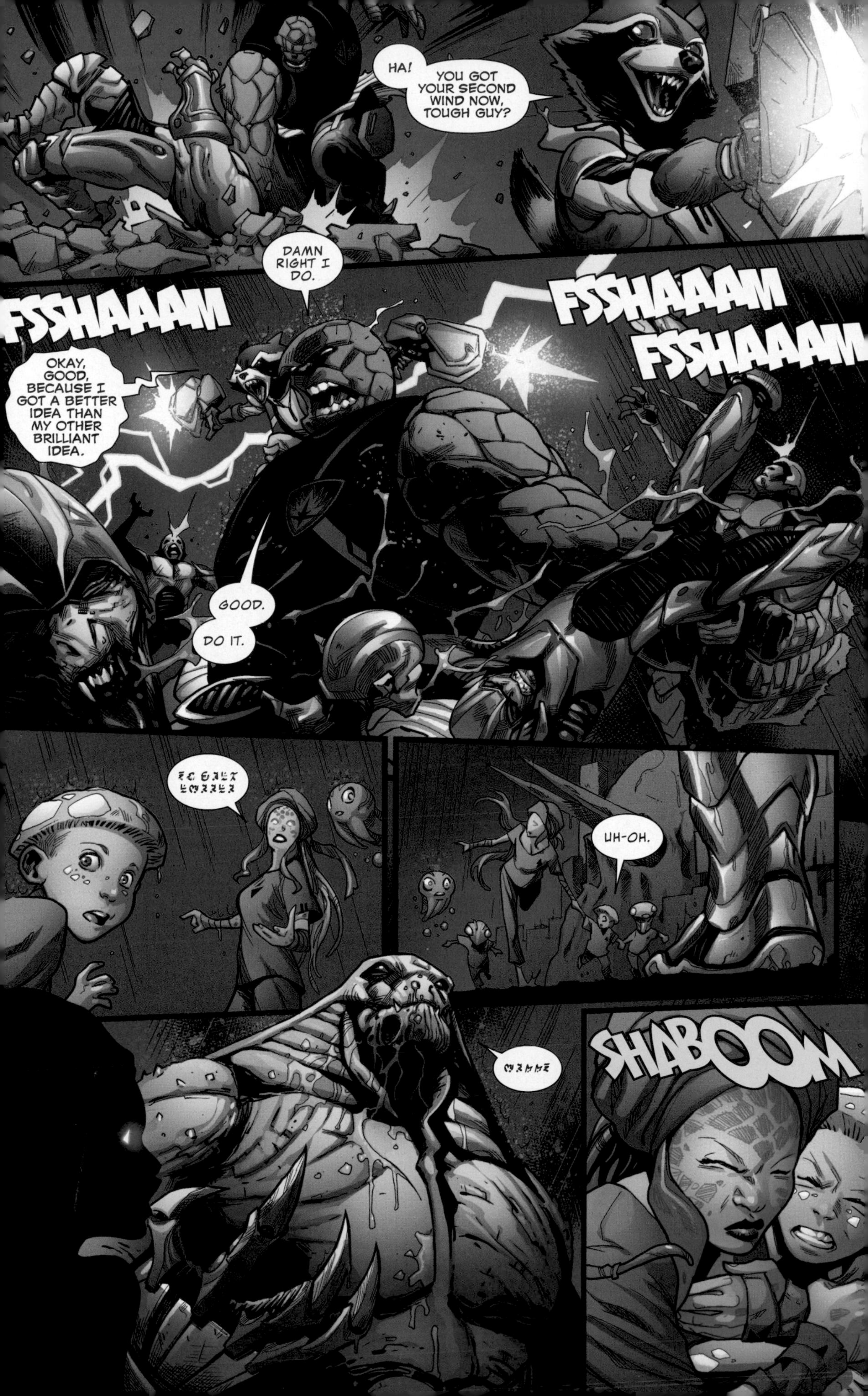
HA!
YOU GOT YOUR SECOND WIND NOW, TOUGH GUY?
DAMN RIGHT I DO.
FSSHAAAM
FSSHAAAM
FSSHAAAM
OKAY, GOOD, BECAUSE I GOT A BETTER IDEA THAN MY OTHER BRILLIANT IDEA.
GOOD.
DO IT.
UH-OH.
SHABOOM

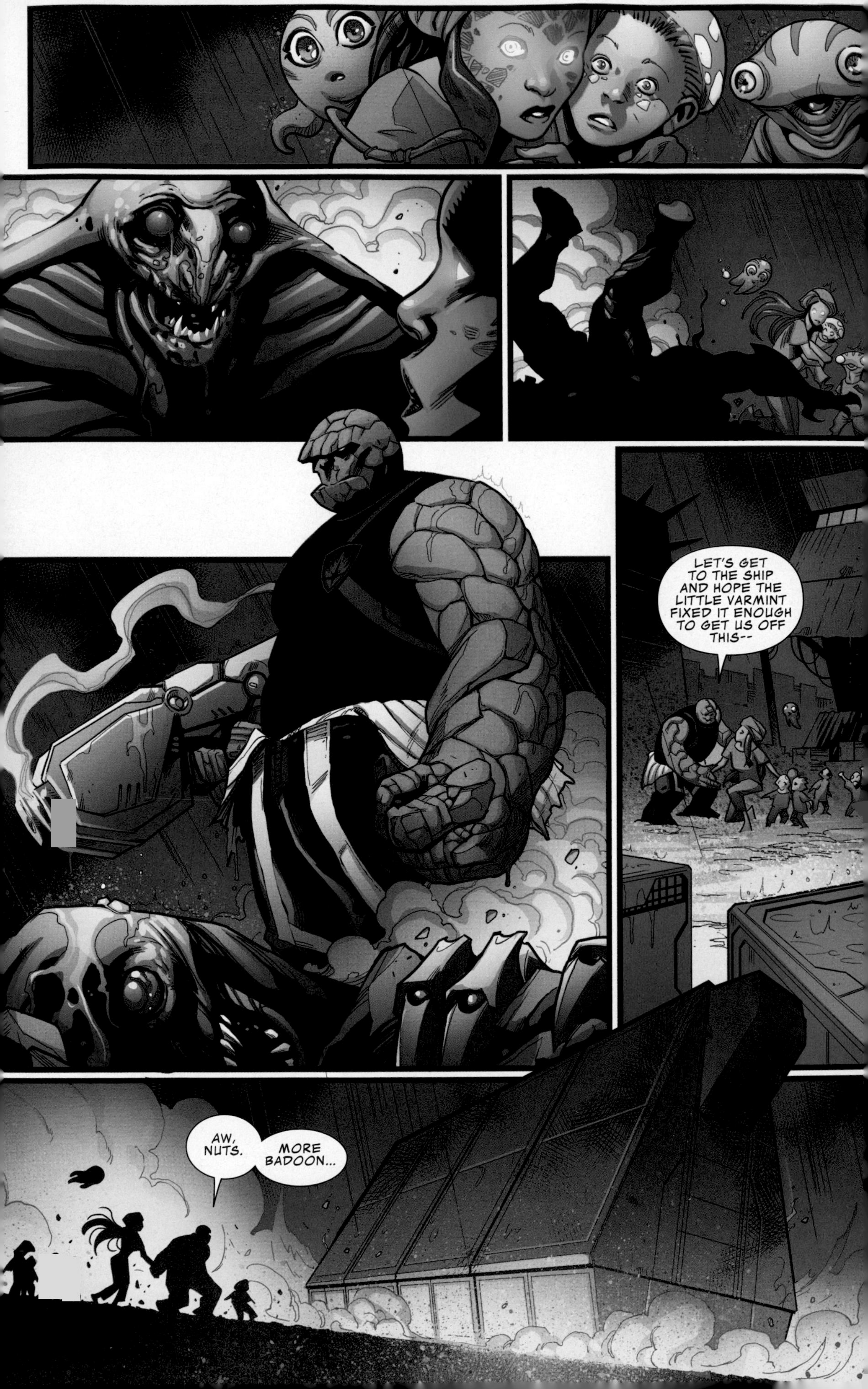
LET'S GET TO THE SHIP AND HOPE THE LITTLE VARMINT FIXED IT ENOUGH TO GET US OFF THIS--
AW, NUTS.
MORE BADOON...

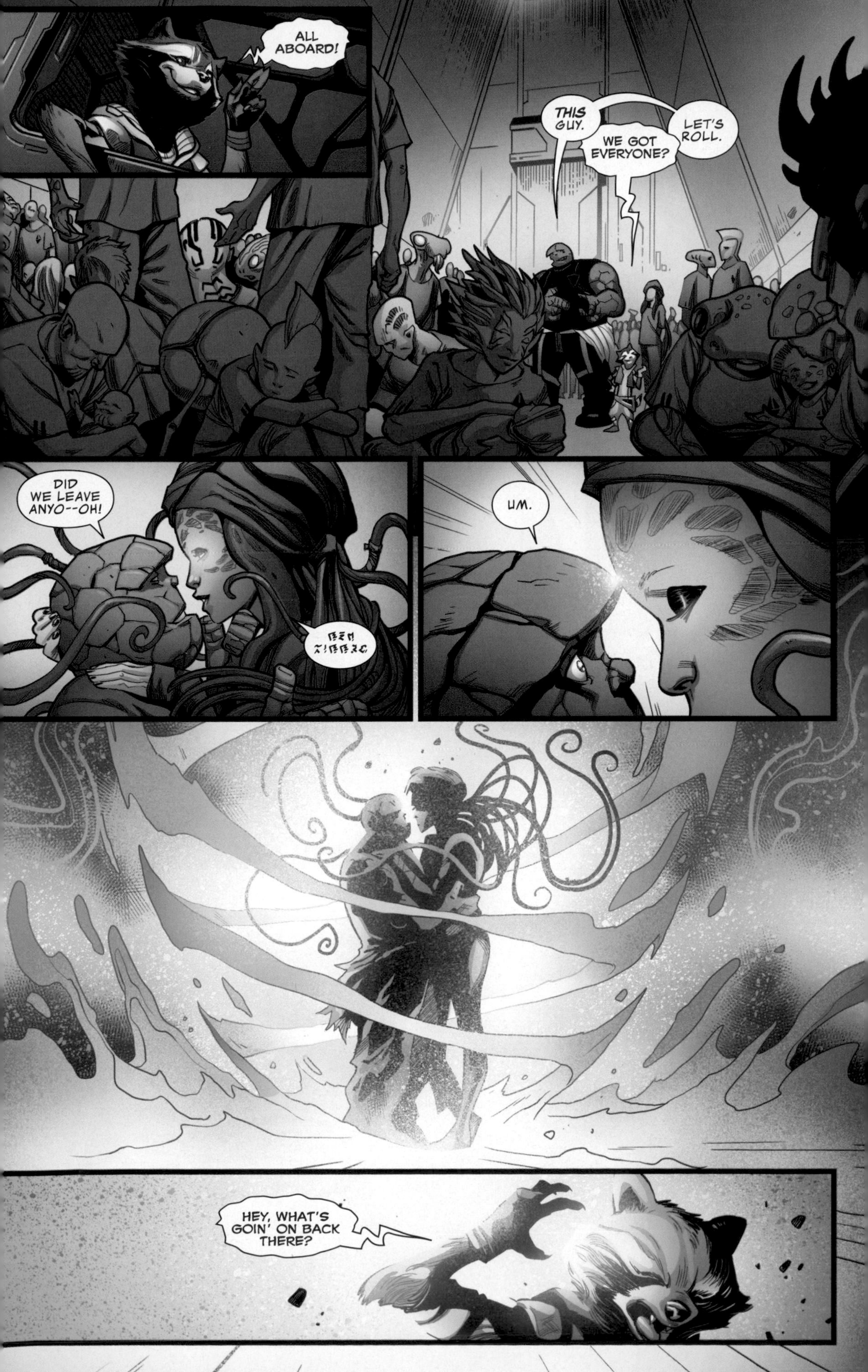
ALL ABOARD!
THIS GUY.
WE GOT EVERYONE?
LET'S ROLL.
DID WE LEAVE ANYO--OH!
UM.
HEY, WHAT'S GOIN' ON BACK THERE?

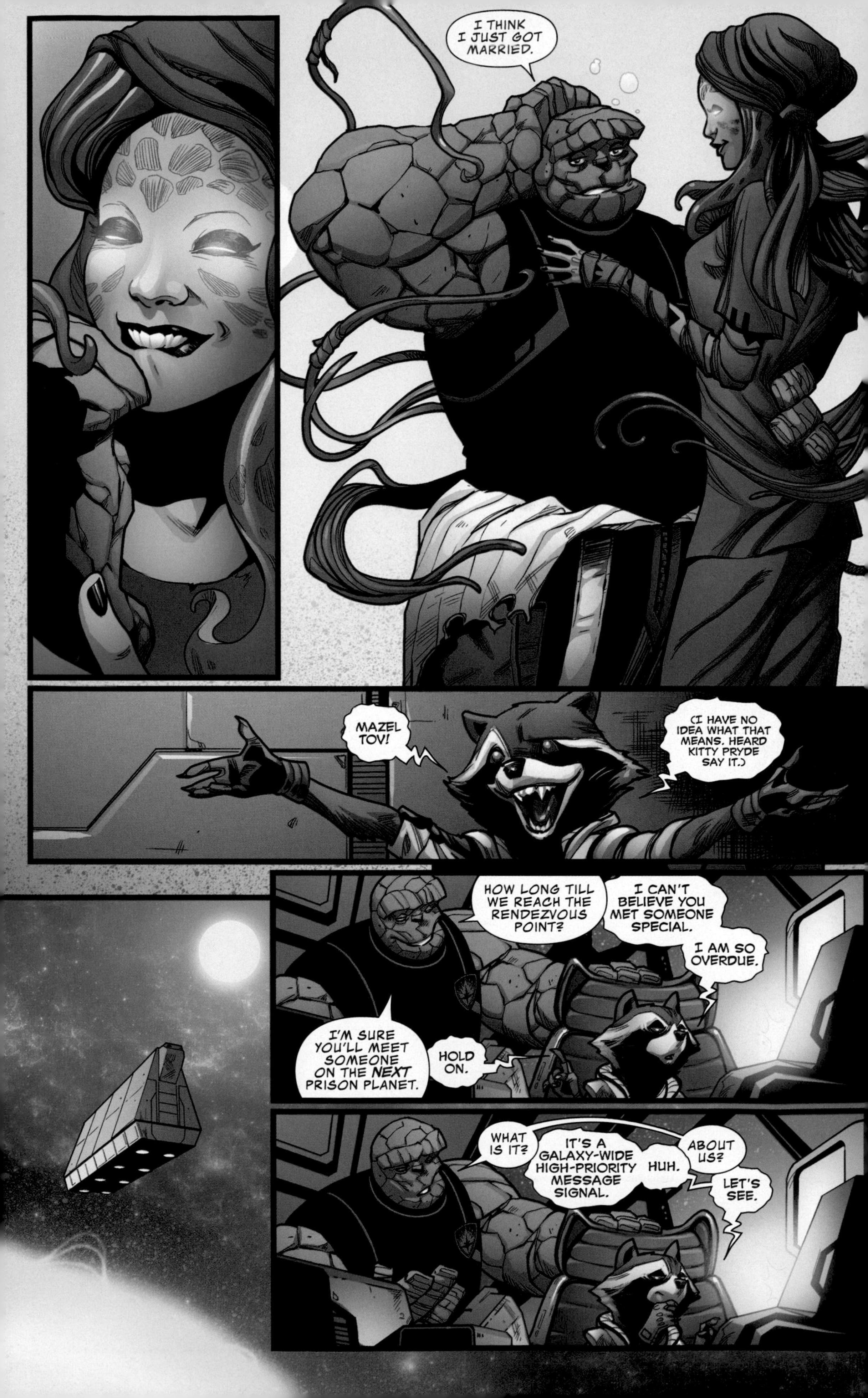
I THINK I JUST GOT MARRIED.
MAZEL TOV!
(I HAVE NO IDEA WHAT THAT MEANS. HEARD KITTY PRYDE SAY IT.)
HOW LONG TILL WE REACH THE RENDEZVOUS POINT?
I CAN'T BELIEVE YOU MET SOMEONE SPECIAL.
I AM SO OVERDUE.
I'M SURE YOU'LL MEET SOMEONE ON THE *NEXT* PRISON PLANET.
HOLD ON.
WHAT IS IT?
IT'S A GALAXY-WIDE HIGH-PRIORITY MESSAGE SIGNAL.
HUH.
ABOUT US?
LET'S SEE.

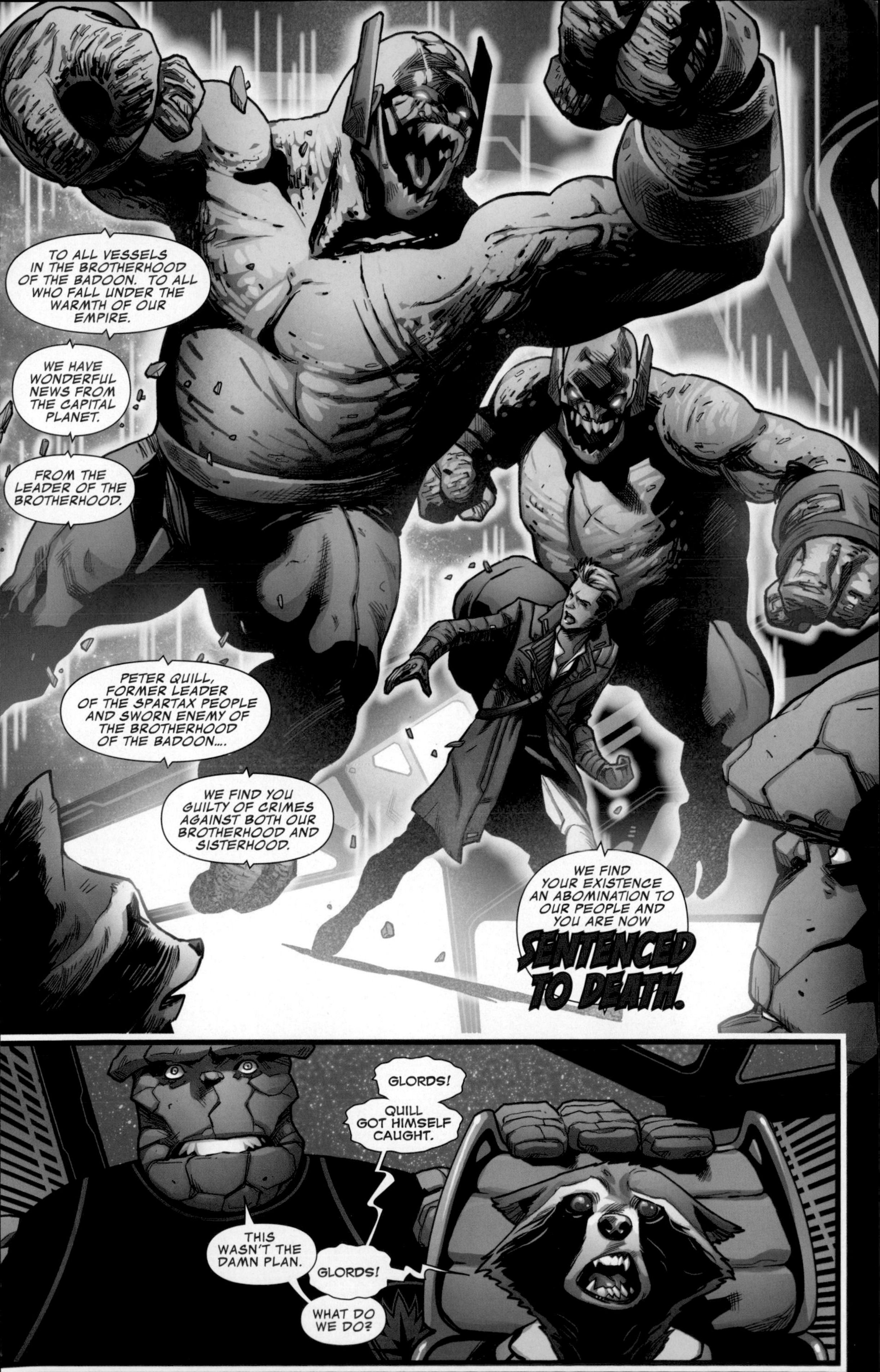

TO ALL VESSELS IN THE BROTHERHOOD OF THE BADOON. TO ALL WHO FALL UNDER THE WARMTH OF OUR EMPIRE.
WE HAVE WONDERFUL NEWS FROM THE CAPITAL PLANET.
FROM THE LEADER OF THE BROTHERHOOD.
PETER QUILL, FORMER LEADER OF THE SPARTAX PEOPLE AND SWORN ENEMY OF THE BROTHERHOOD OF THE BADOON....
WE FIND YOU GUILTY OF CRIMES AGAINST BOTH OUR BROTHERHOOD AND SISTERHOOD.
WE FIND YOUR EXISTENCE AN ABOMINATION TO OUR PEOPLE AND YOU ARE NOW SENTENCED TO DEATH.
GLORDS!
QUILL GOT HIMSELF CAUGHT.
THIS WASN'T THE DAMN PLAN.
GLORDS!
WHAT DO WE DO?

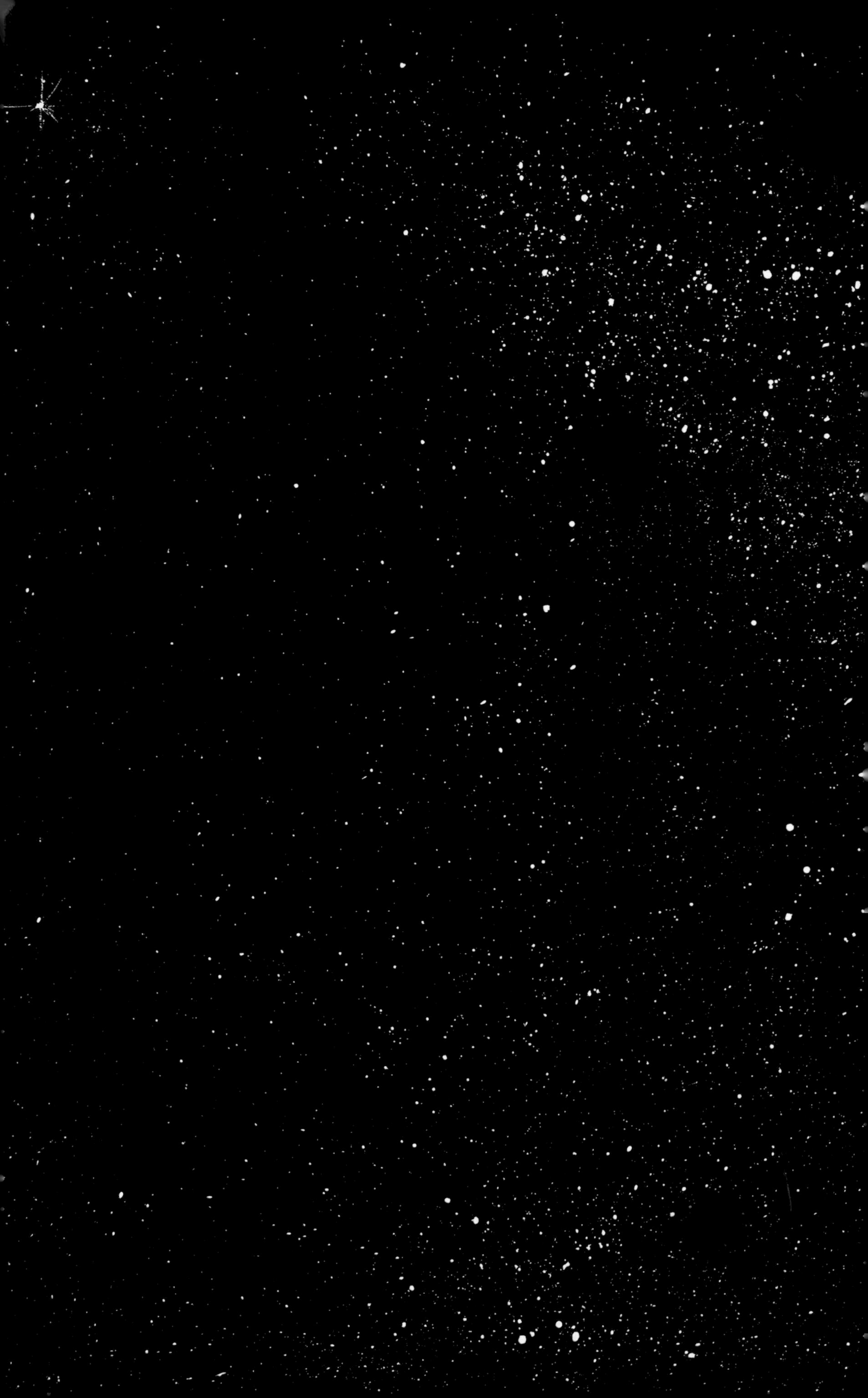

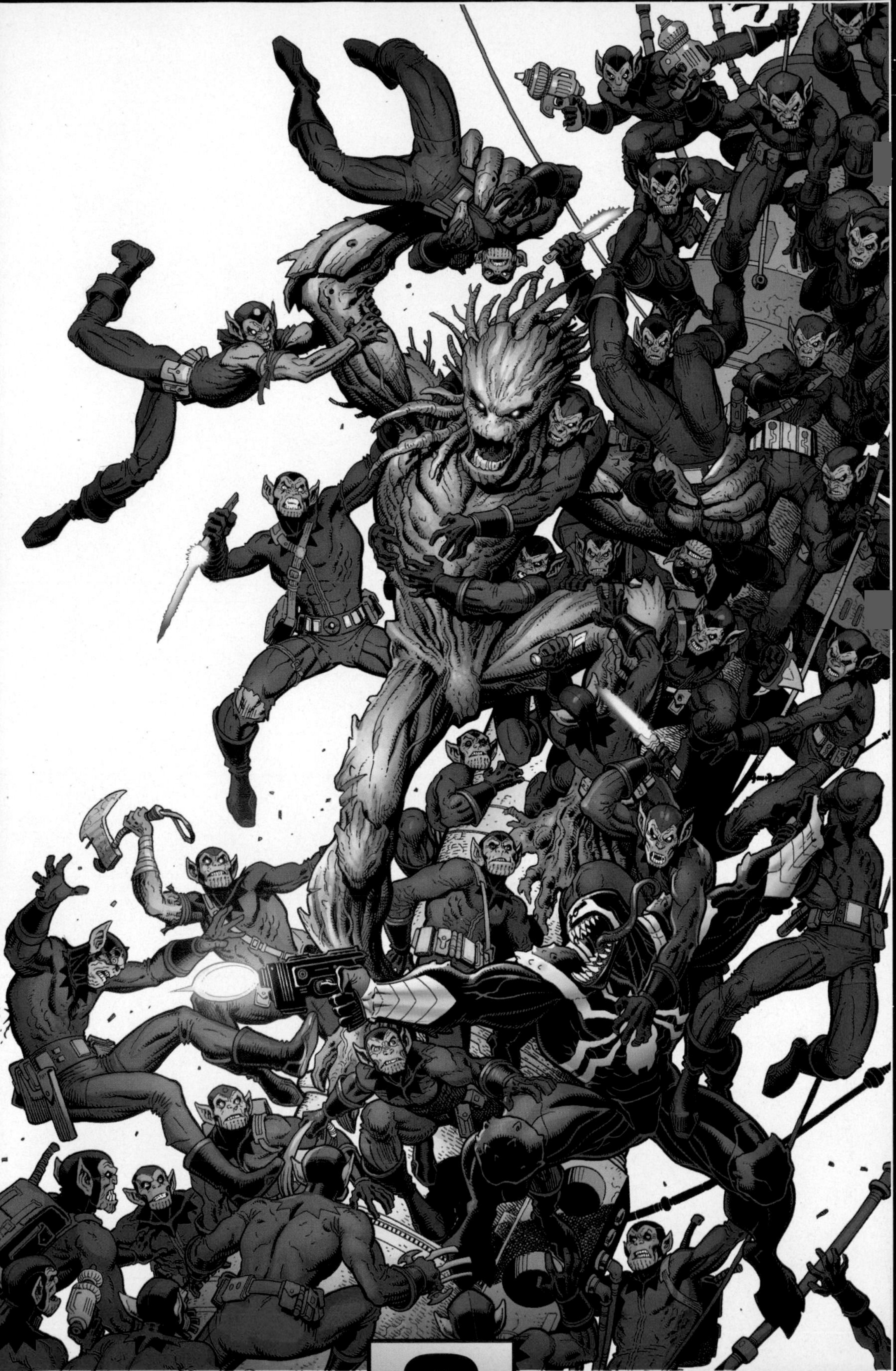

8

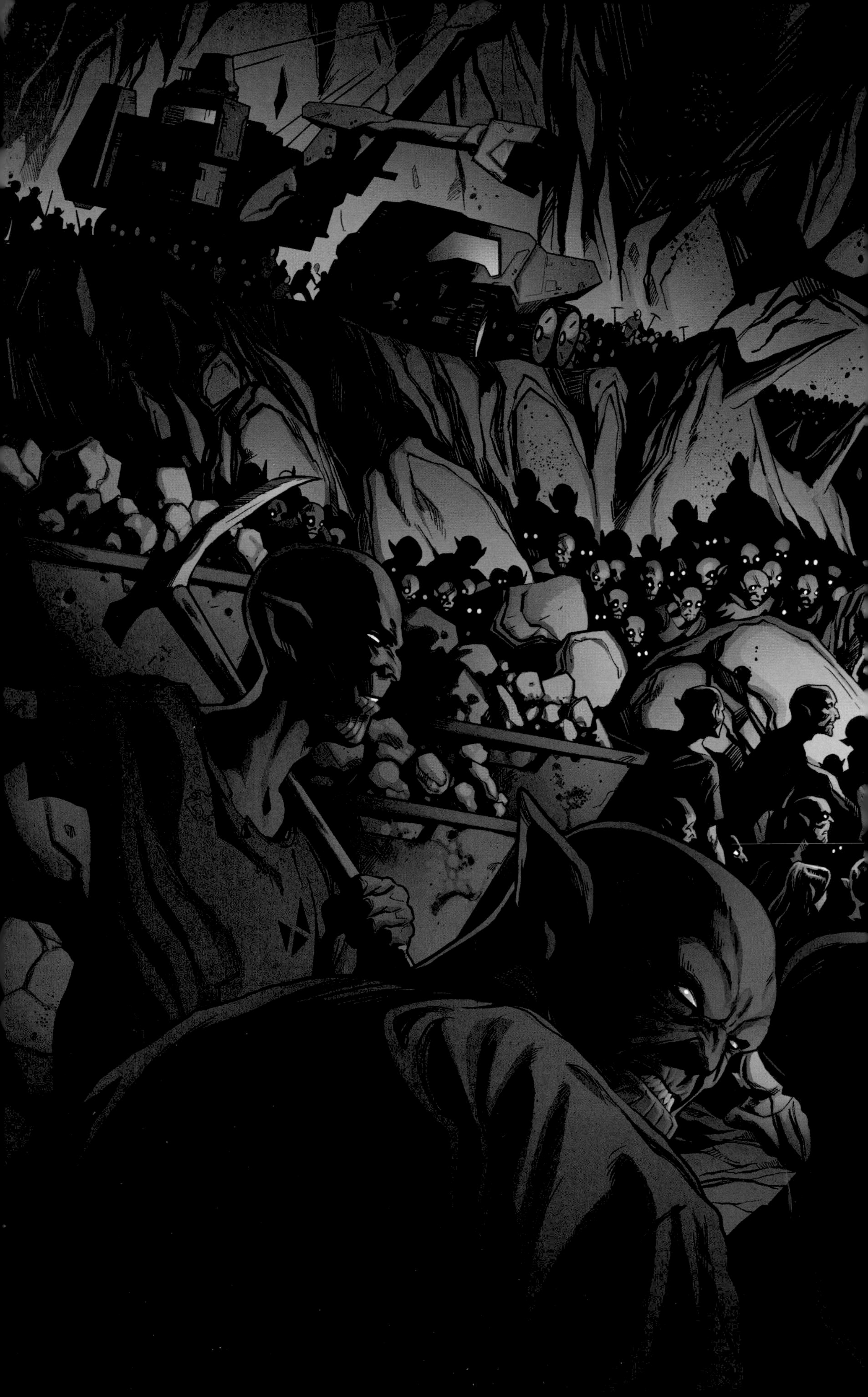

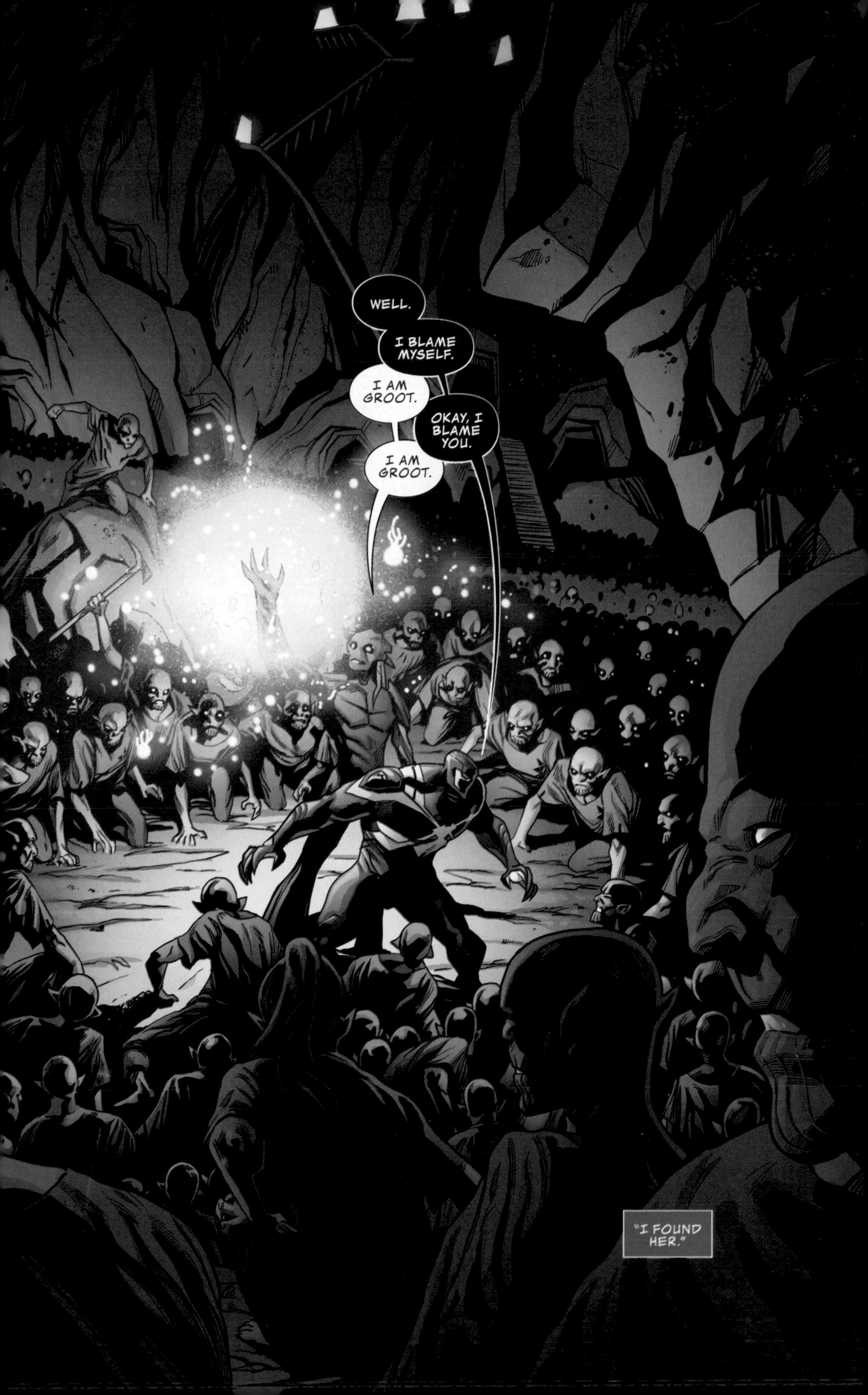
WELL.
I BLAME MYSELF.
I AM GROOT.
OKAY, I BLAME YOU.
I AM GROOT.
"I FOUND HER."

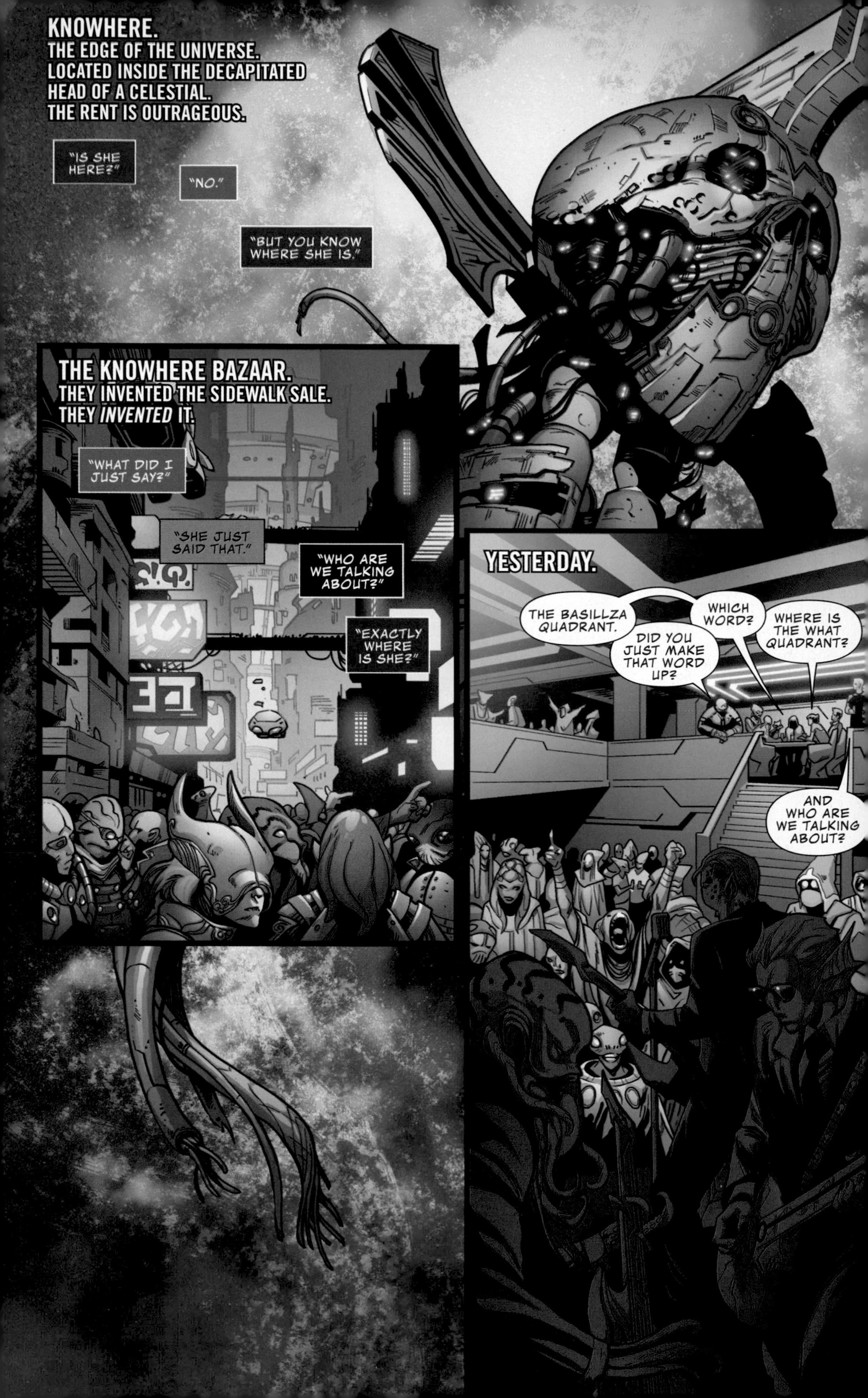
KNOWHERE.
THE EDGE OF THE UNIVERSE.
LOCATED INSIDE THE DECAPITATED HEAD OF A CELESTIAL.
THE RENT IS OUTRAGEOUS.
"IS SHE HERE?"
"NO."
"BUT YOU KNOW WHERE SHE IS."
THE KNOWHERE BAZAAR.
THEY INVENTED THE SIDEWALK SALE.
THEY INVENTED IT.
"WHAT DID I JUST SAY?"
"SHE JUST SAID THAT."
"WHO ARE WE TALKING ABOUT?"
"EXACTLY WHERE IS SHE?"
YESTERDAY.
THE BASILLZA QUADRANT.
DID YOU JUST MAKE THAT WORD UP?
WHICH WORD?
WHERE IS THE WHAT QUADRANT?
AND WHO ARE WE TALKING ABOUT?

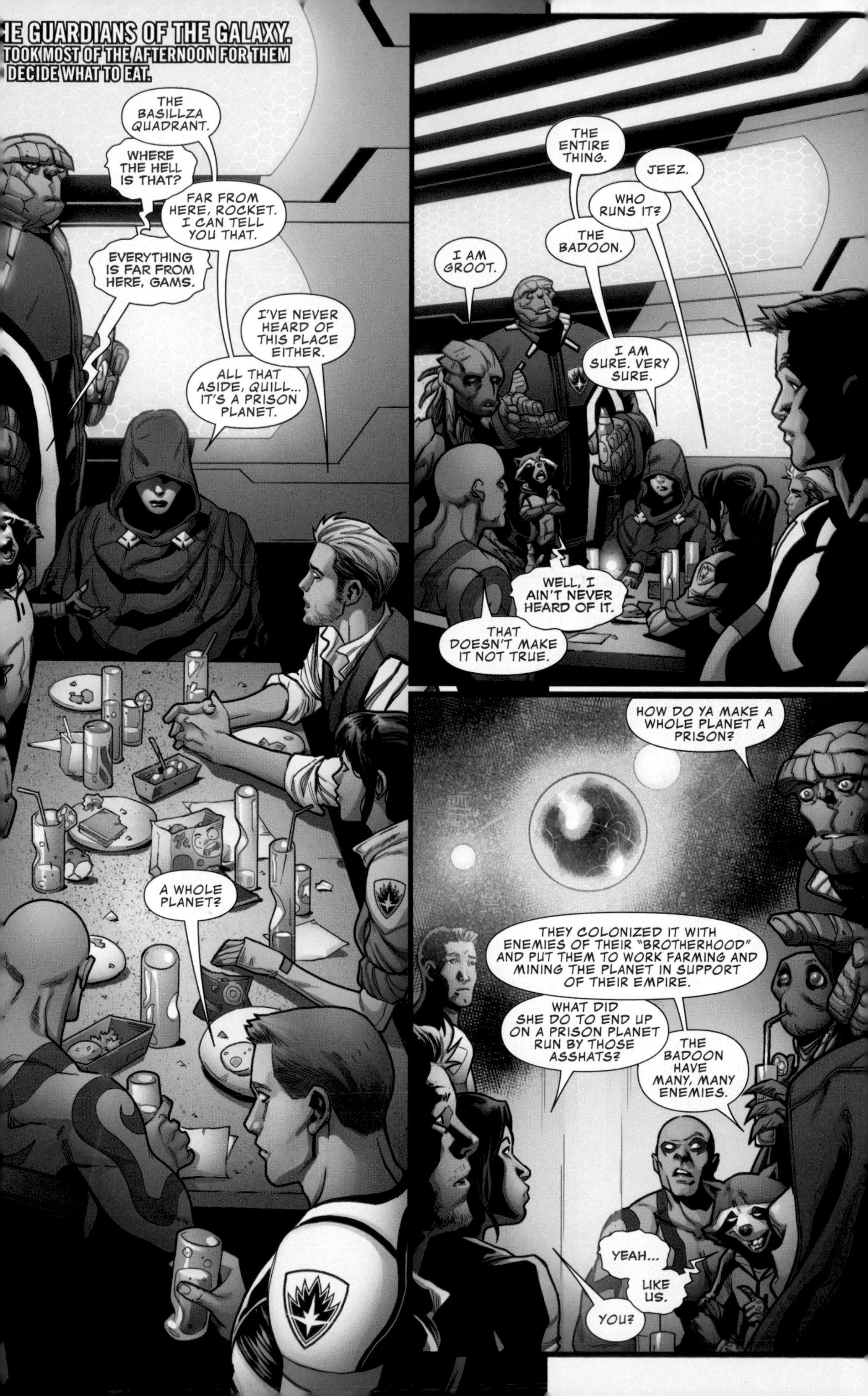

IE GUARDIANS OF THE GALAXY.
TOOK MOST OF THE AFTERNOON FOR THEM
DECIDE WHAT TO EAT.
THE BASILLZA QUADRANT.
WHERE THE HELL IS THAT?
FAR FROM HERE, ROCKET. I CAN TELL YOU THAT.
EVERYTHING IS FAR FROM HERE, GAMS.
I'VE NEVER HEARD OF THIS PLACE EITHER.
ALL THAT ASIDE, QUILL... IT'S A PRISON PLANET.
A WHOLE PLANET?
THE ENTIRE THING.
JEEZ.
WHO RUNS IT?
THE BADOON.
I AM GROOT.
I AM SURE. VERY SURE.
WELL, I AIN'T NEVER HEARD OF IT.
THAT DOESN'T MAKE IT NOT TRUE.
HOW DO YA MAKE A WHOLE PLANET A PRISON?
THEY COLONIZED IT WITH ENEMIES OF THEIR "BROTHERHOOD" AND PUT THEM TO WORK FARMING AND MINING THE PLANET IN SUPPORT OF THEIR EMPIRE.
WHAT DID SHE DO TO END UP ON A PRISON PLANET RUN BY THOSE ASSHATS?
THE BADOON HAVE MANY, MANY ENEMIES.
YEAH...
LIKE US.
YOU?

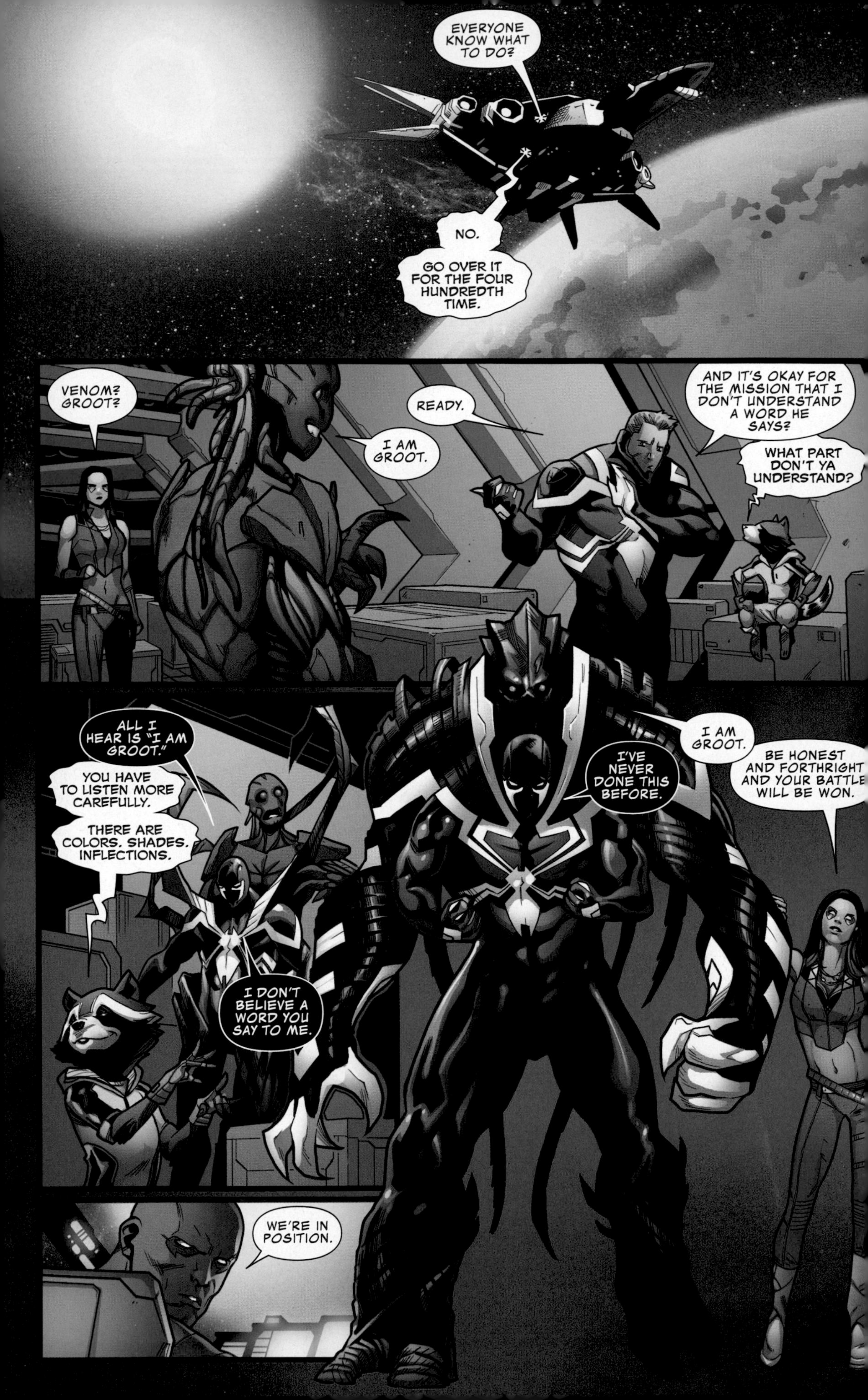
EVERYONE KNOW WHAT TO DO?
NO.
GO OVER IT FOR THE FOUR HUNDREDTH TIME.
VENOM? GROOT?
I AM GROOT.
READY.
AND IT'S OKAY FOR THE MISSION THAT I DON'T UNDERSTAND A WORD HE SAYS?
WHAT PART DON'T YA UNDERSTAND?
ALL I HEAR IS "I AM GROOT."
YOU HAVE TO LISTEN MORE CAREFULLY.
THERE ARE COLORS. SHADES. INFLECTIONS.
I DON'T BELIEVE A WORD YOU SAY TO ME.
I AM GROOT.
I'VE NEVER DONE THIS BEFORE.
BE HONEST AND FORTHRIGHT AND YOUR BATTLE WILL BE WON.
WE'RE IN POSITION.

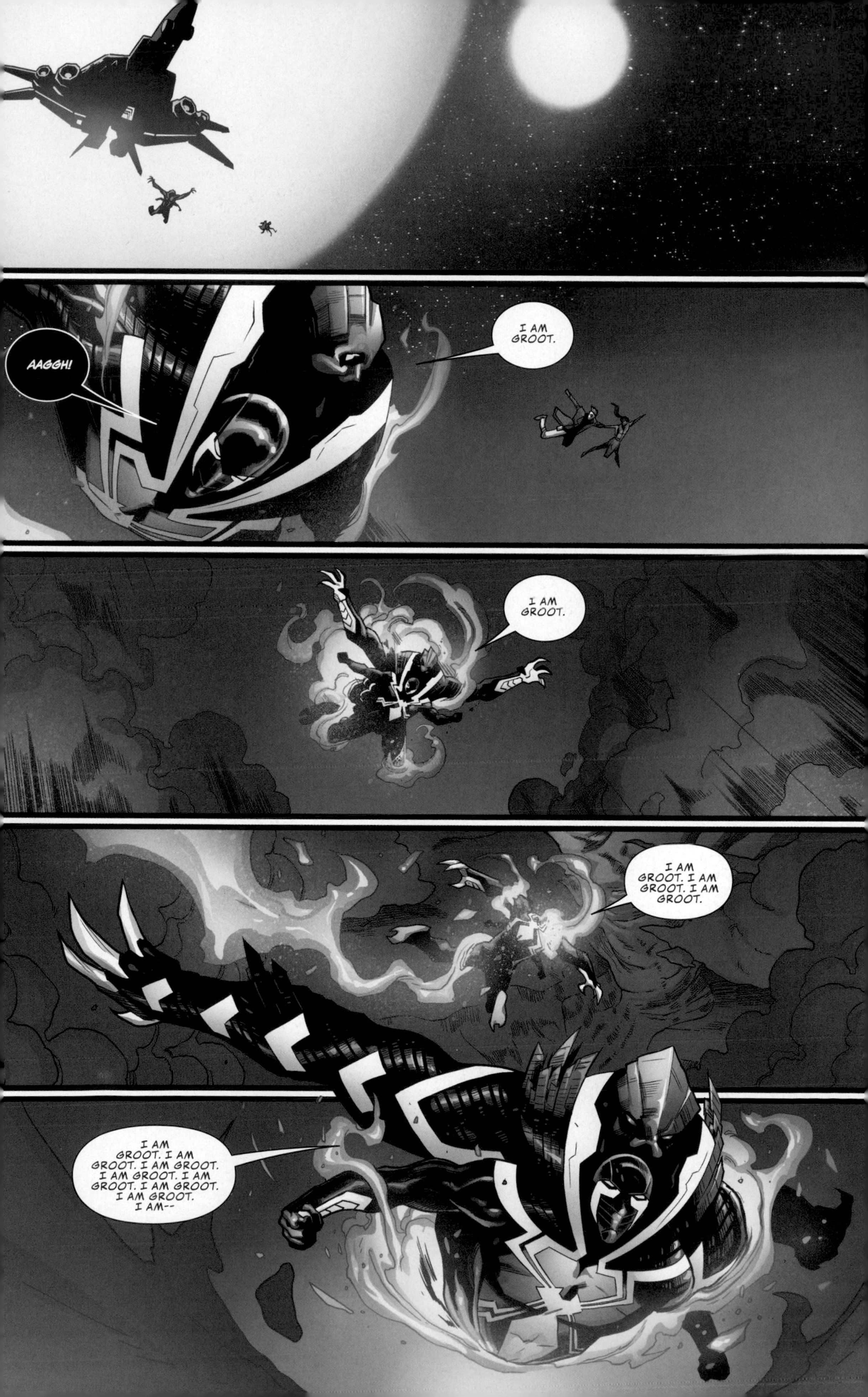
AAGGH!
I AM GROOT.
I AM GROOT.
I AM GROOT. I AM GROOT. I AM GROOT.
I AM GROOT. I AM GROOT. I AM GROOT. I AM GROOT. I AM GROOT. I AM GROOT. I AM GROOT. I AM--

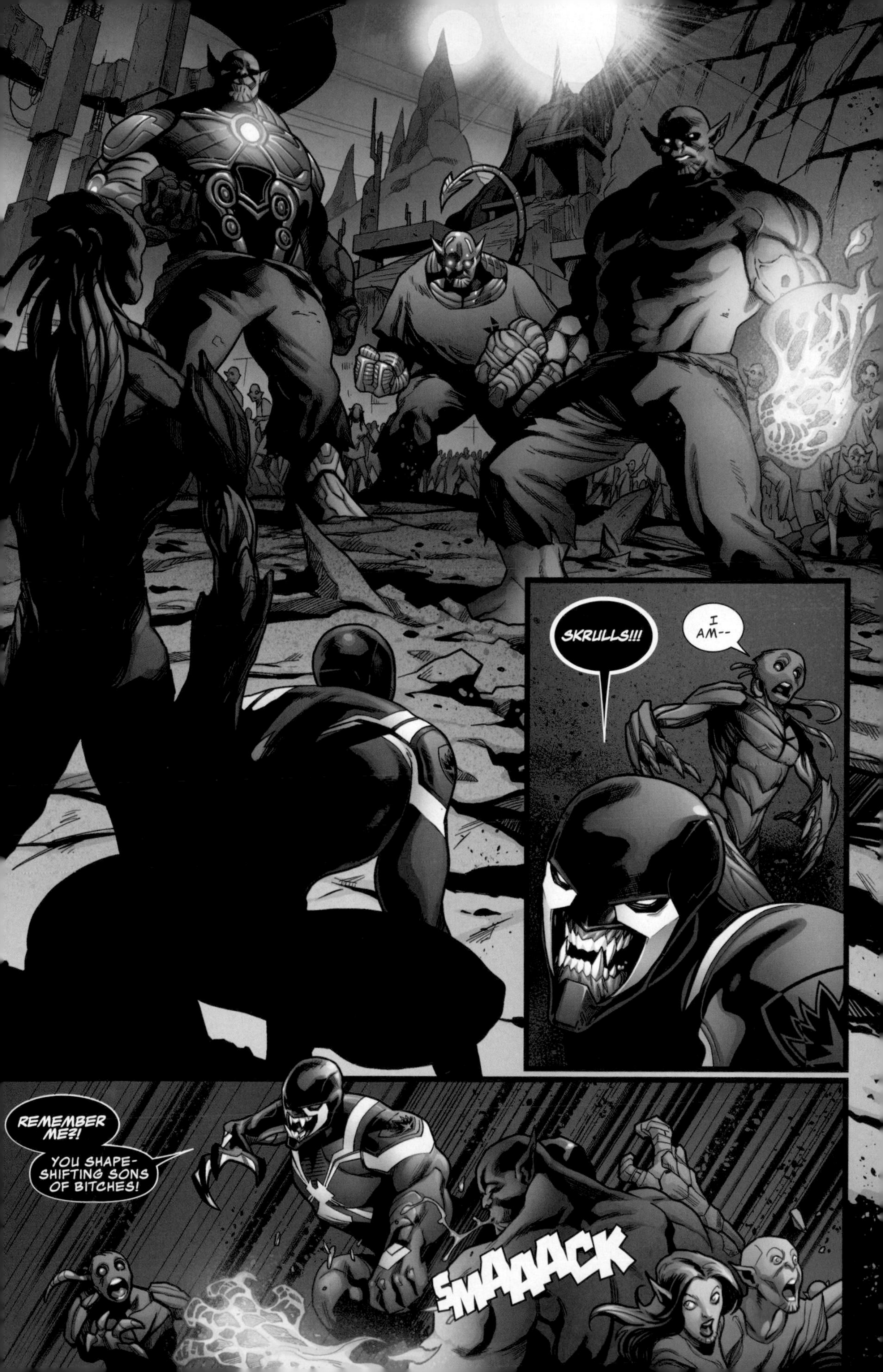
SKRULLS!!!
I AM--
REMEMBER ME?!
YOU SHAPE-SHIFTING SONS OF BITCHES!
SMAAACK

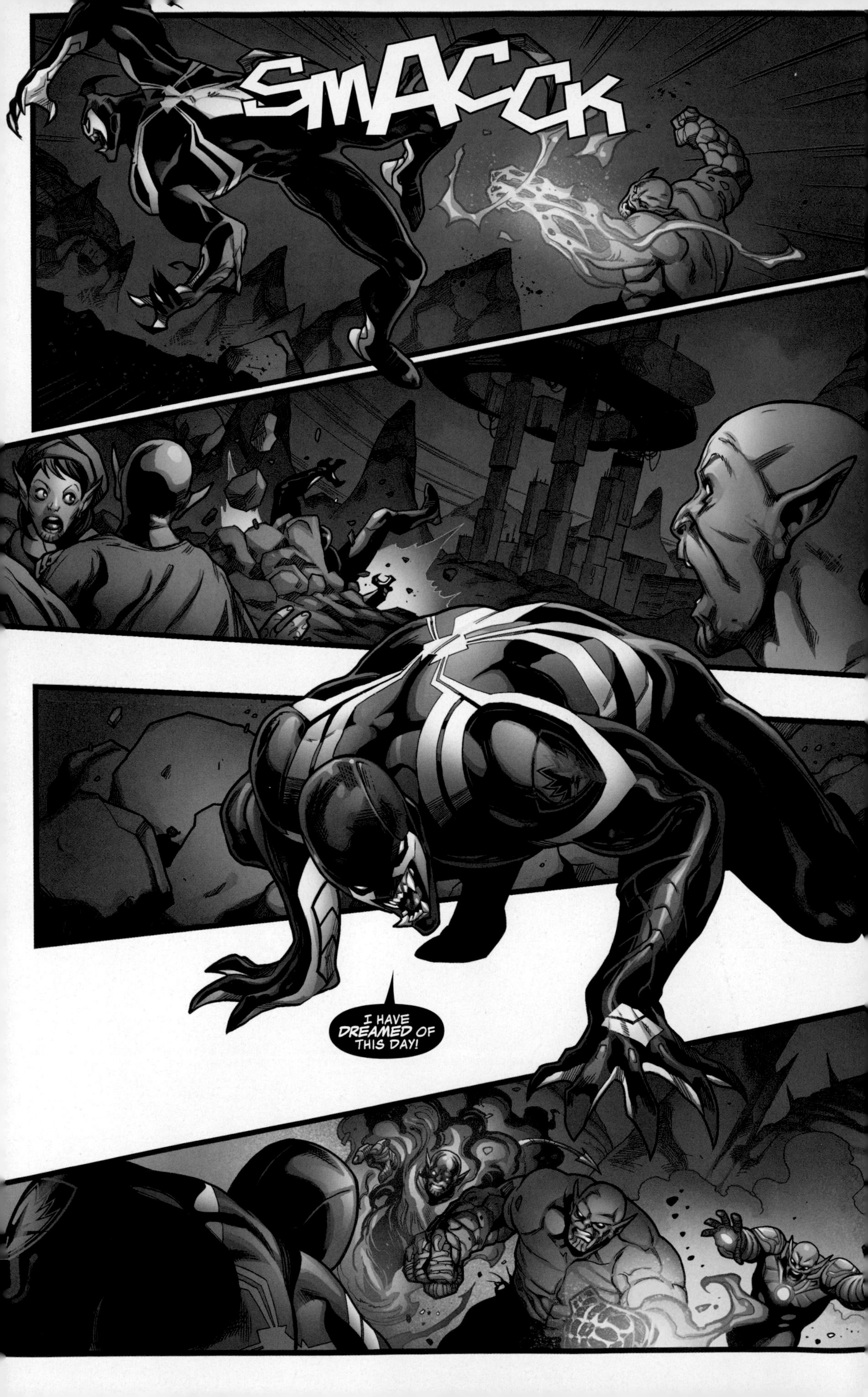
SMACCK
I HAVE DREAMED OF THIS DAY!

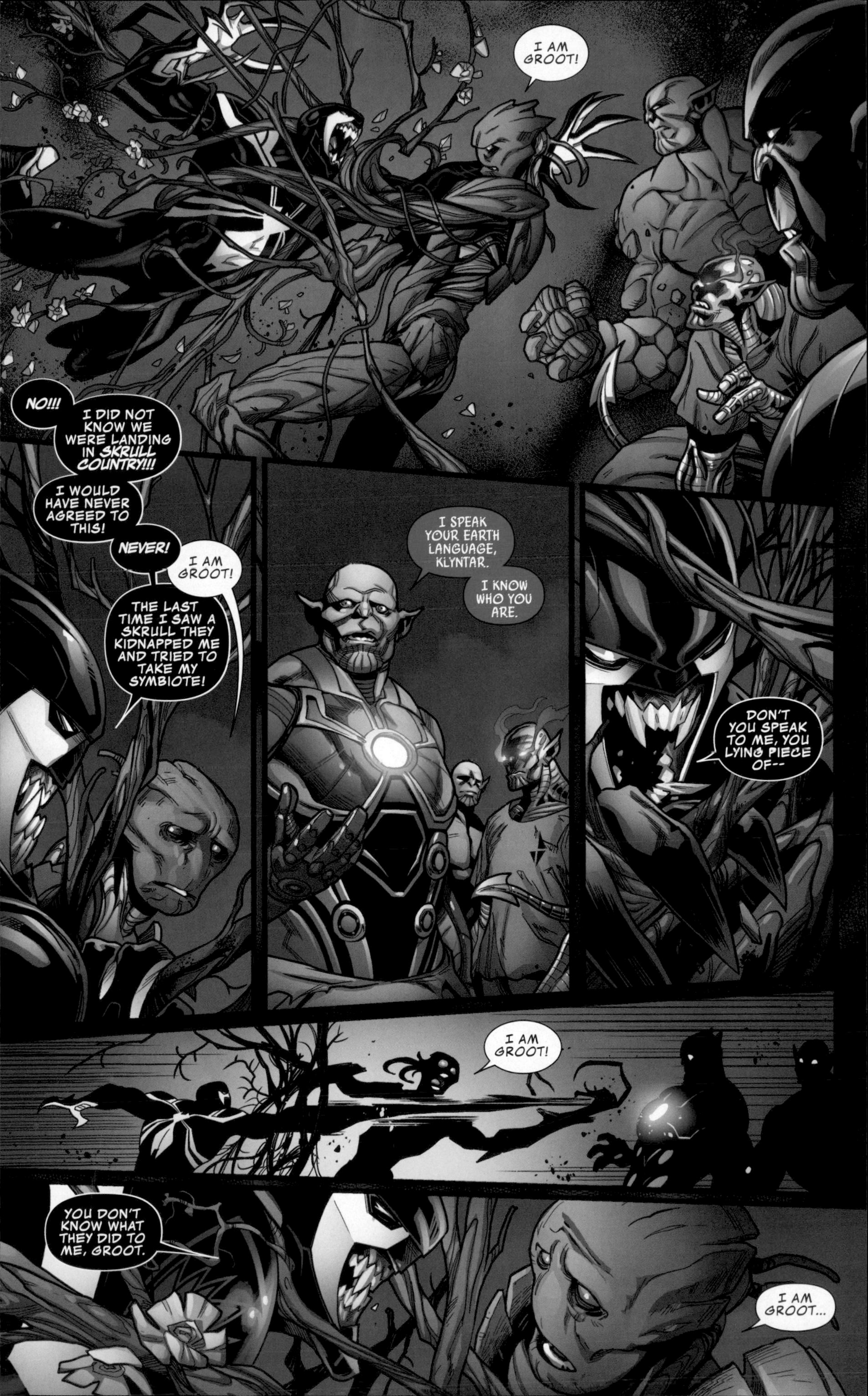
I AM GROOT!
NO!!!
I DID NOT KNOW WE WERE LANDING IN SKRULL COUNTRY!!!
I WOULD HAVE NEVER AGREED TO THIS!
NEVER!
I AM GROOT!
THE LAST TIME I SAW A SKRULL THEY KIDNAPPED ME AND TRIED TO TAKE MY SYMBIOTE!
I SPEAK YOUR EARTH LANGUAGE, KLYNTAR.
I KNOW WHO YOU ARE.
DON'T YOU SPEAK TO ME, YOU LYING PIECE OF--
I AM GROOT!
YOU DON'T KNOW WHAT THEY DID TO ME, GROOT.
I AM GROOT...

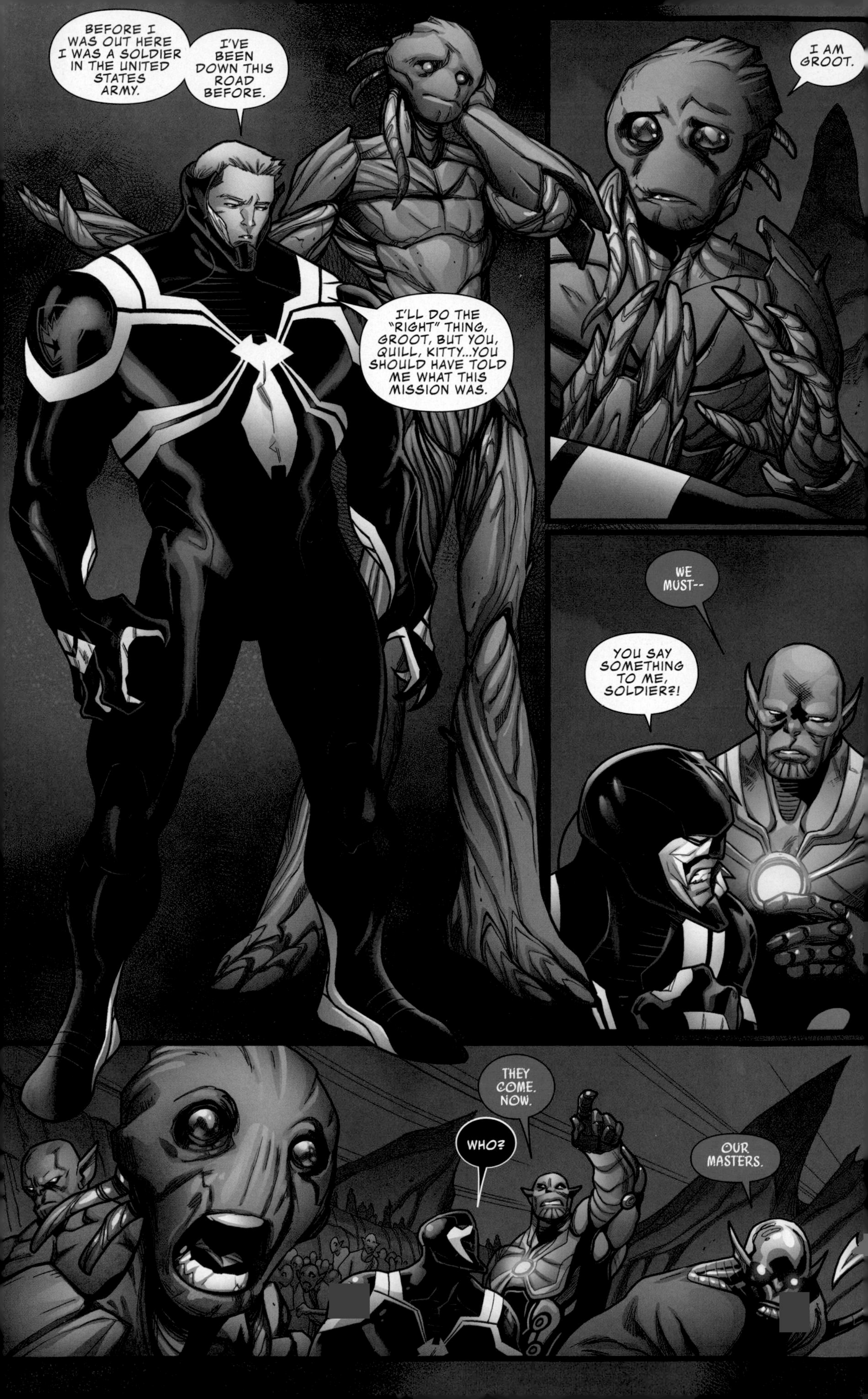
BEFORE I WAS OUT HERE I WAS A SOLDIER IN THE UNITED STATES ARMY.
I'VE BEEN DOWN THIS ROAD BEFORE.
I'LL DO THE "RIGHT" THING, GROOT, BUT YOU, QUILL, KITTY...YOU SHOULD HAVE TOLD ME WHAT THIS MISSION WAS.
I AM GROOT.
WE MUST--
YOU SAY SOMETHING TO ME, SOLDIER?!
THEY COME. NOW.
WHO?
OUR MASTERS.

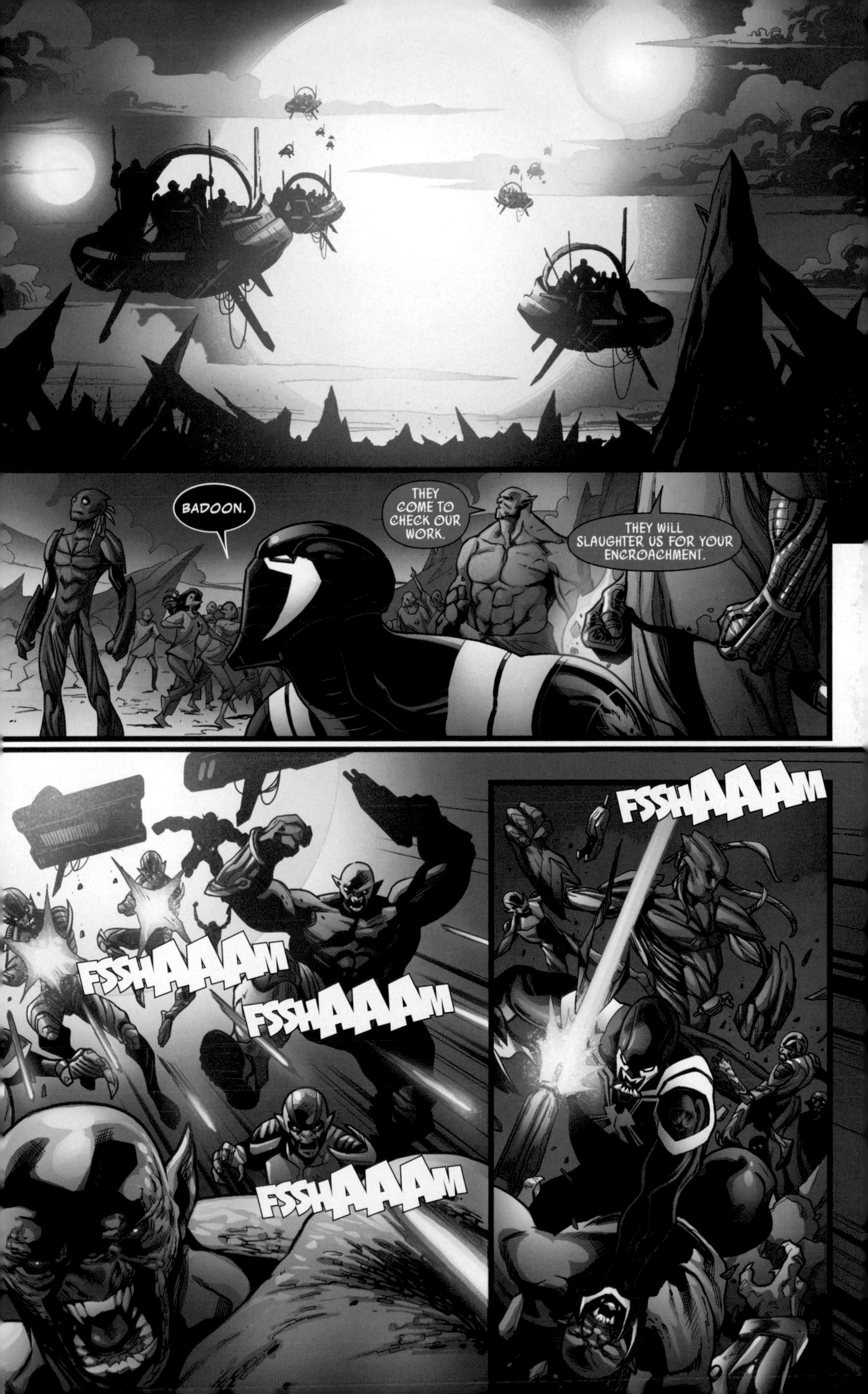
BADOON.
THEY COME TO CHECK OUR WORK.
THEY WILL SLAUGHTER US FOR YOUR ENCROACHMENT.
FSSHAAAAM
FSSHAAAM
FSSHAAAM
FSSHAAAM

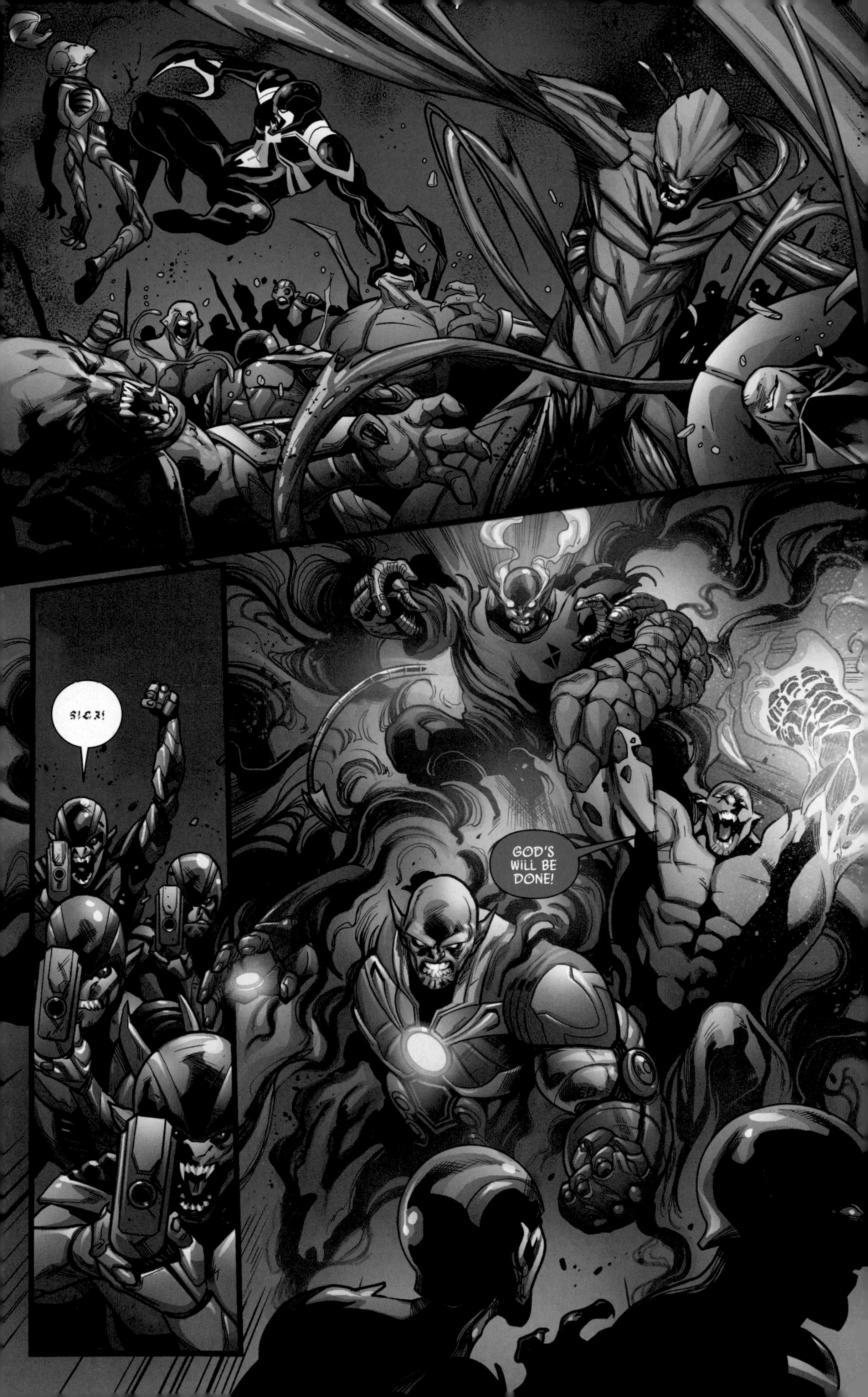
GOD'S WILL BE DONE!

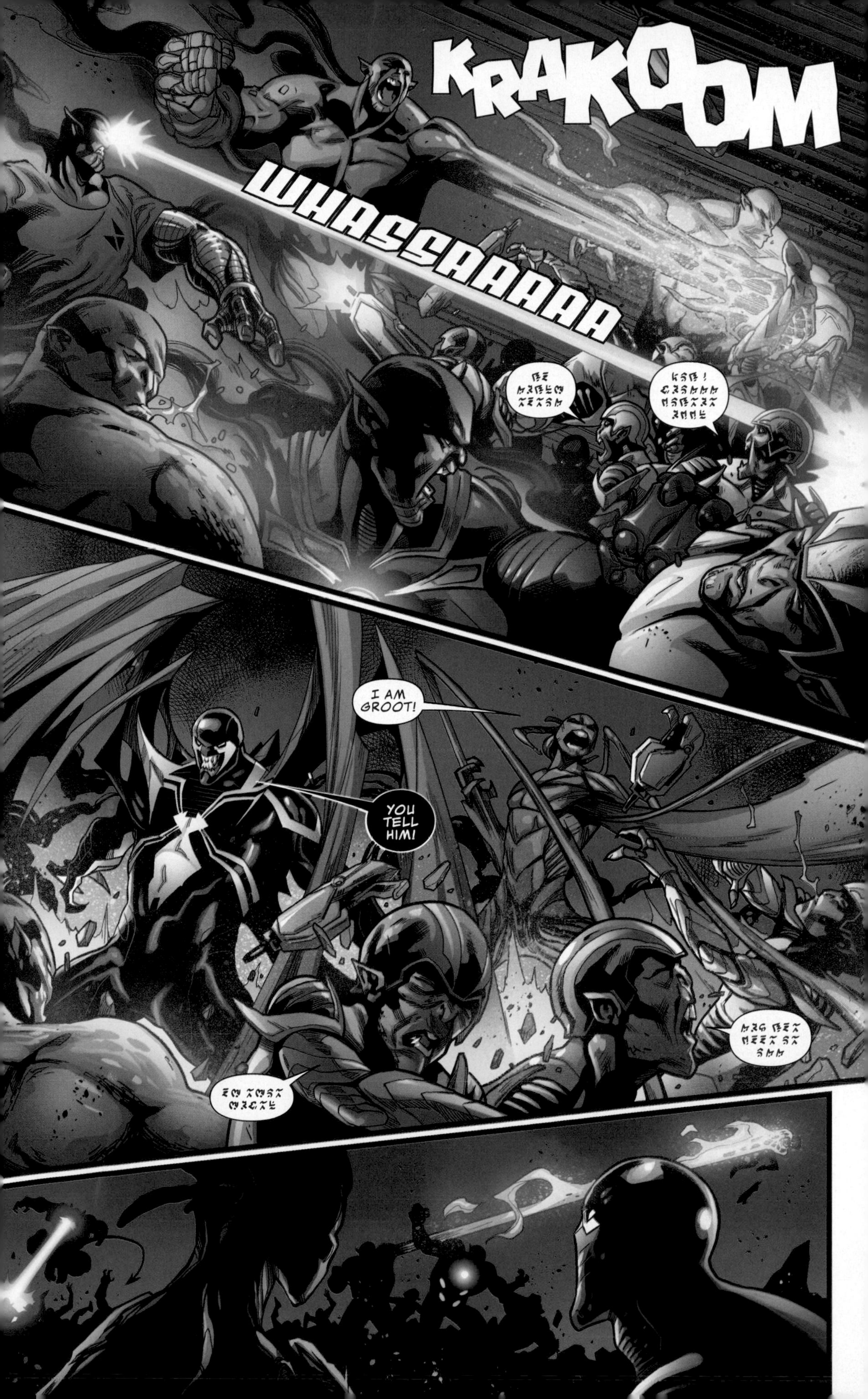
KRAKOOOM
WHASSAAAAA
I AM GROOT!
YOU TELL HIM!

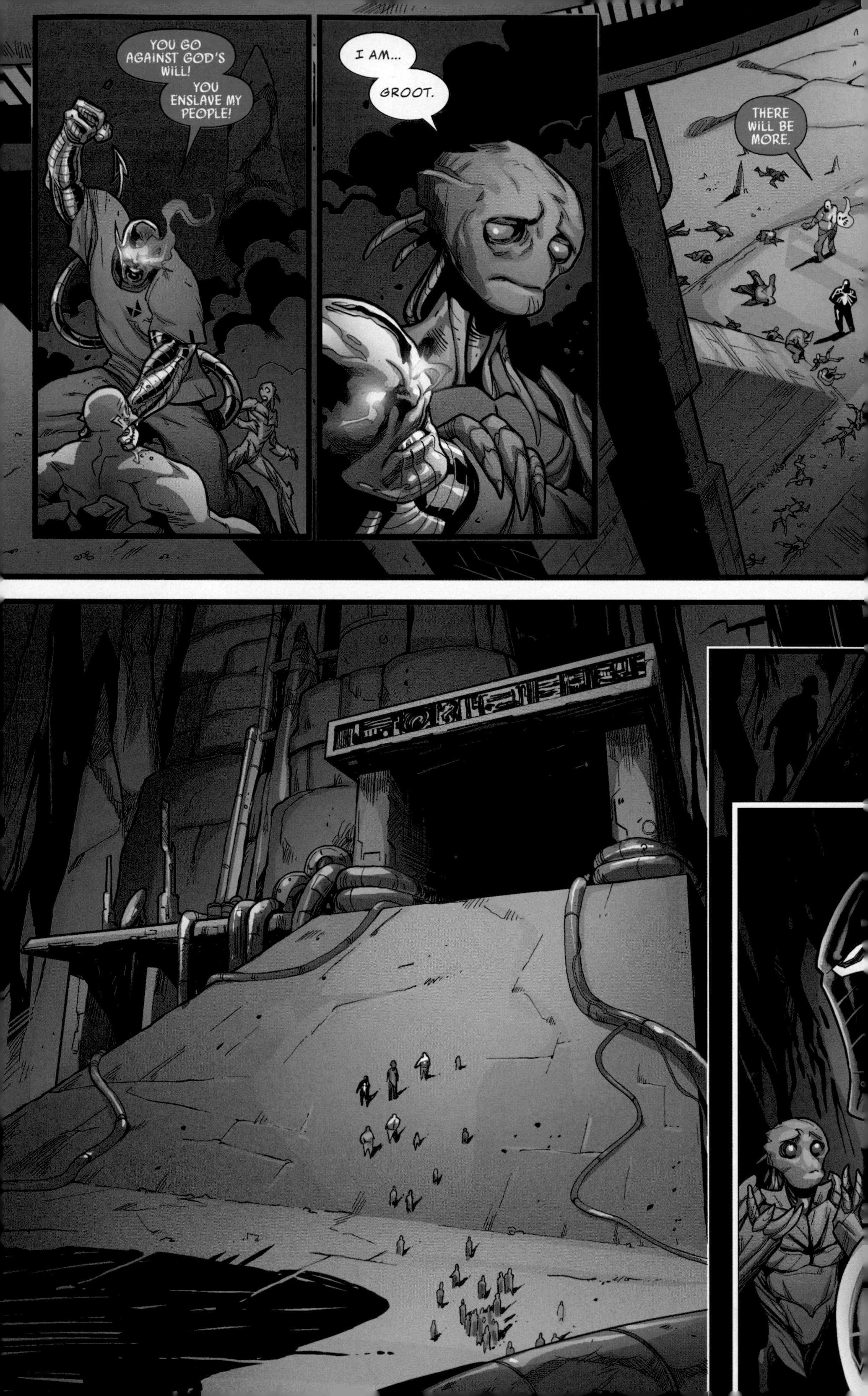
YOU GO AGAINST GOD'S WILL!
YOU ENSLAVE MY PEOPLE!
I AM...
GROOT.
THERE WILL BE MORE.

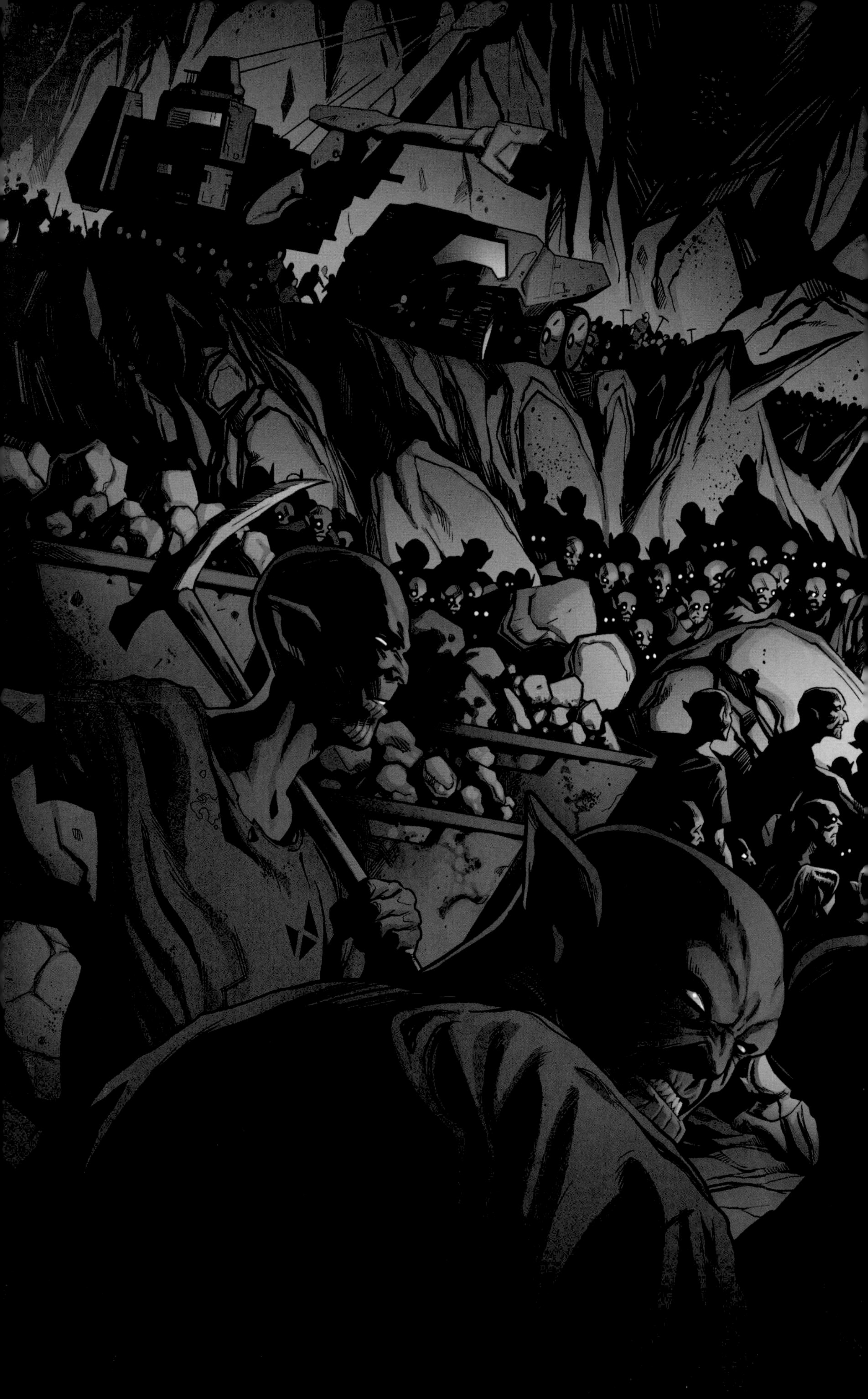

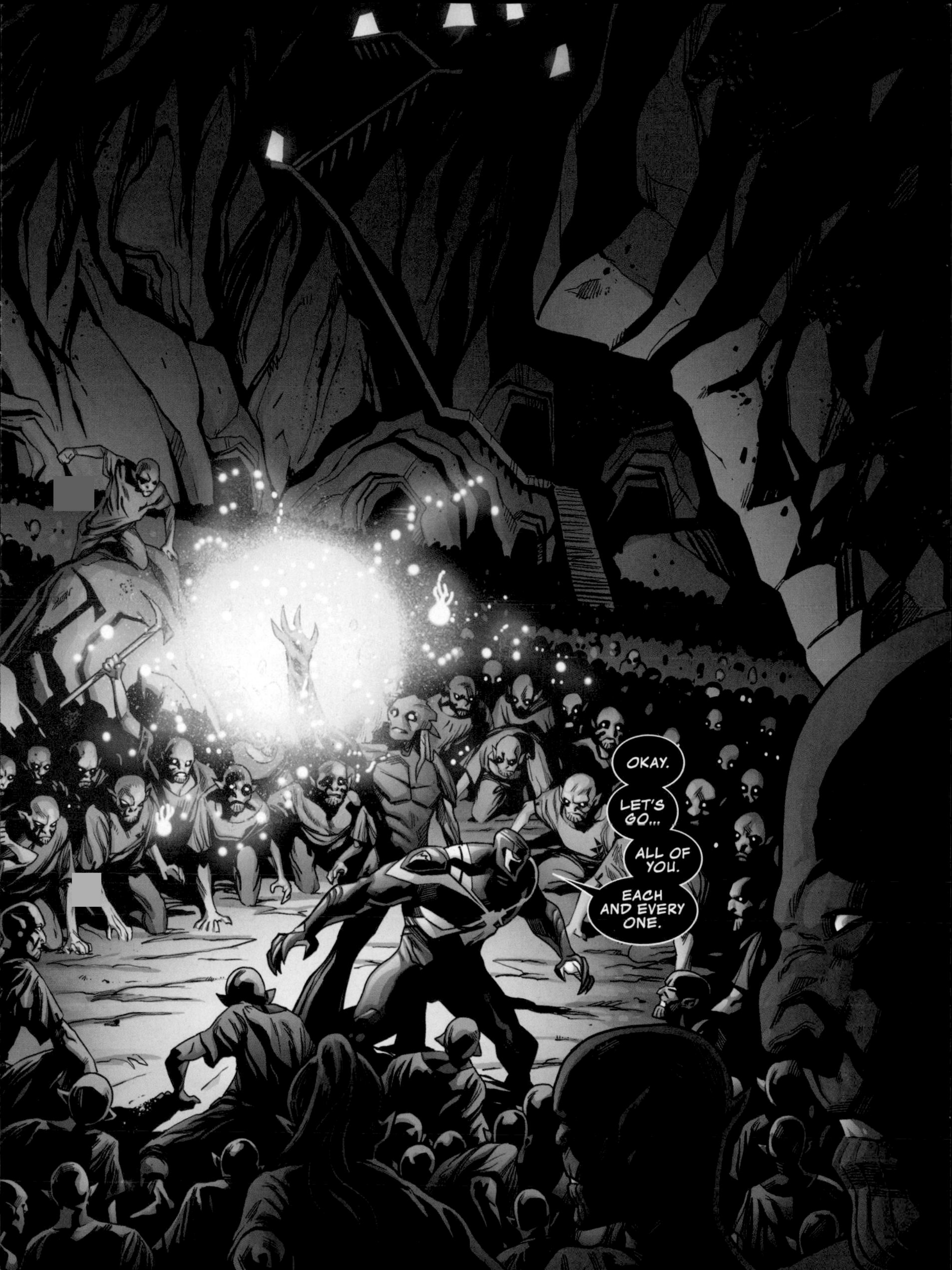
OKAY.
LET'S GO...
ALL OF YOU.
EACH AND EVERY ONE.

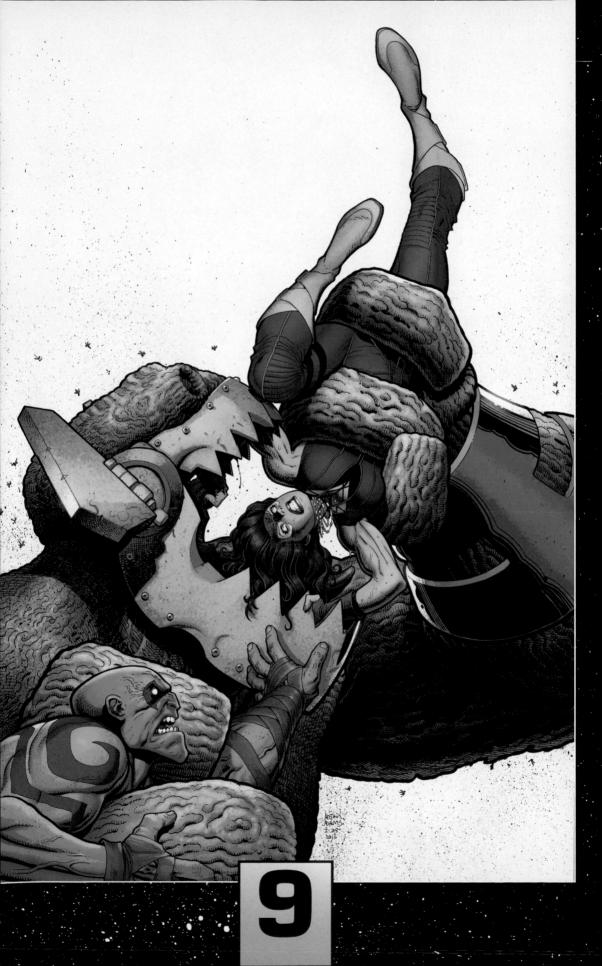

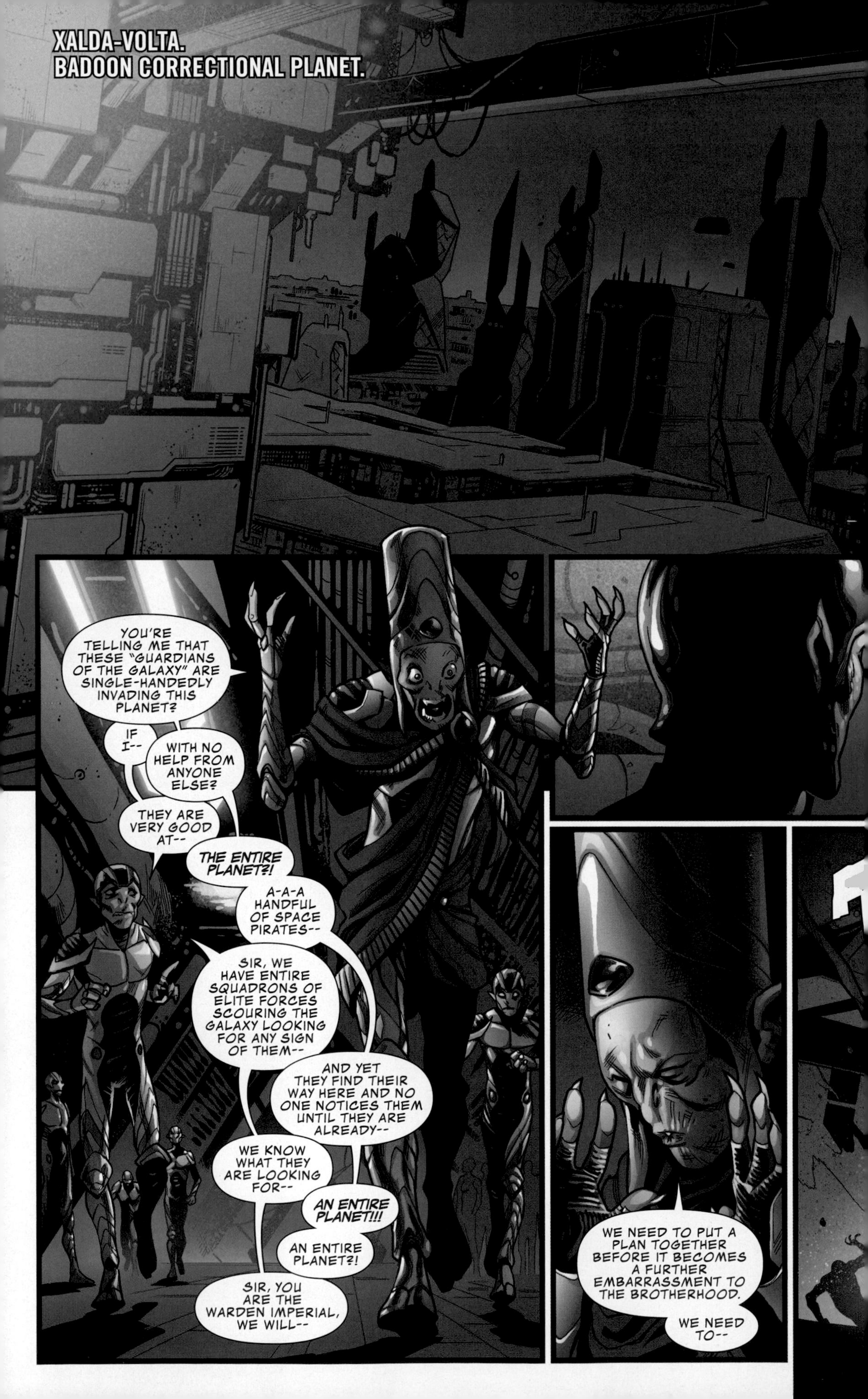
XALDA-VOLTA.
BADOON CORRECTIONAL PLANET.
YOU'RE TELLING ME THAT THESE "GUARDIANS OF THE GALAXY" ARE SINGLE-HANDEDLY INVADING THIS PLANET?
IF I--
WITH NO HELP FROM ANYONE ELSE?
THEY ARE VERY GOOD AT--
THE ENTIRE PLANET?!
A-A-A HANDFUL OF SPACE PIRATES--
SIR, WE HAVE ENTIRE SQUADRONS OF ELITE FORCES SCOURING THE GALAXY LOOKING FOR ANY SIGN OF THEM--
AND YET THEY FIND THEIR WAY HERE AND NO ONE NOTICES THEM UNTIL THEY ARE ALREADY--
WE KNOW WHAT THEY ARE LOOKING FOR--
AN ENTIRE PLANET!!!
AN ENTIRE PLANET?!
SIR, YOU ARE THE WARDEN IMPERIAL, WE WILL--
WE NEED TO PUT A PLAN TOGETHER BEFORE IT BECOMES A FURTHER EMBARRASSMENT TO THE BROTHERHOOD.
WE NEED TO--

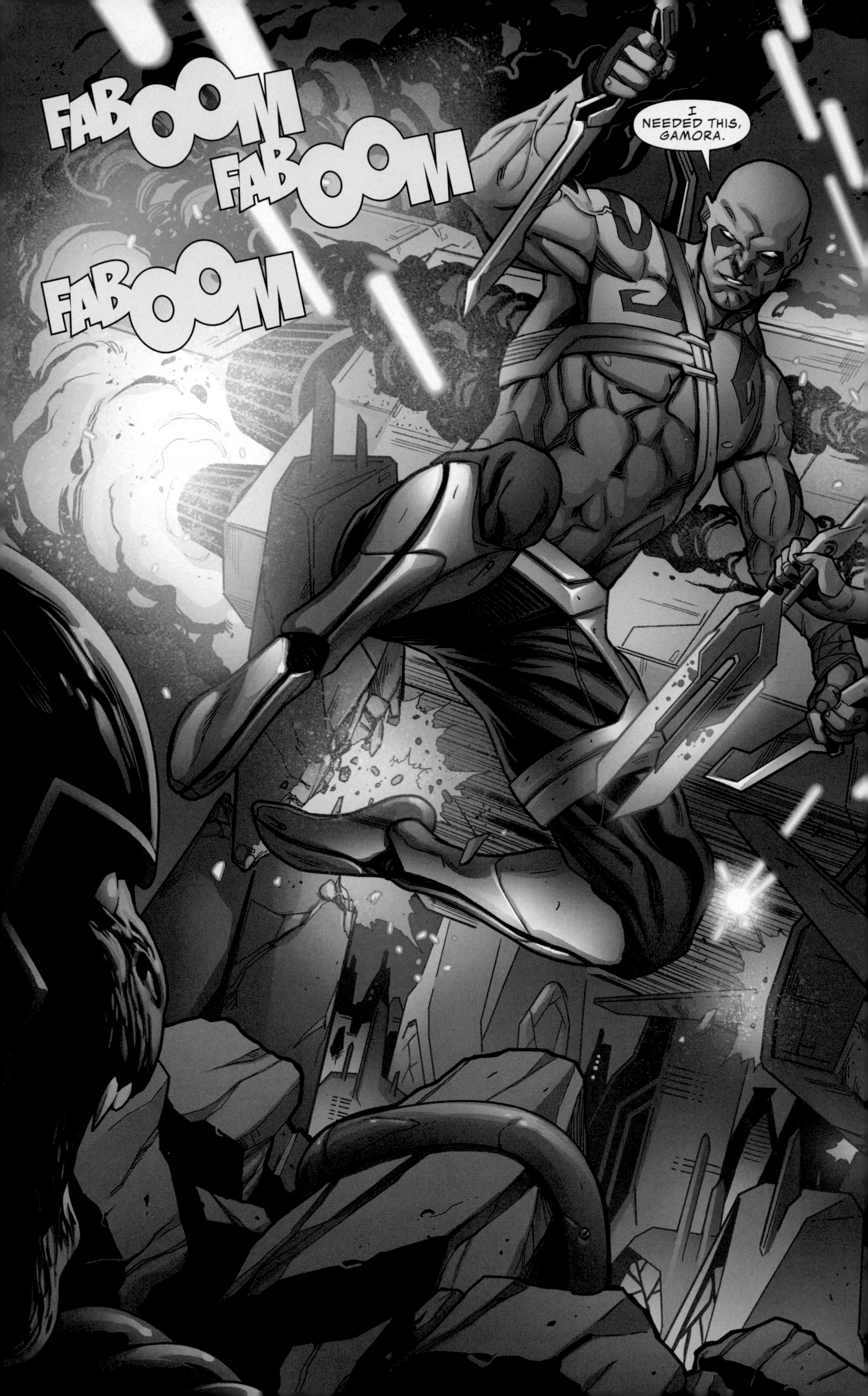
FABOOM
FABOOM
FABOOM
I NEEDED THIS, GAMORA.

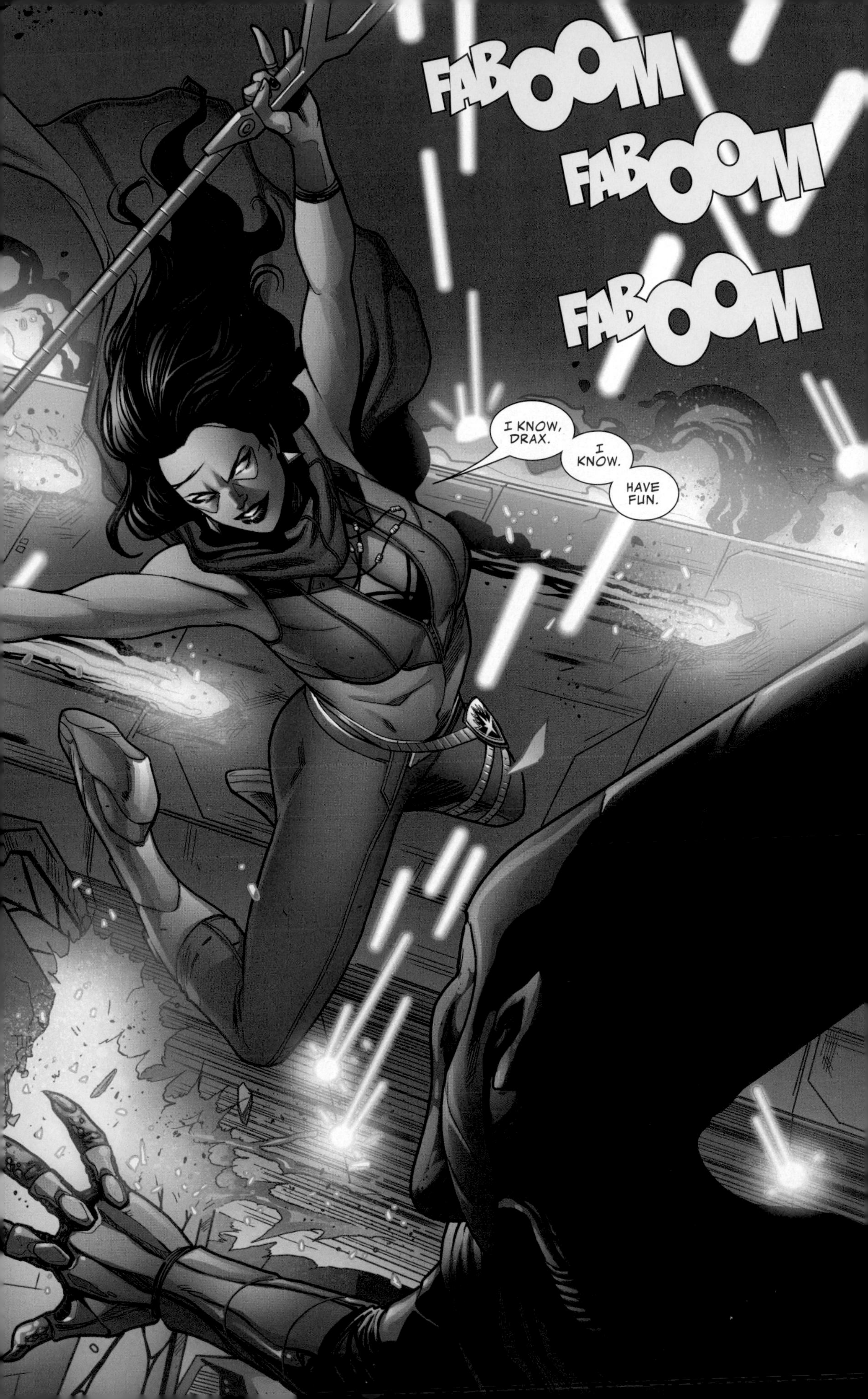
FABOOM
FABOOM
FABOOM
I KNOW, DRAX.
I KNOW.
HAVE FUN.

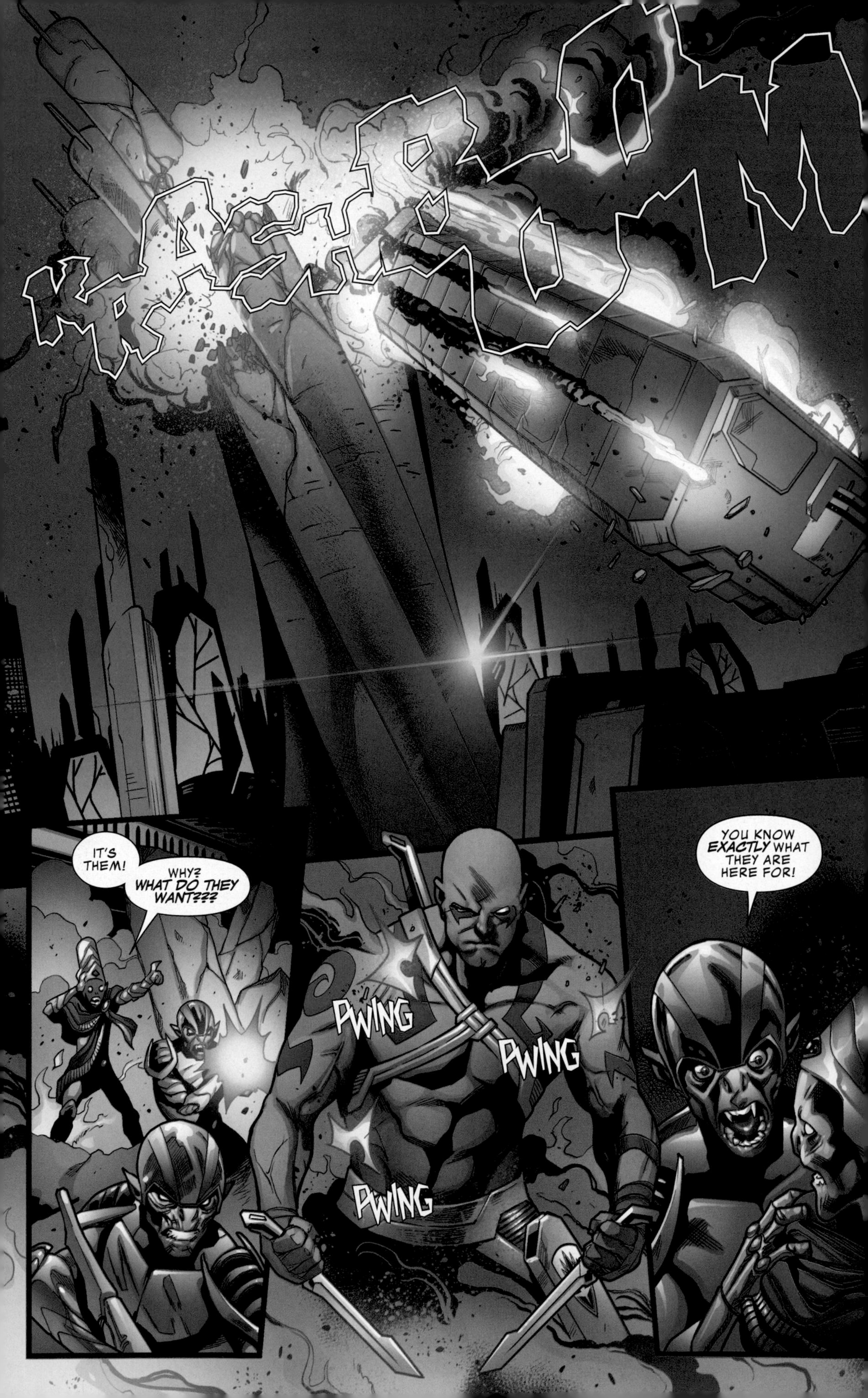
KA-BOOM
IT'S THEM!
WHY? WHAT DO THEY WANT???
PWING
PWING
PWING
YOU KNOW EXACTLY WHAT THEY ARE HERE FOR!

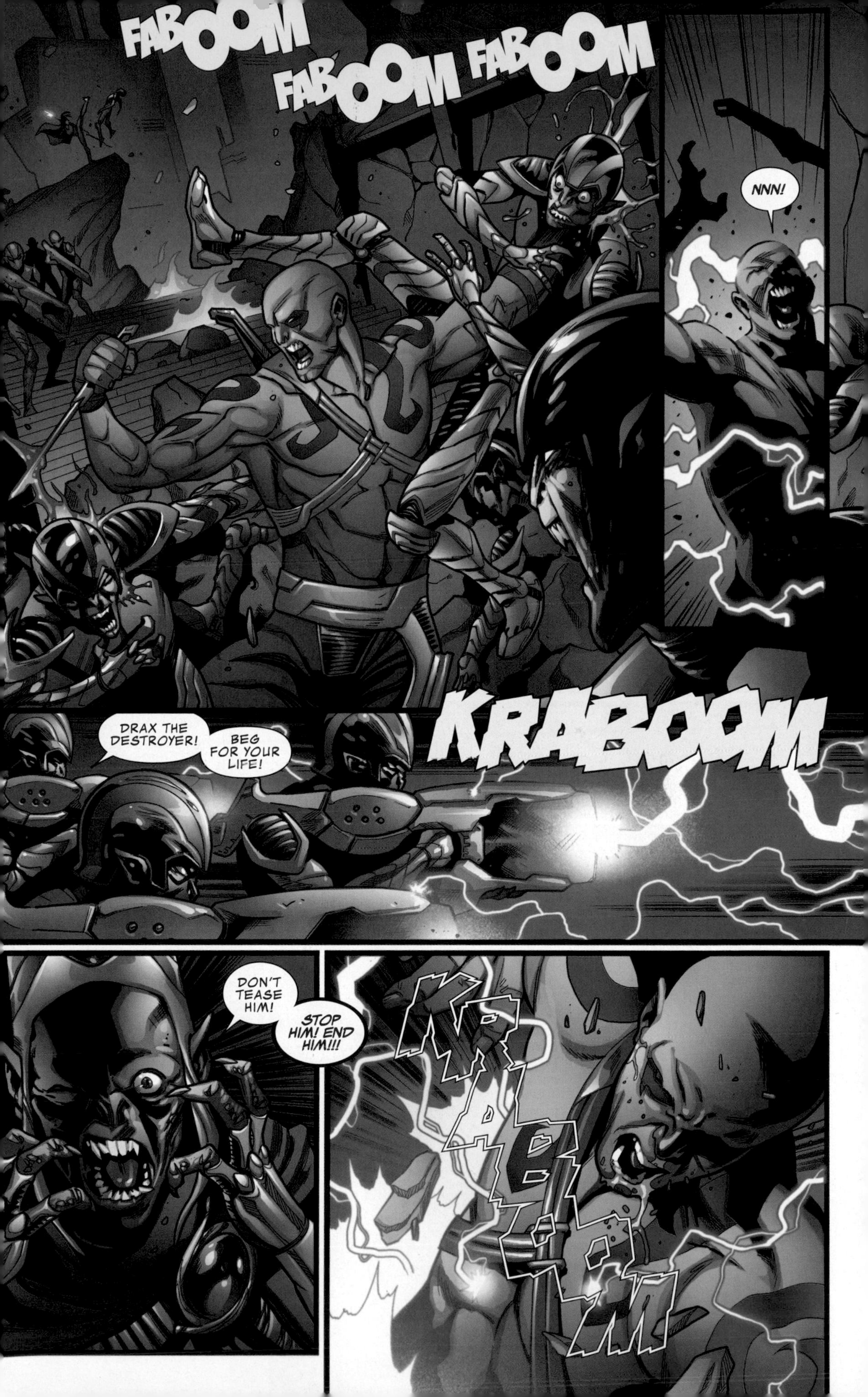
FABOOM
FABOOM FABOOM
NNN!
KRABOOM
DRAX THE DESTROYER!
BEG FOR YOUR LIFE!
DON'T TEASE HIM!
STOP HIM! END HIM!!!
KRAKOOM

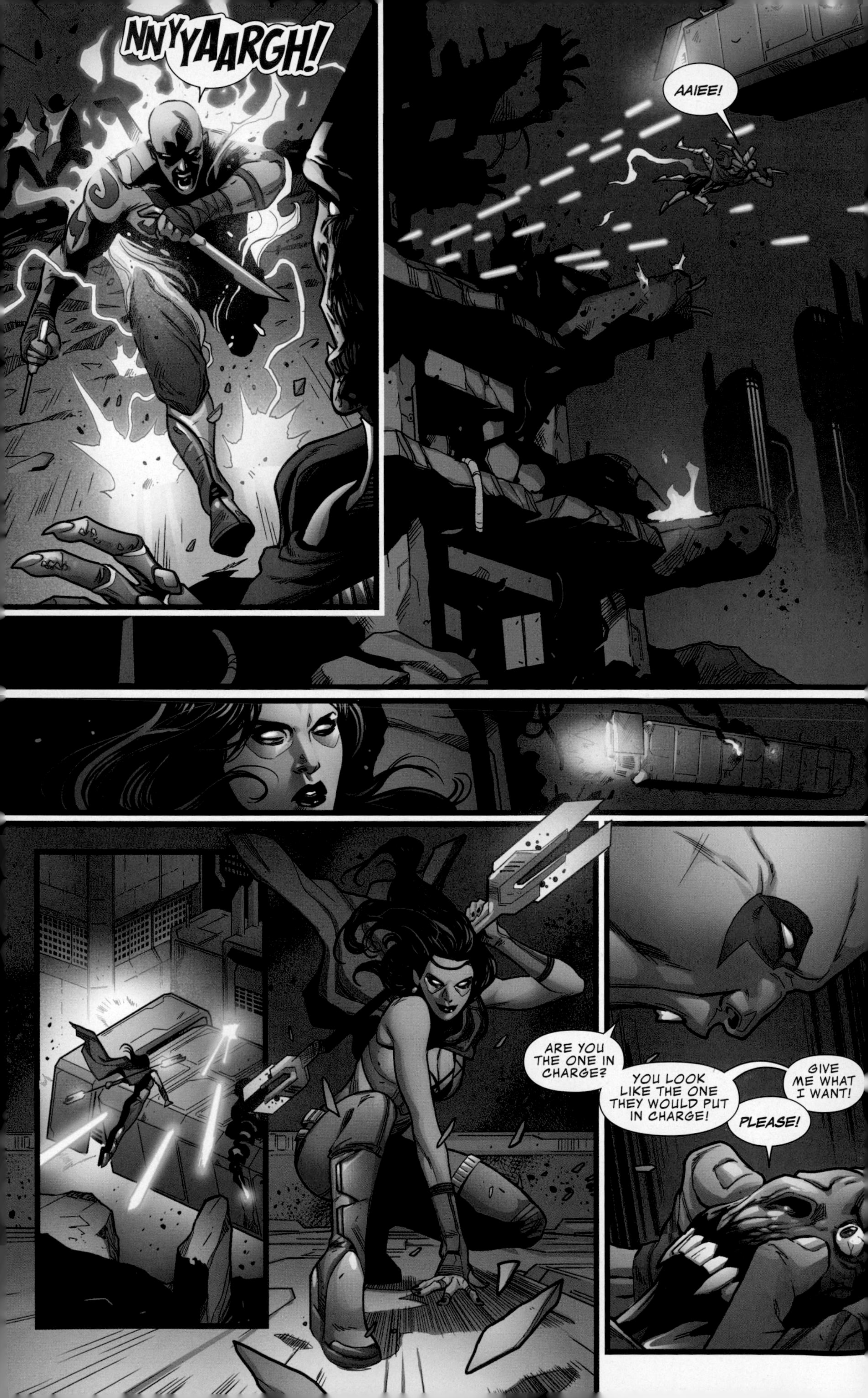
NNYYAARGH!
AAIEE!
ARE YOU THE ONE IN CHARGE?
YOU LOOK LIKE THE ONE THEY WOULD PUT IN CHARGE!
GIVE ME WHAT I WANT!
PLEASE!

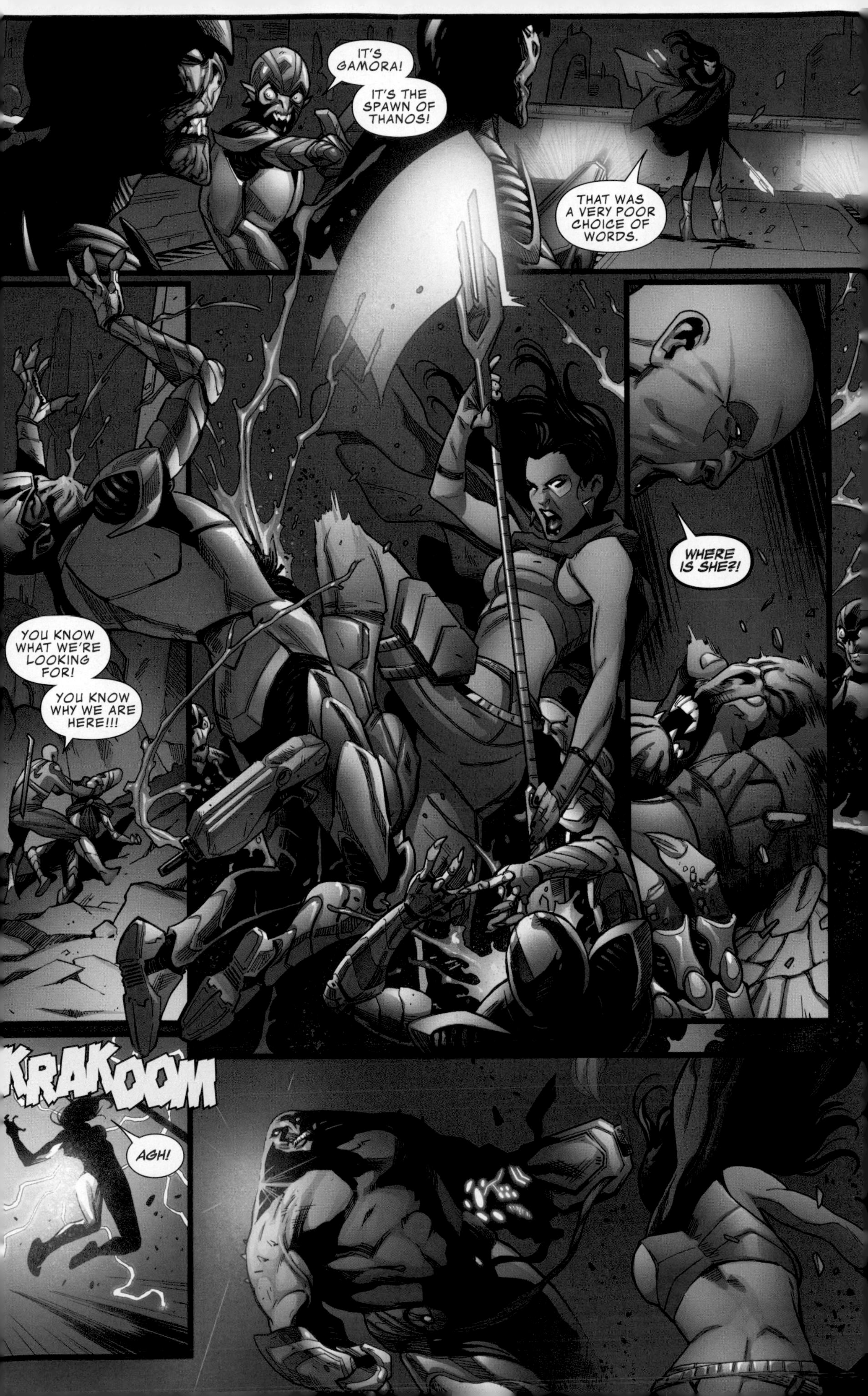
IT'S GAMORA!
IT'S THE SPAWN OF THANOS!
THAT WAS A VERY POOR CHOICE OF WORDS.
WHERE IS SHE?!
YOU KNOW WHAT WE'RE LOOKING FOR!
YOU KNOW WHY WE ARE HERE!!!
KRAKOOM
AGH!

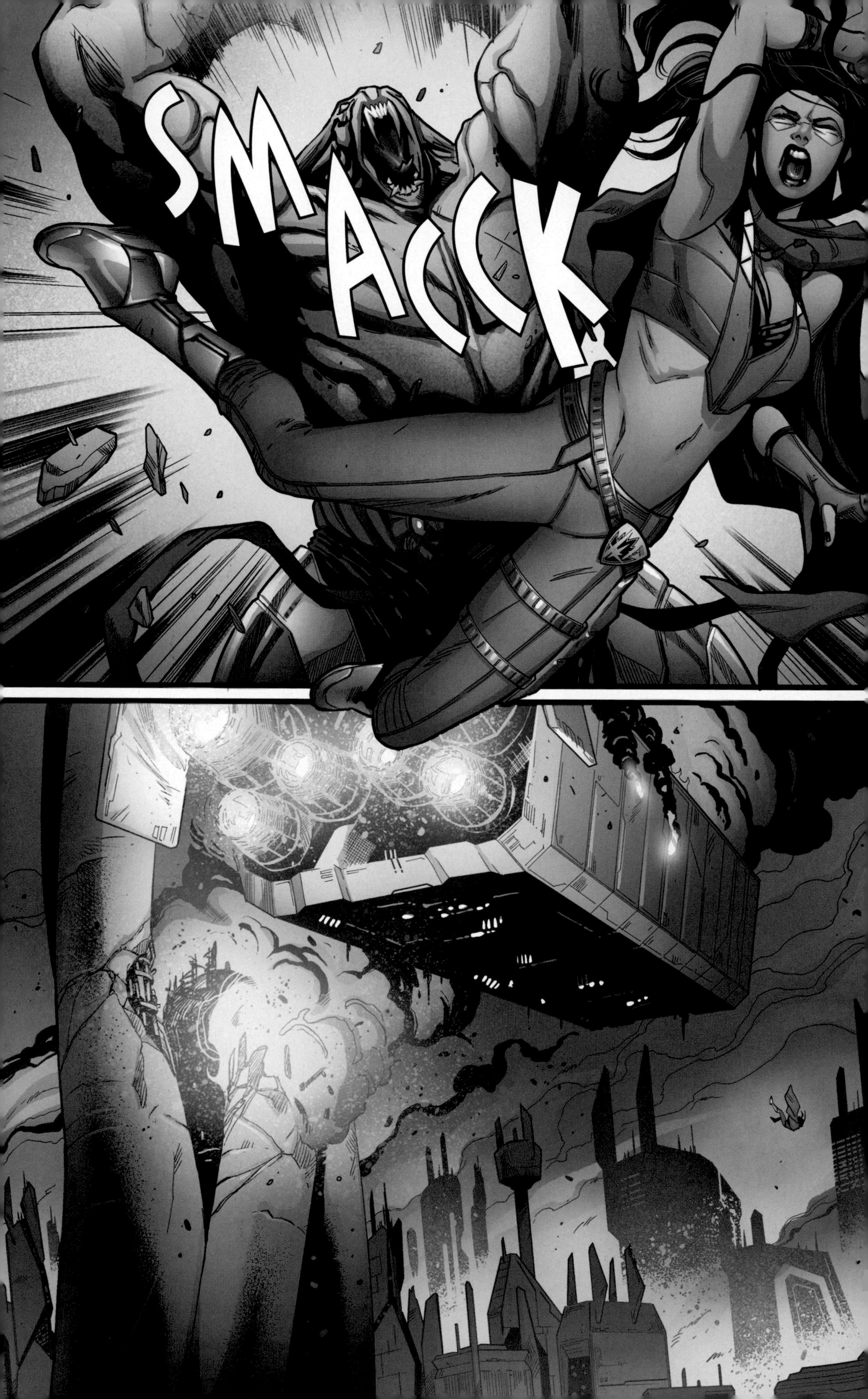
SMACCK

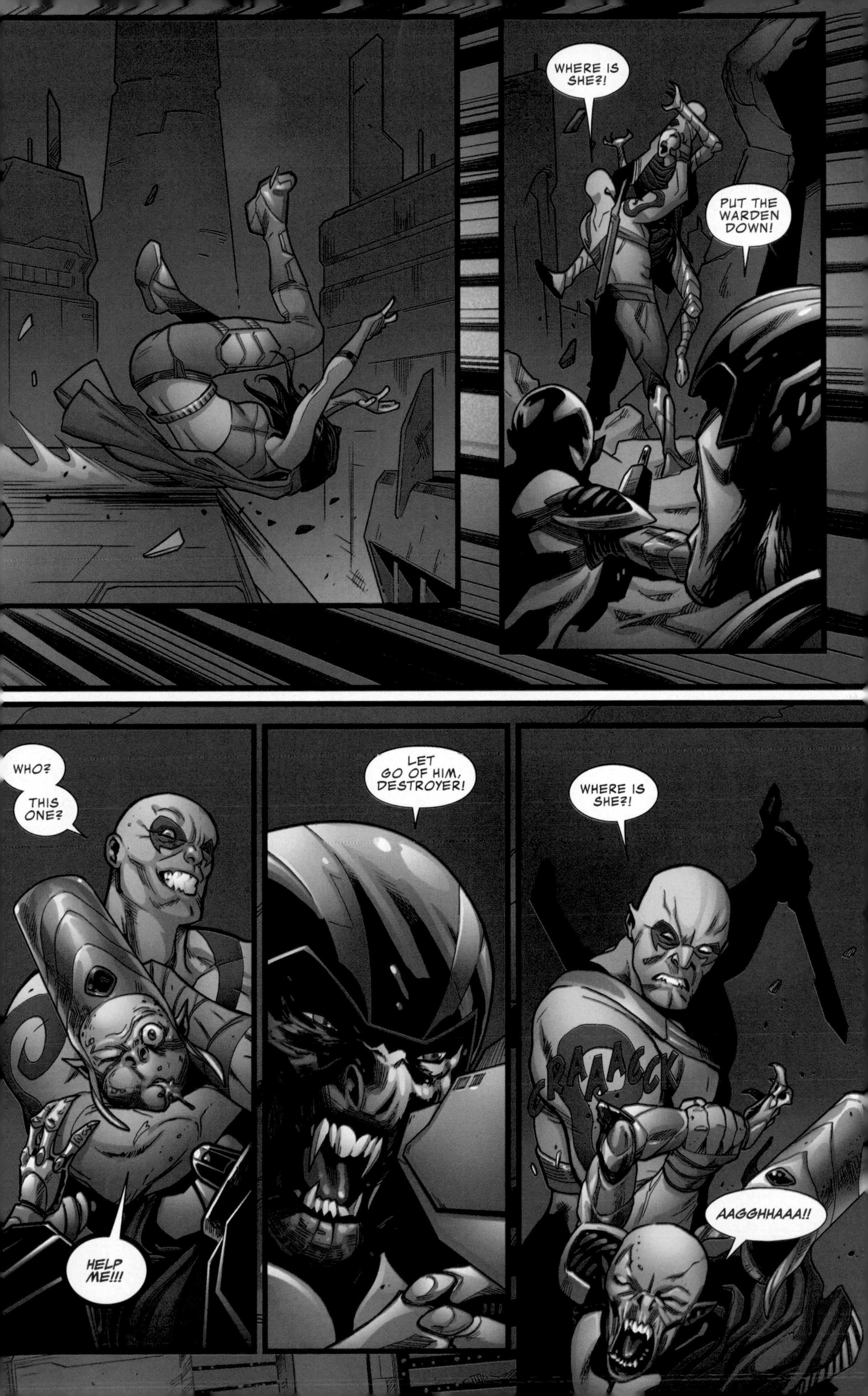
WHERE IS SHE?!
PUT THE WARDEN DOWN!
WHO?
THIS ONE?
HELP ME!!!
LET GO OF HIM, DESTROYER!
WHERE IS SHE?!
CRAAACK
AAGGHHAAA!!

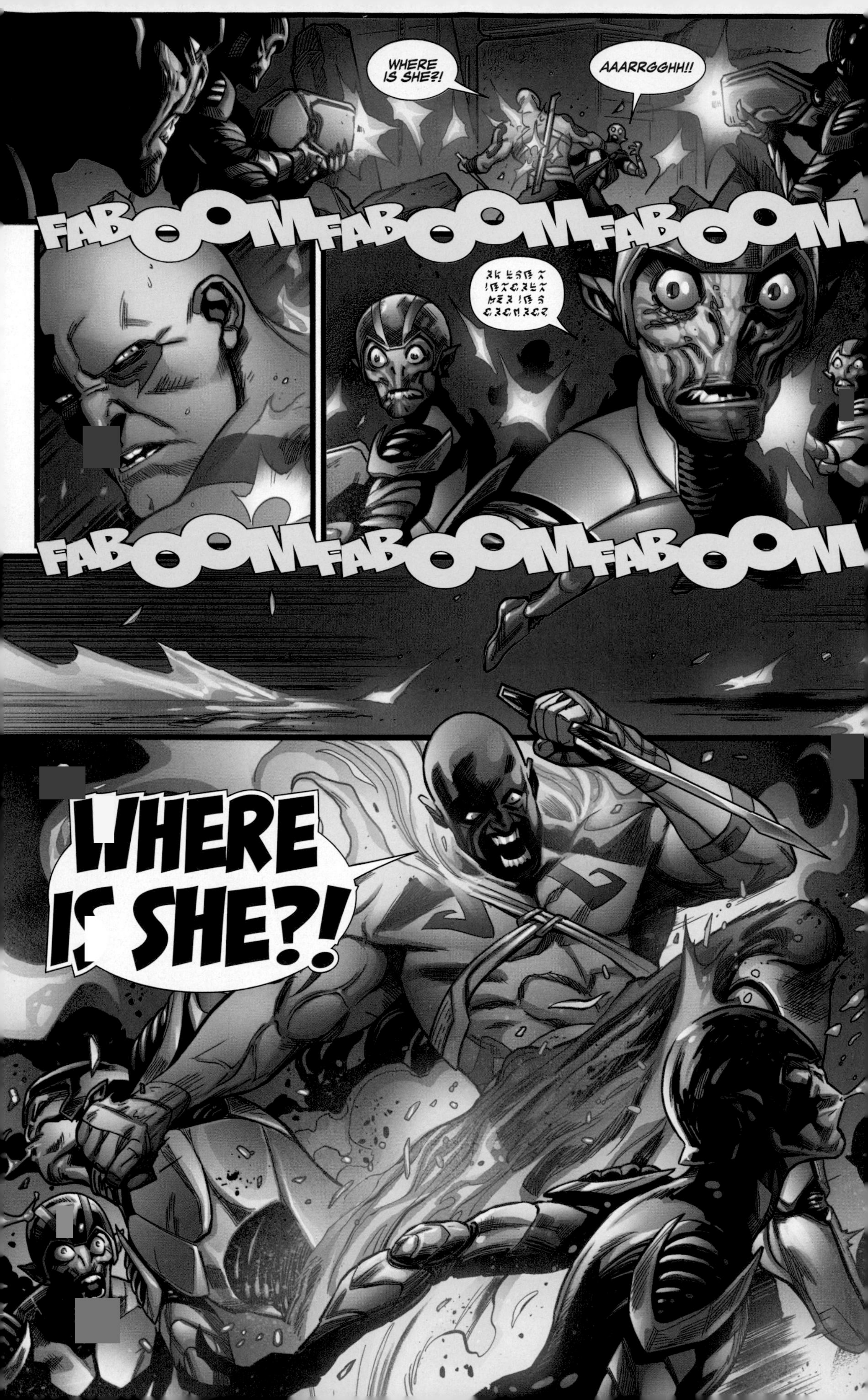
WHERE IS SHE?!
AAARRGGHH!!
FABOOM FABOOM FABOOM
FABOOM FABOOM FABOOM
WHERE IS SHE?!

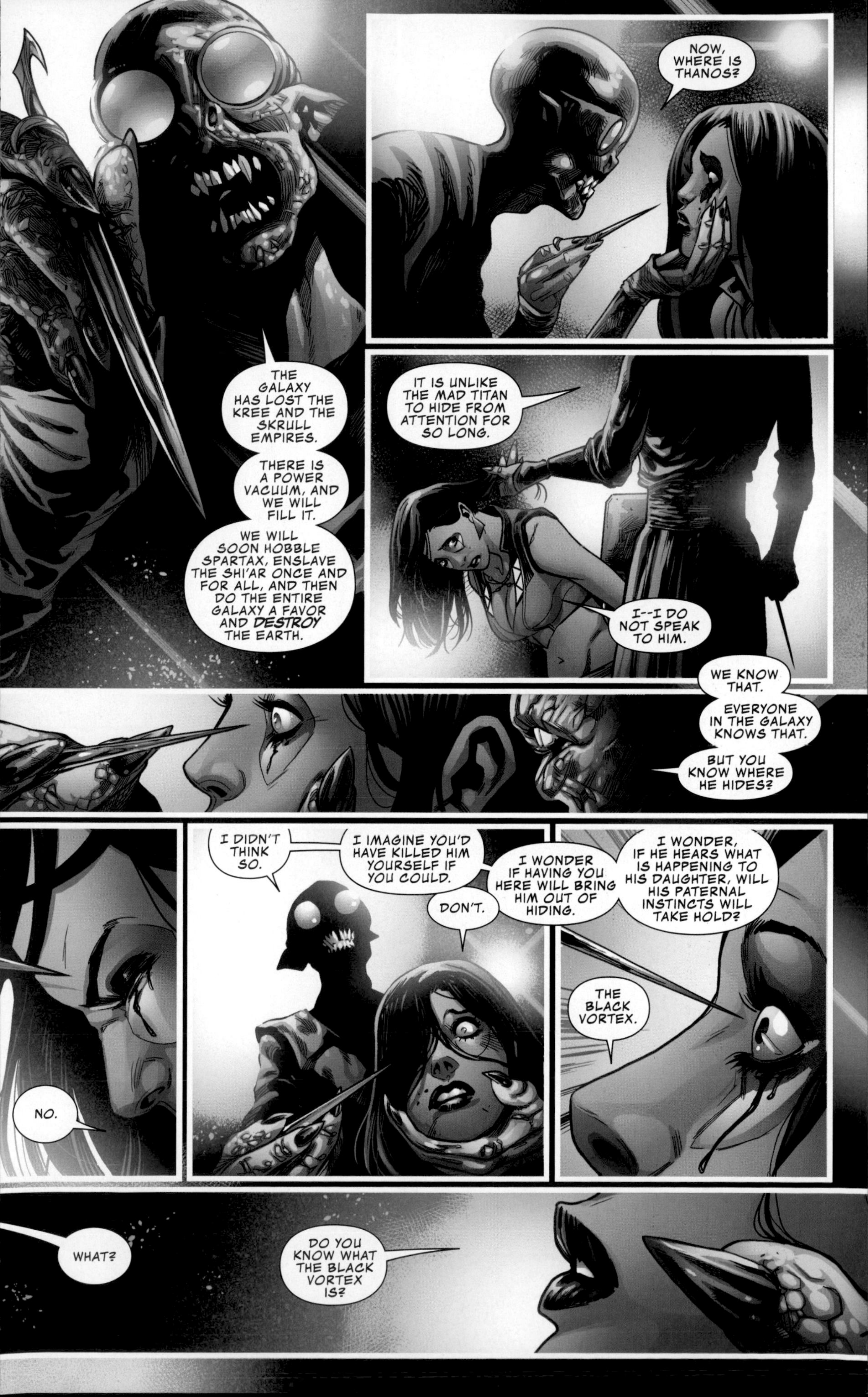
NOW, WHERE IS THANOS?
THE GALAXY HAS LOST THE KREE AND THE SKRULL EMPIRES.
THERE IS A POWER VACUUM, AND WE WILL FILL IT.
WE WILL SOON HOBBLE SPARTAX, ENSLAVE THE SHI'AR ONCE AND FOR ALL, AND THEN DO THE ENTIRE GALAXY A FAVOR AND DESTROY THE EARTH.
IT IS UNLIKE THE MAD TITAN TO HIDE FROM ATTENTION FOR SO LONG.
I--I DO NOT SPEAK TO HIM.
WE KNOW THAT.
EVERYONE IN THE GALAXY KNOWS THAT.
BUT YOU KNOW WHERE HE HIDES?
NO.
I DIDN'T THINK SO.
I IMAGINE YOU'D HAVE KILLED HIM YOURSELF IF YOU COULD.
DON'T.
I WONDER IF HAVING YOU HERE WILL BRING HIM OUT OF HIDING.
I WONDER, IF HE HEARS WHAT IS HAPPENING TO HIS DAUGHTER, WILL HIS PATERNAL INSTINCTS WILL TAKE HOLD?
THE BLACK VORTEX.
WHAT?
DO YOU KNOW WHAT THE BLACK VORTEX IS?

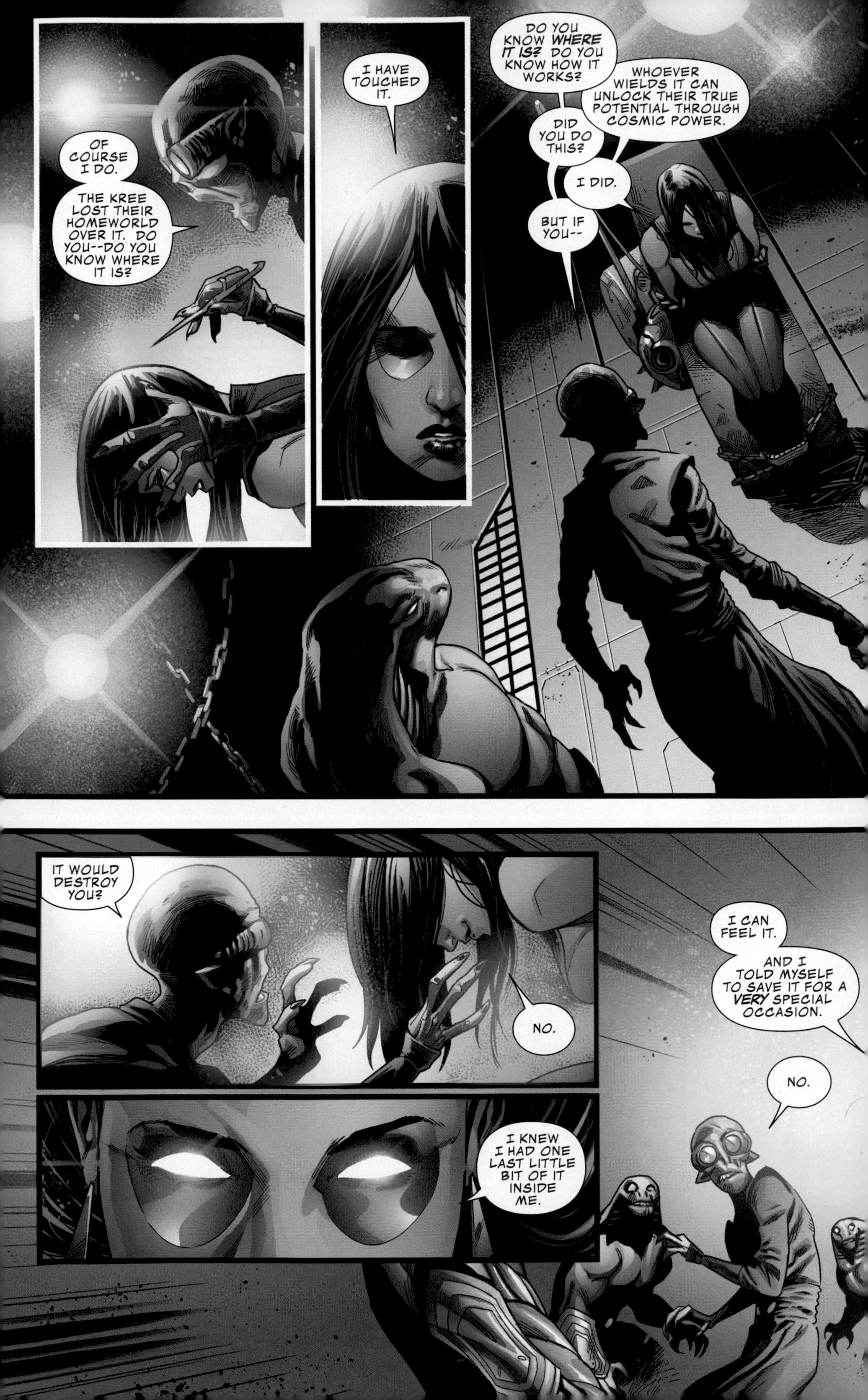
OF COURSE I DO.
THE KREE LOST THEIR HOMEWORLD OVER IT. DO YOU--DO YOU KNOW WHERE IT IS?
I HAVE TOUCHED IT.
DO YOU KNOW WHERE IT IS? DO YOU KNOW HOW IT WORKS?
WHOEVER WIELDS IT CAN UNLOCK THEIR TRUE POTENTIAL THROUGH COSMIC POWER.
DID YOU DO THIS?
I DID.
BUT IF YOU--
IT WOULD DESTROY YOU?
NO.
I KNEW I HAD ONE LAST LITTLE BIT OF IT INSIDE ME.
I CAN FEEL IT.
AND I TOLD MYSELF TO SAVE IT FOR A VERY SPECIAL OCCASION.
NO.

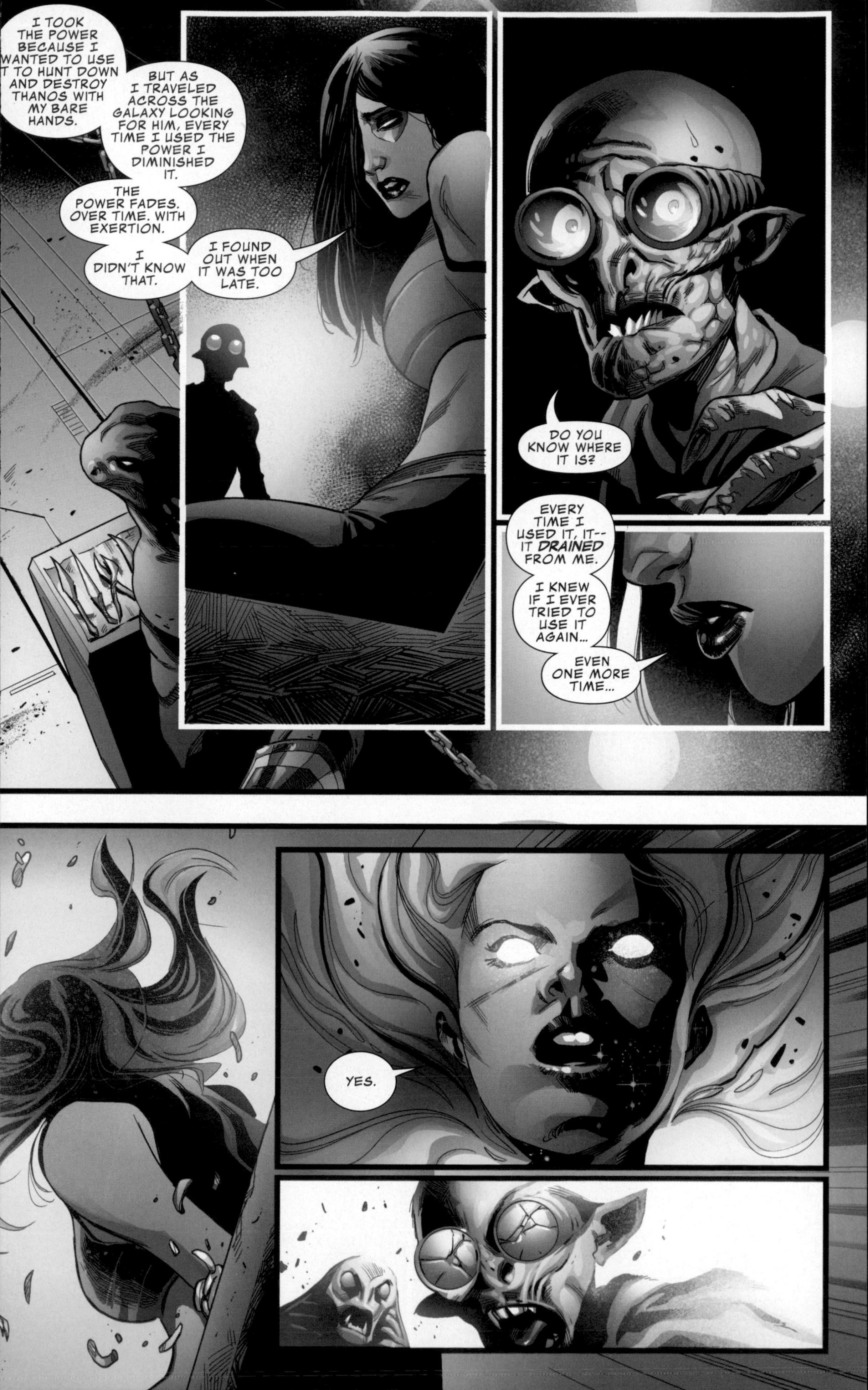
I TOOK THE POWER BECAUSE I WANTED TO USE IT TO HUNT DOWN AND DESTROY THANOS WITH MY BARE HANDS.
BUT AS I TRAVELED ACROSS THE GALAXY LOOKING FOR HIM, EVERY TIME I USED THE POWER I DIMINISHED IT.
THE POWER FADES. OVER TIME. WITH EXERTION.
I DIDN'T KNOW THAT.
I FOUND OUT WHEN IT WAS TOO LATE.
DO YOU KNOW WHERE IT IS?
EVERY TIME I USED IT, IT-- IT DRAINED FROM ME.
I KNEW IF I EVER TRIED TO USE IT AGAIN...
EVEN ONE MORE TIME...
YES.

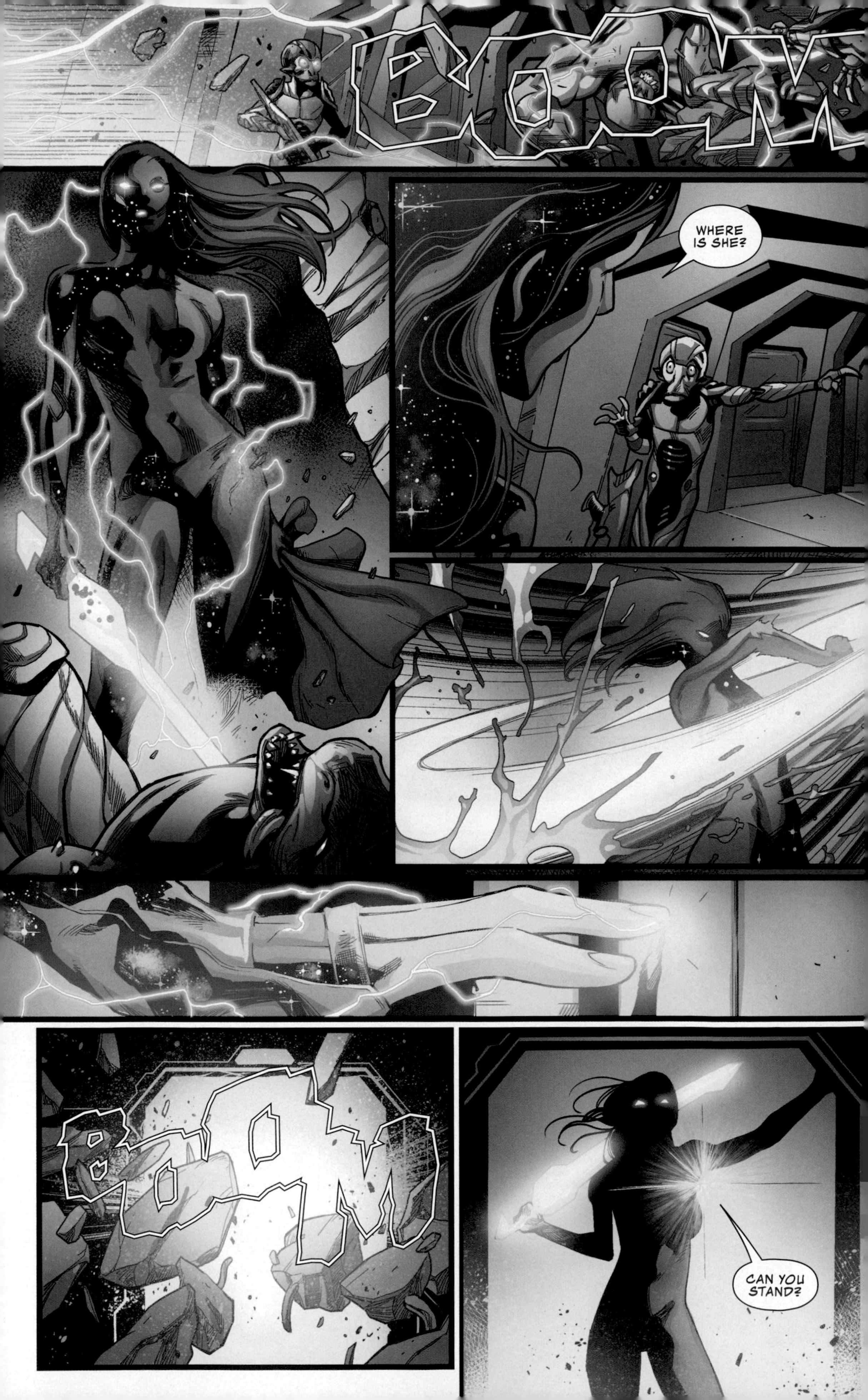
BOOM
WHERE IS SHE?
BOOM
CAN YOU STAND?

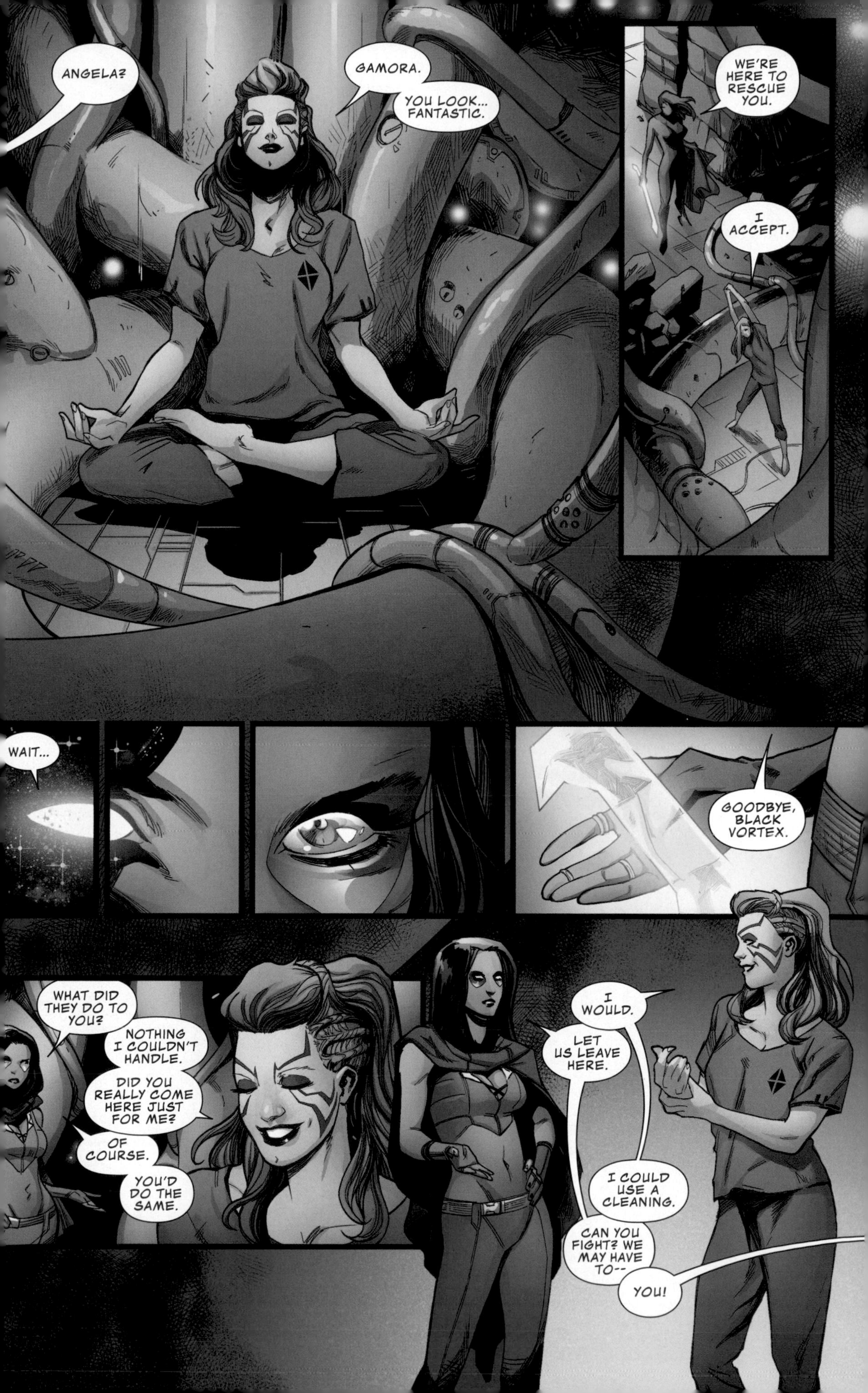
ANGELA?
GAMORA.
YOU LOOK... FANTASTIC.
WE'RE HERE TO RESCUE YOU.
I ACCEPT.
WAIT...
GOODBYE, BLACK VORTEX.
WHAT DID THEY DO TO YOU?
NOTHING I COULDN'T HANDLE.
DID YOU REALLY COME HERE JUST FOR ME?
OF COURSE.
YOU'D DO THE SAME.
I WOULD.
LET US LEAVE HERE.
I COULD USE A CLEANING.
CAN YOU FIGHT? WE MAY HAVE TO--
YOU!

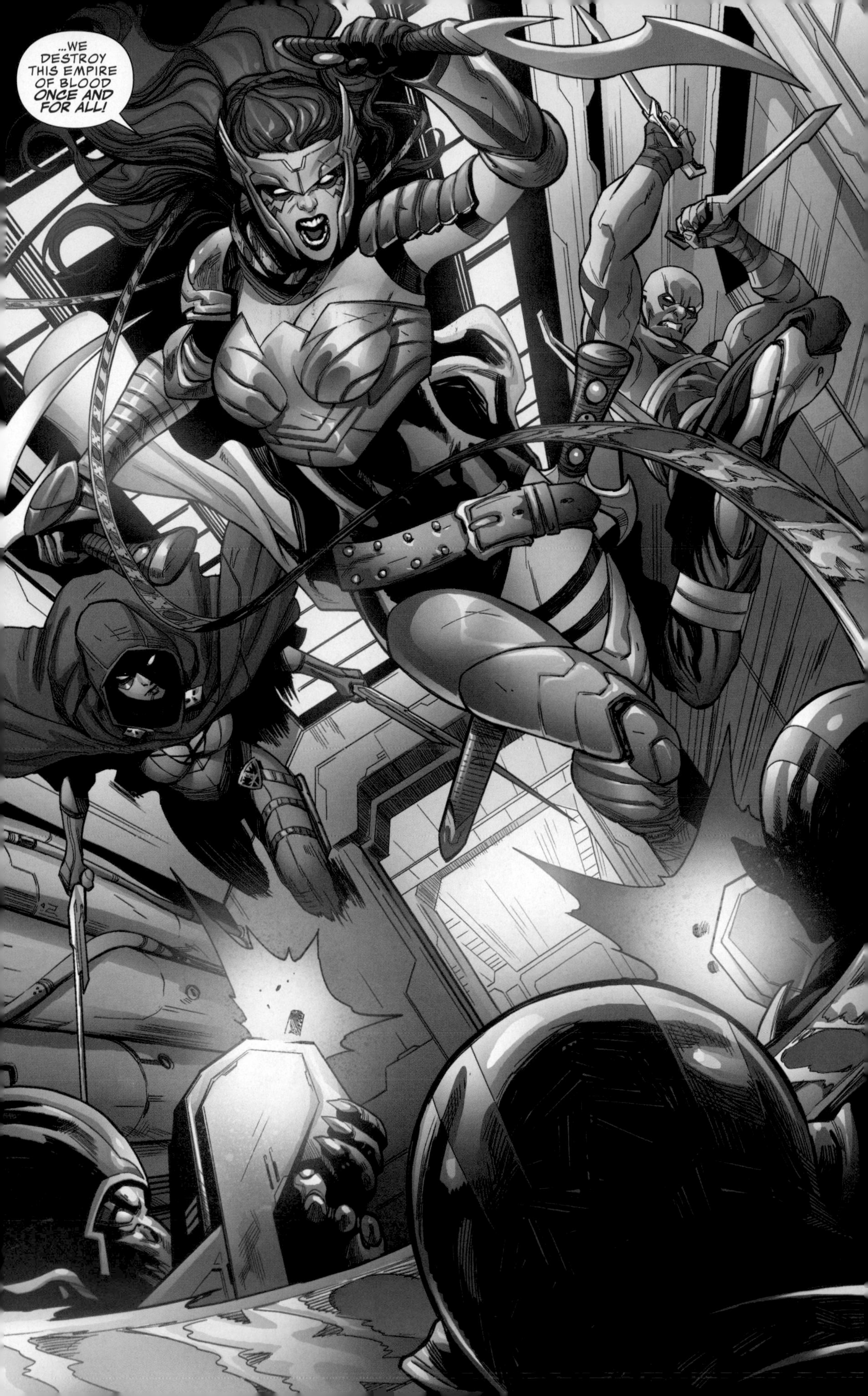
...WE DESTROY THIS EMPIRE OF BLOOD ONCE AND FOR ALL!

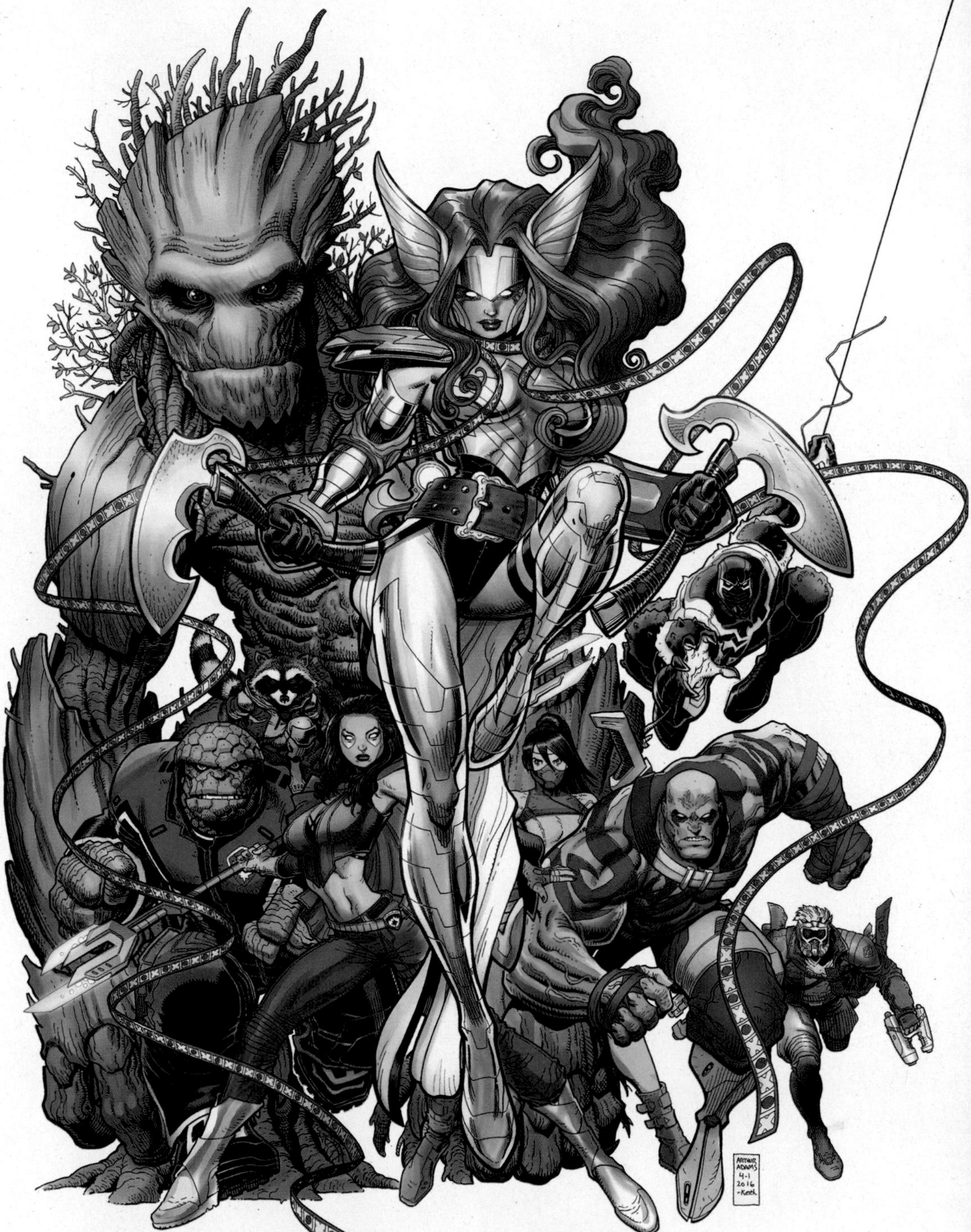
ARTHUR ADAMS
4-1
2016
+Keith

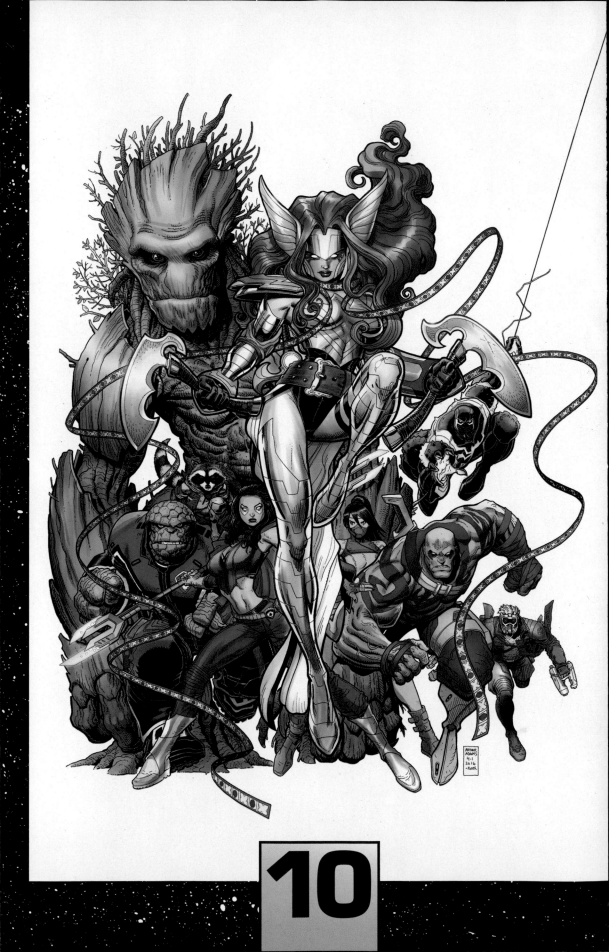

# 10

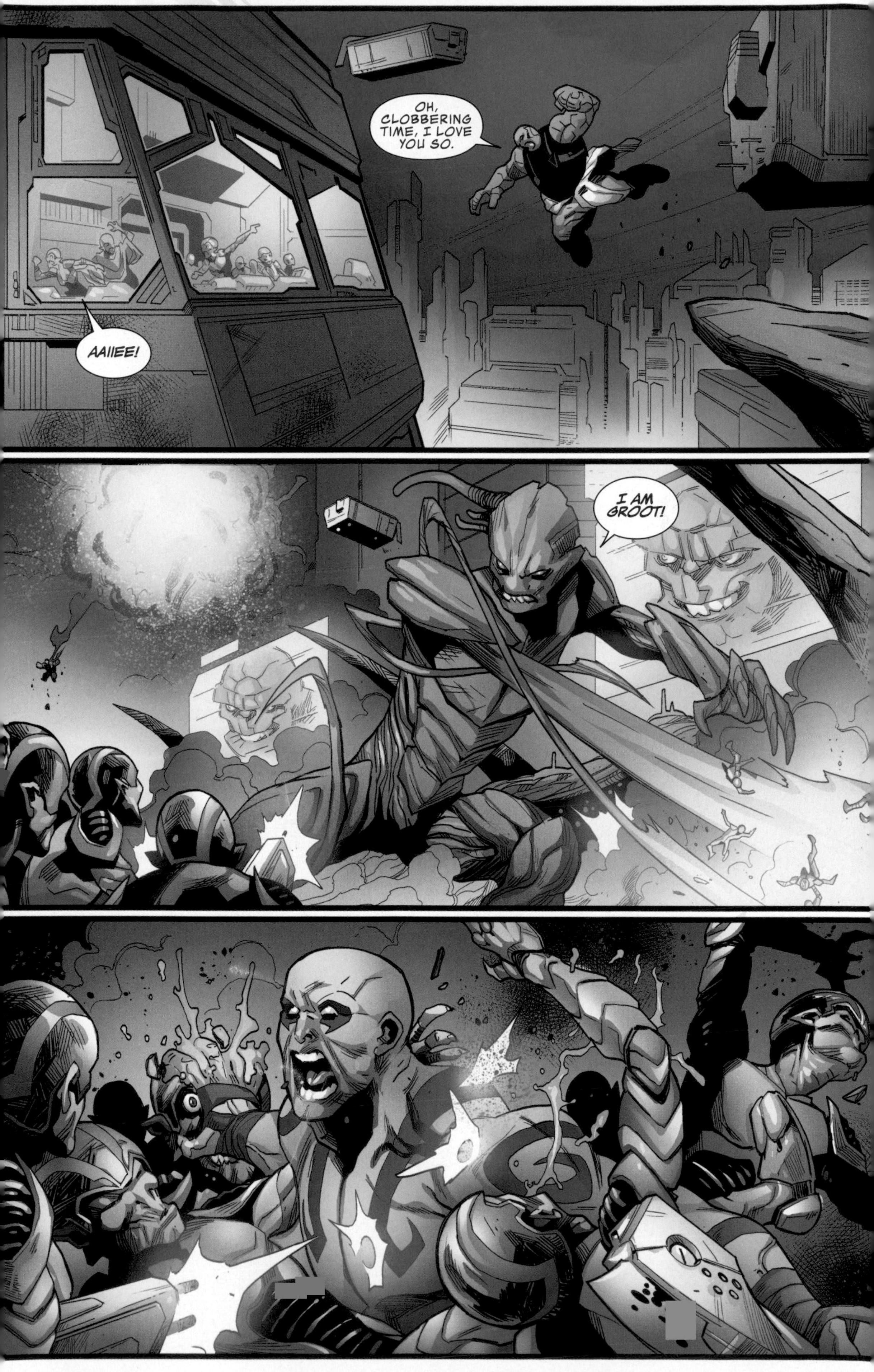

OH, CLOBBERING TIME, I LOVE YOU SO.
AAIIEE!
I AM GROOT!

**NEXT: CIVIL WAR II**

#6 VARIANT BY
**GREG HILDEBRANT**

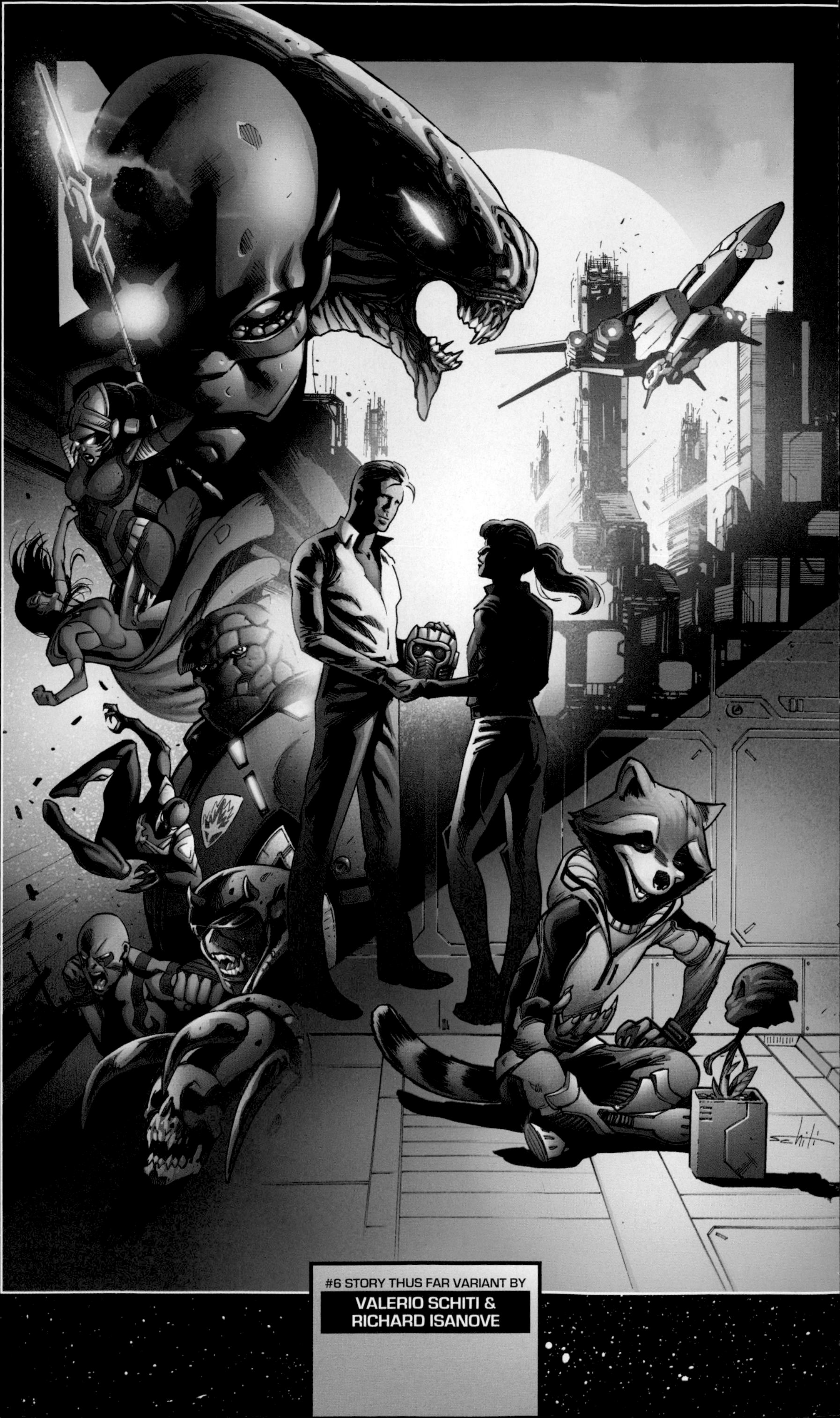

#6 STORY THUS FAR VARIANT BY

**VALERIO SCHITI & RICHARD ISANOVE**

#6 WOMAN OF POWER
VARIANT BY
**SIYA OUM**

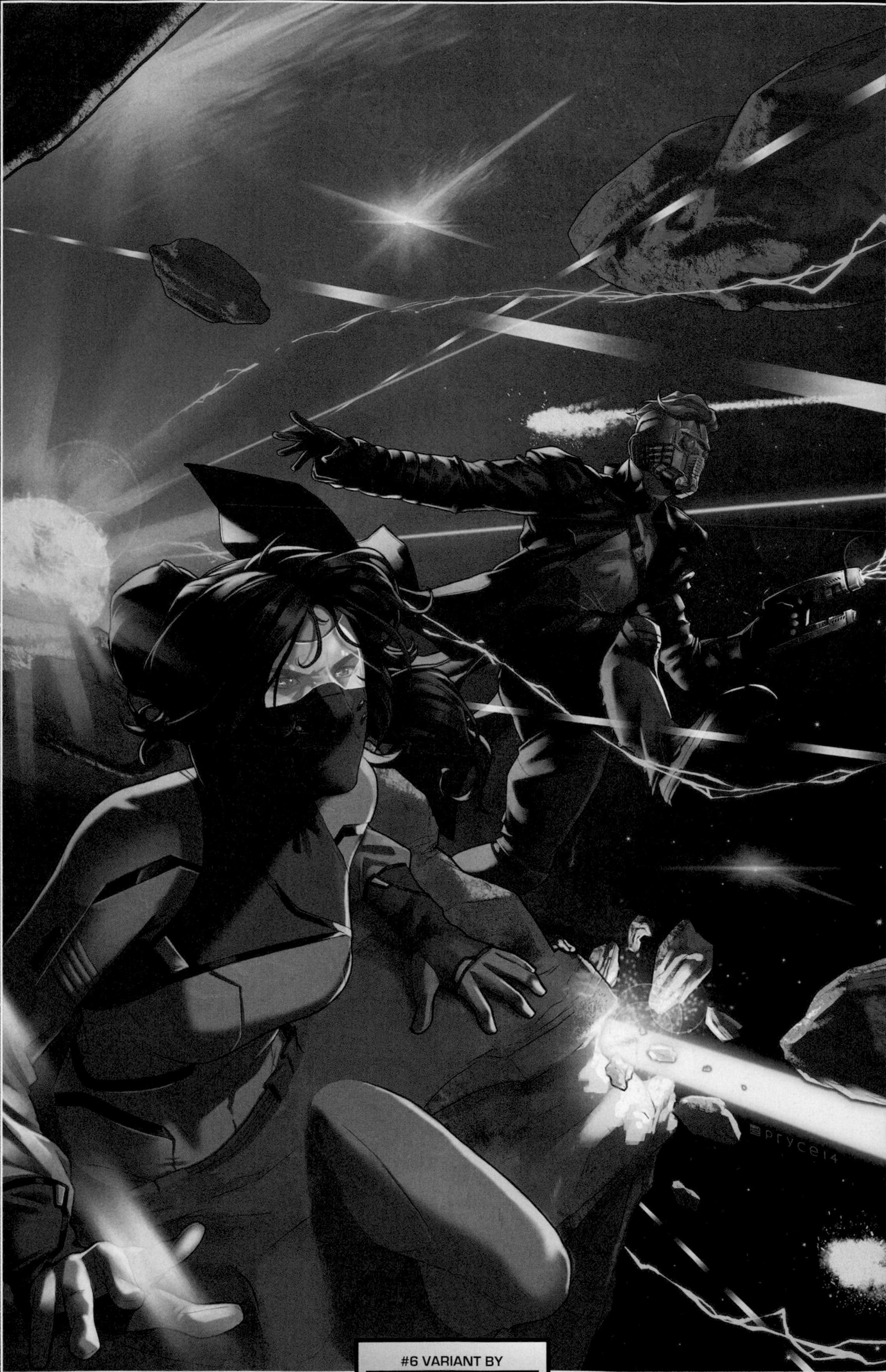
pryce14

#6 VARIANT BY
**JAMAL CAMPBELL**

# GUARDIANS OF THE GALAXY
## A MARVEL COMICS EVENT

# CIVIL WAR

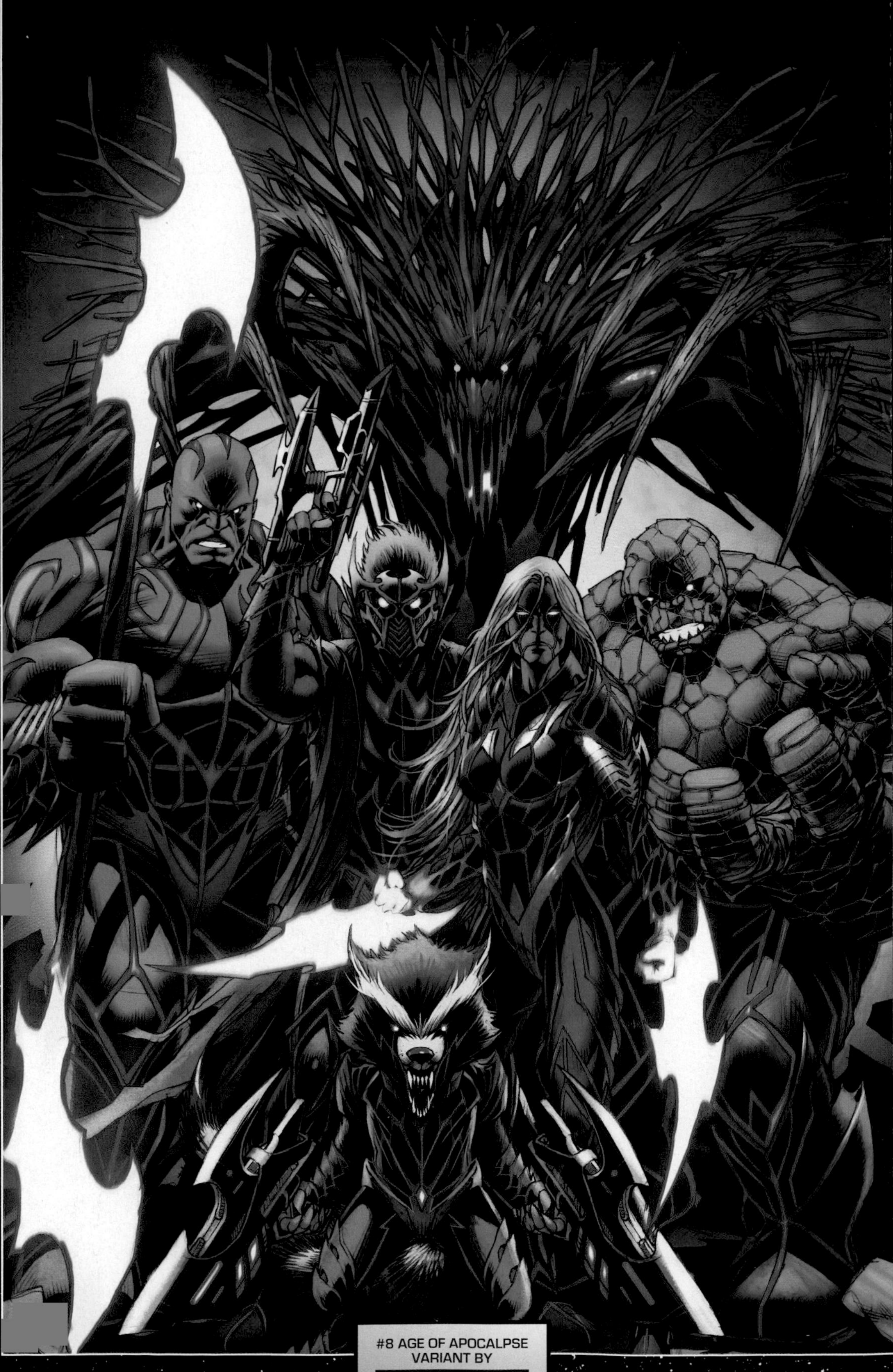

#8 AGE OF APOCALPSE VARIANT BY

ARTHUR ADAMS & JASON KEITH

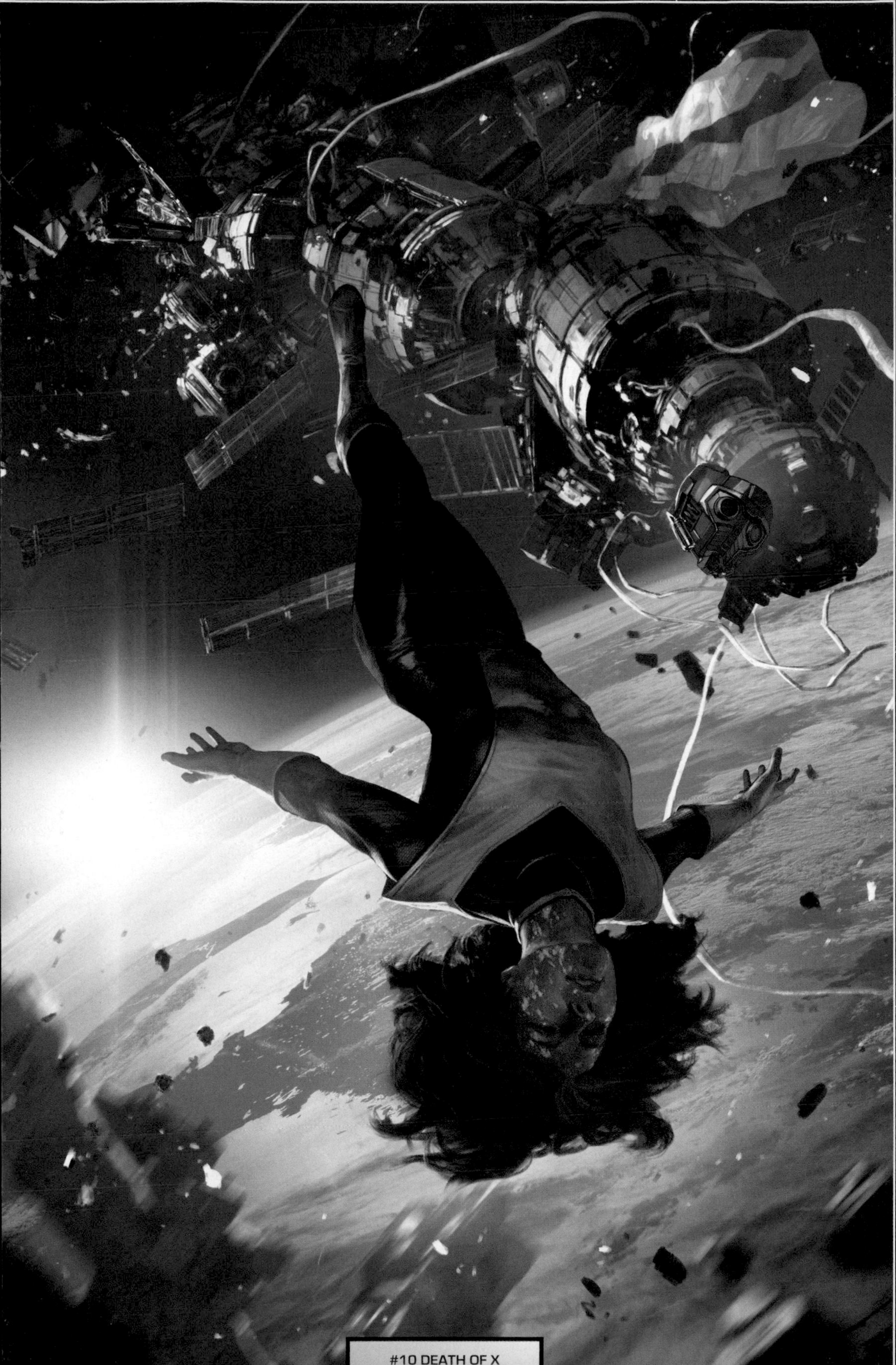

#10 DEATH OF X
VARIANT BY
**SKAN SRISUWAN**

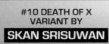

MOCK COSTUME DESIGNS BY
VALERIO SCHITI

# GAMORA

SAME HELMET OF THE MOVIE

LOGO

BOTTOM

TOP

IN

OUT

# STAR LORD

CHARACTER DESIGNS BY
**VALERIO SCHITI**

FROM THE DESK OF
ARTHUR ADAMS

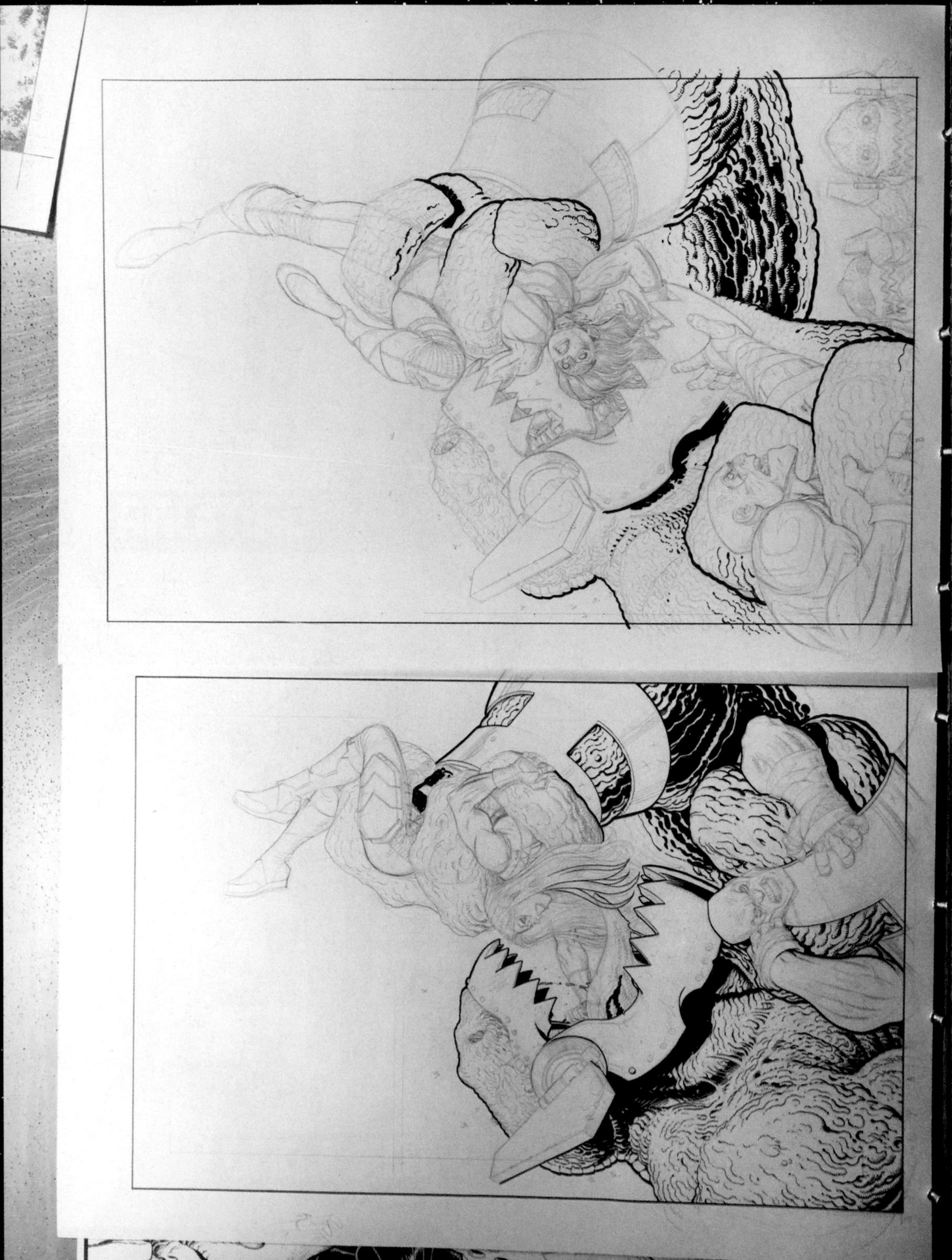

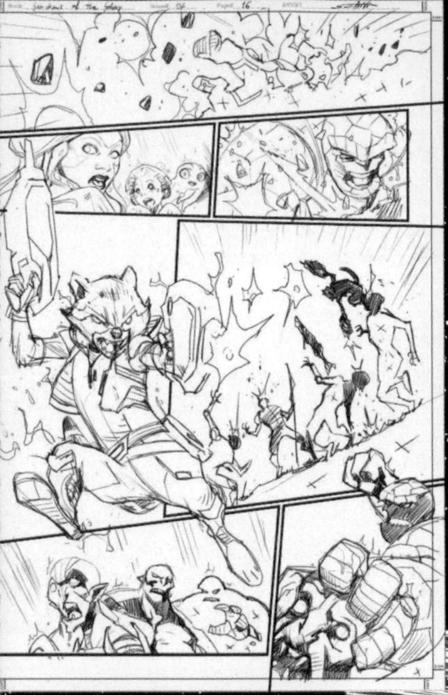

#7, PAGE 15 ART PROCESS BY

**VALERIO SCHITI**

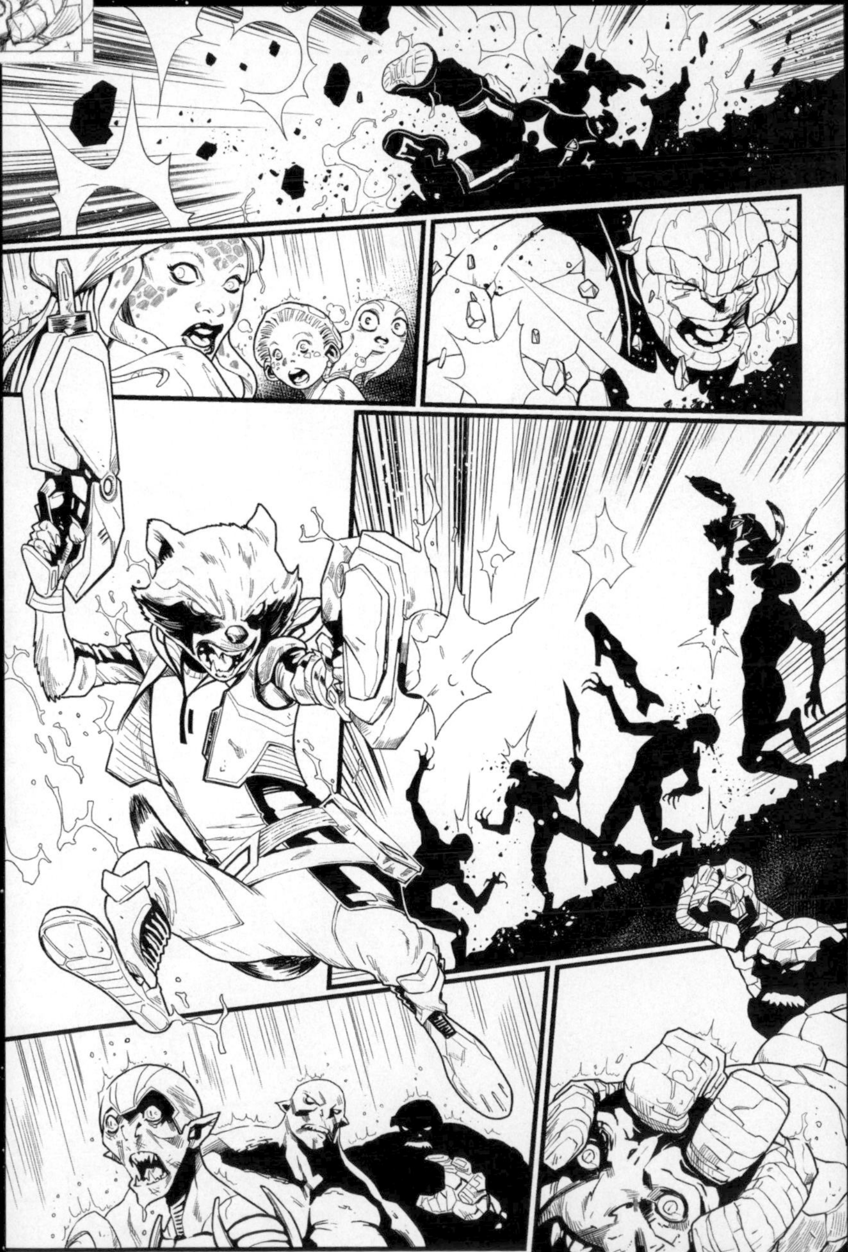

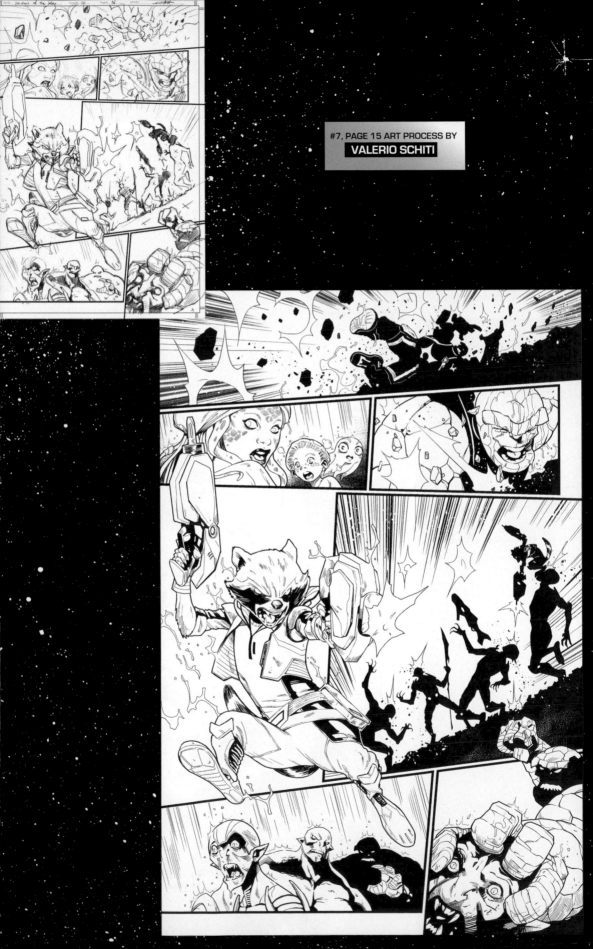

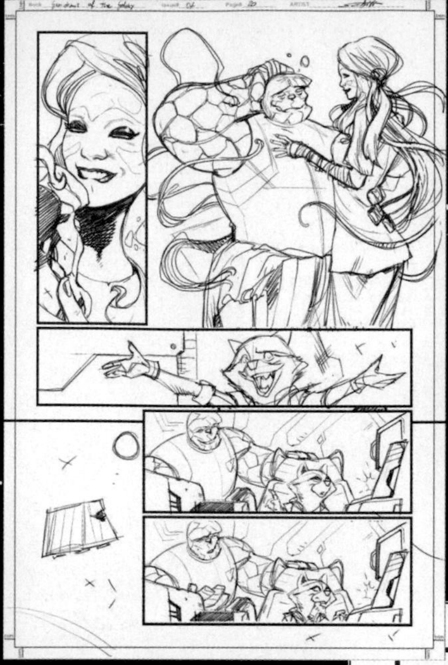

#7, PAGE 19 ART PROCESS BY

**VALERIO SCHITI**

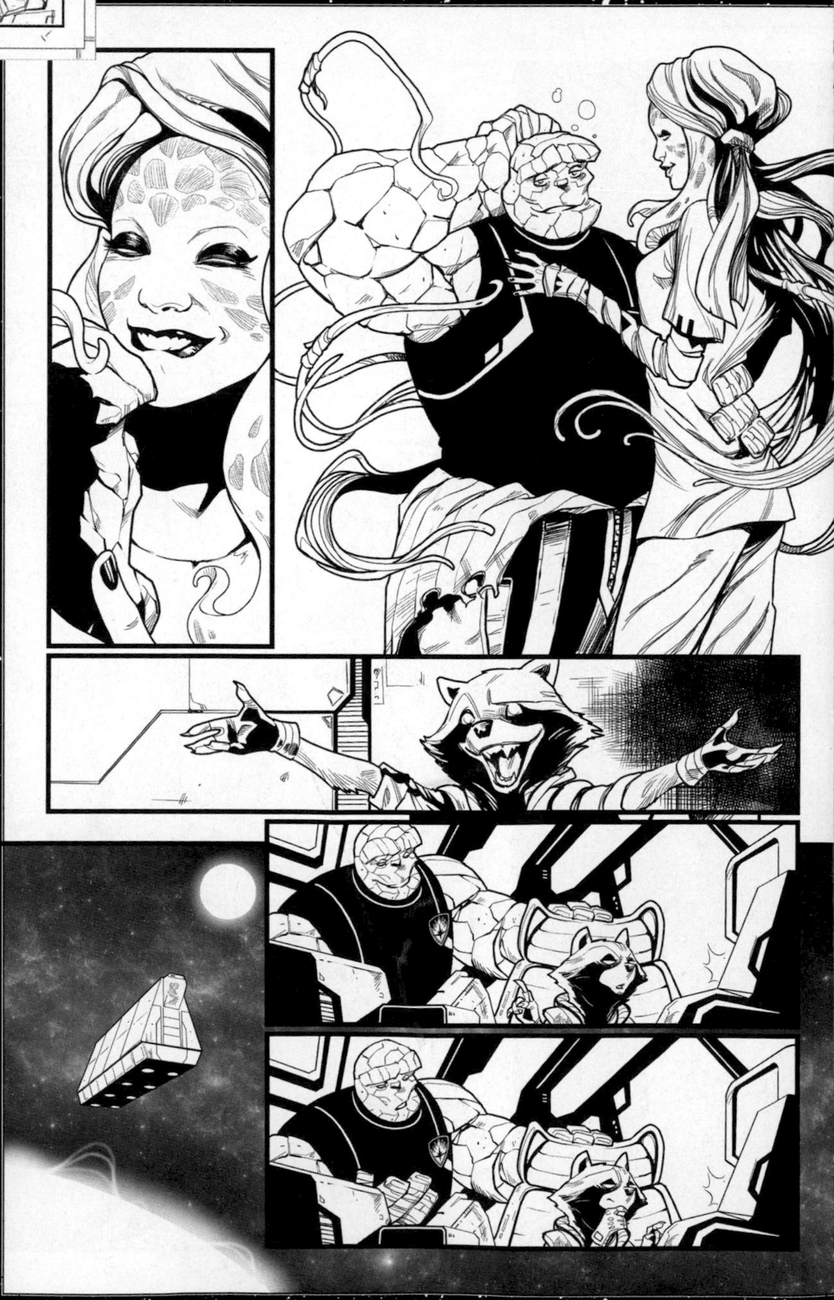

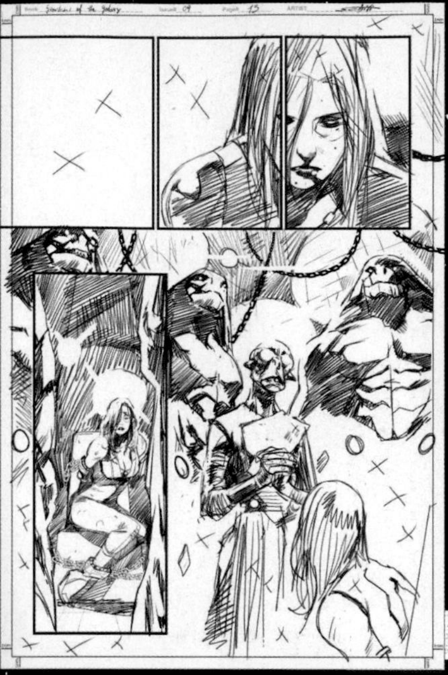

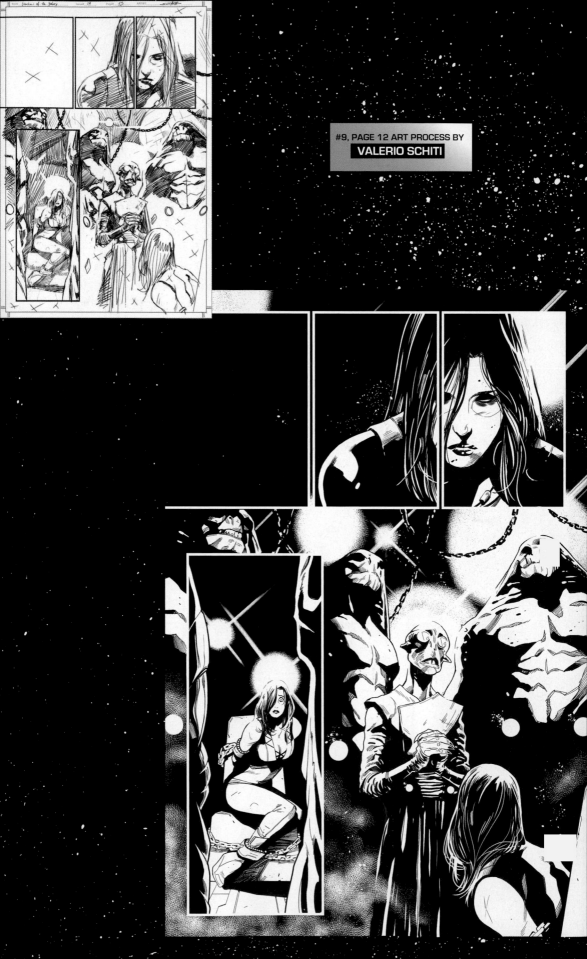

#9, PAGE 12 ART PROCESS BY
VALERIO SCHITI

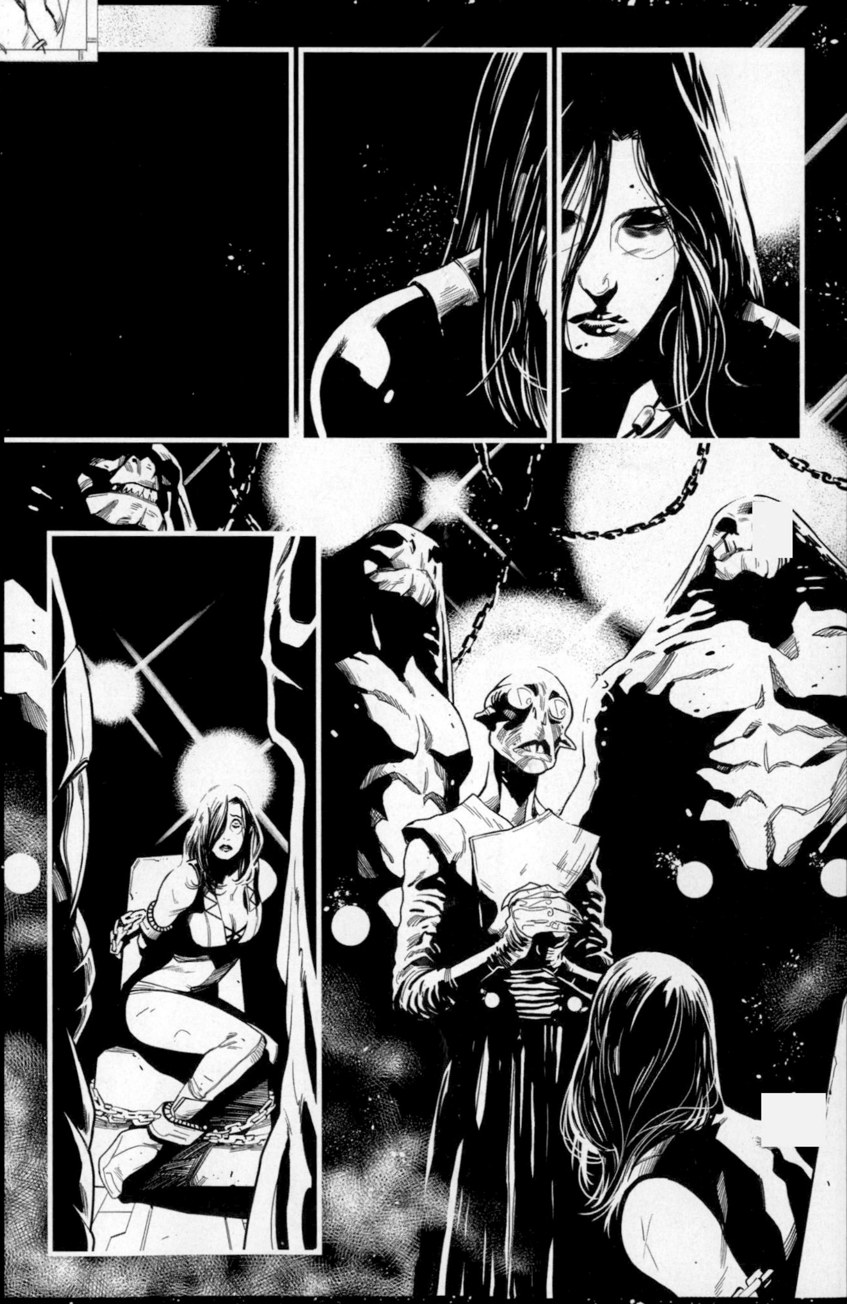

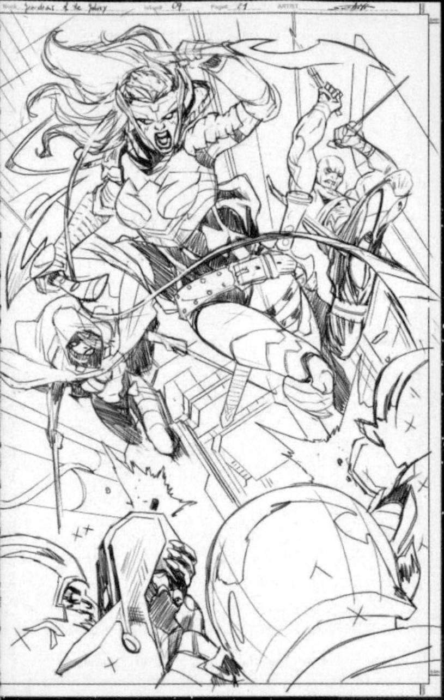

#9, PAGE 20 ART PROCESS BY

**VALERIO SCHITI**

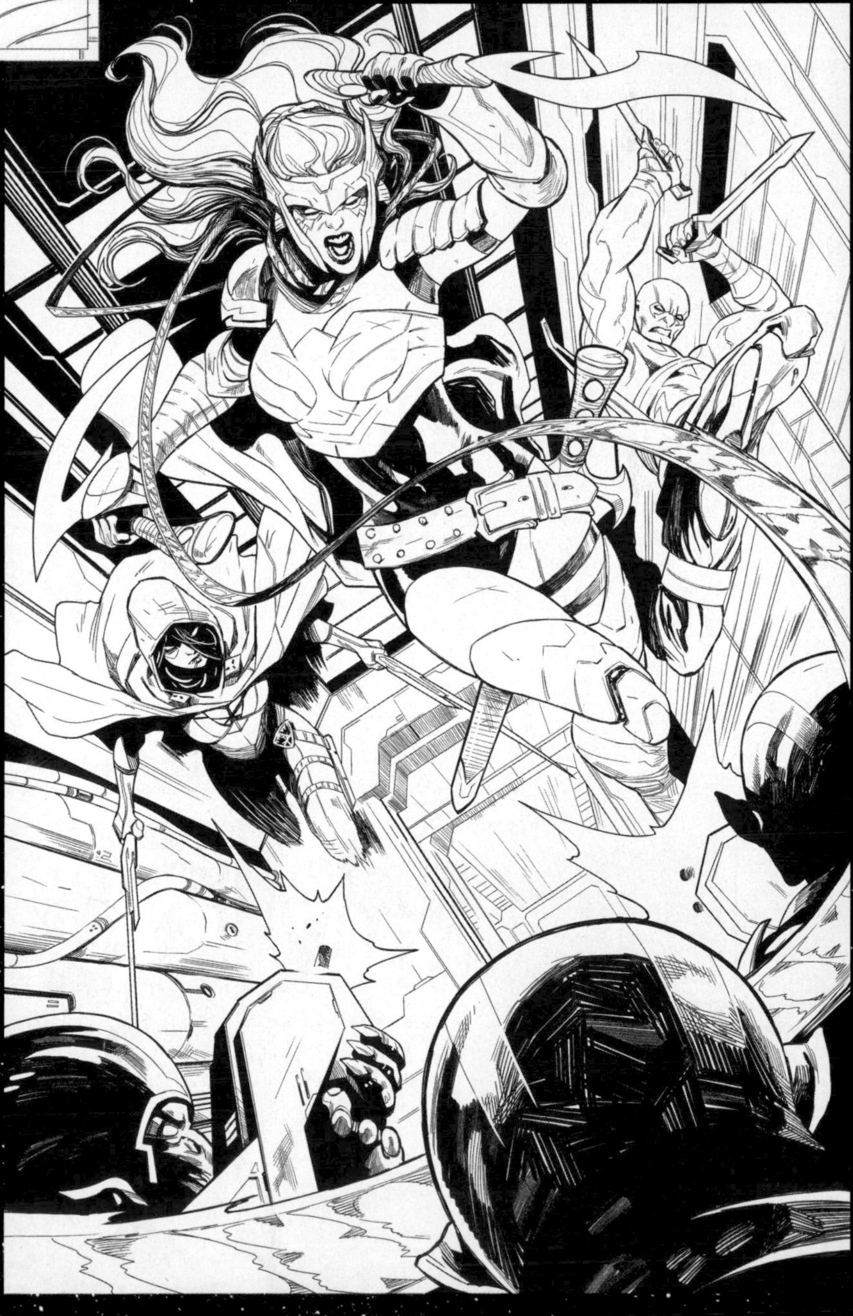

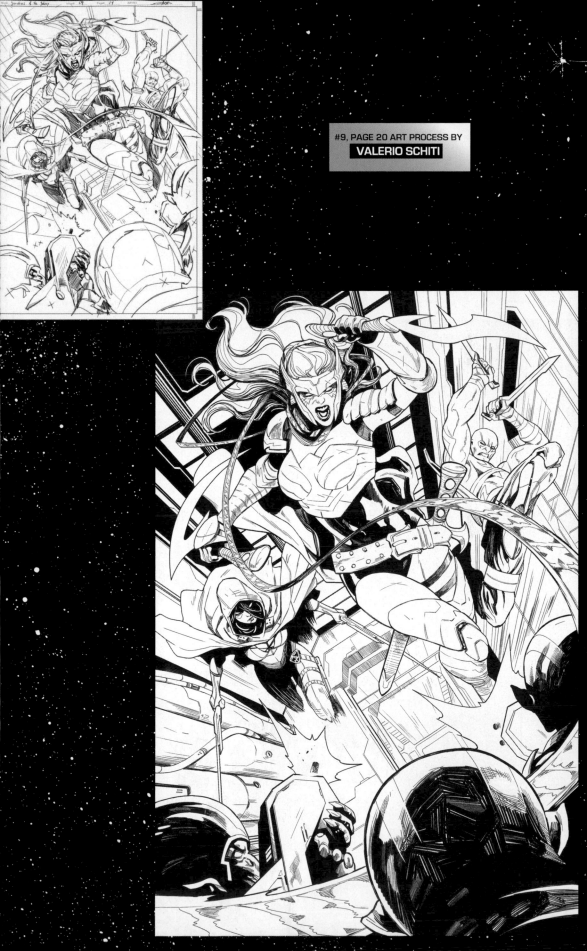

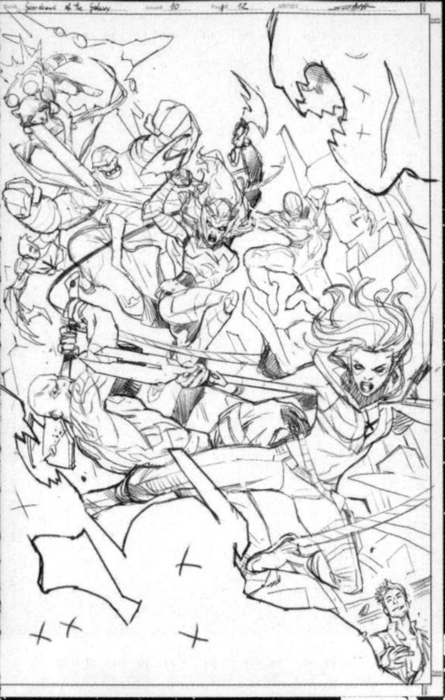

#10, PAGE 11 ART PROCESS BY

**VALERIO SCHITI**

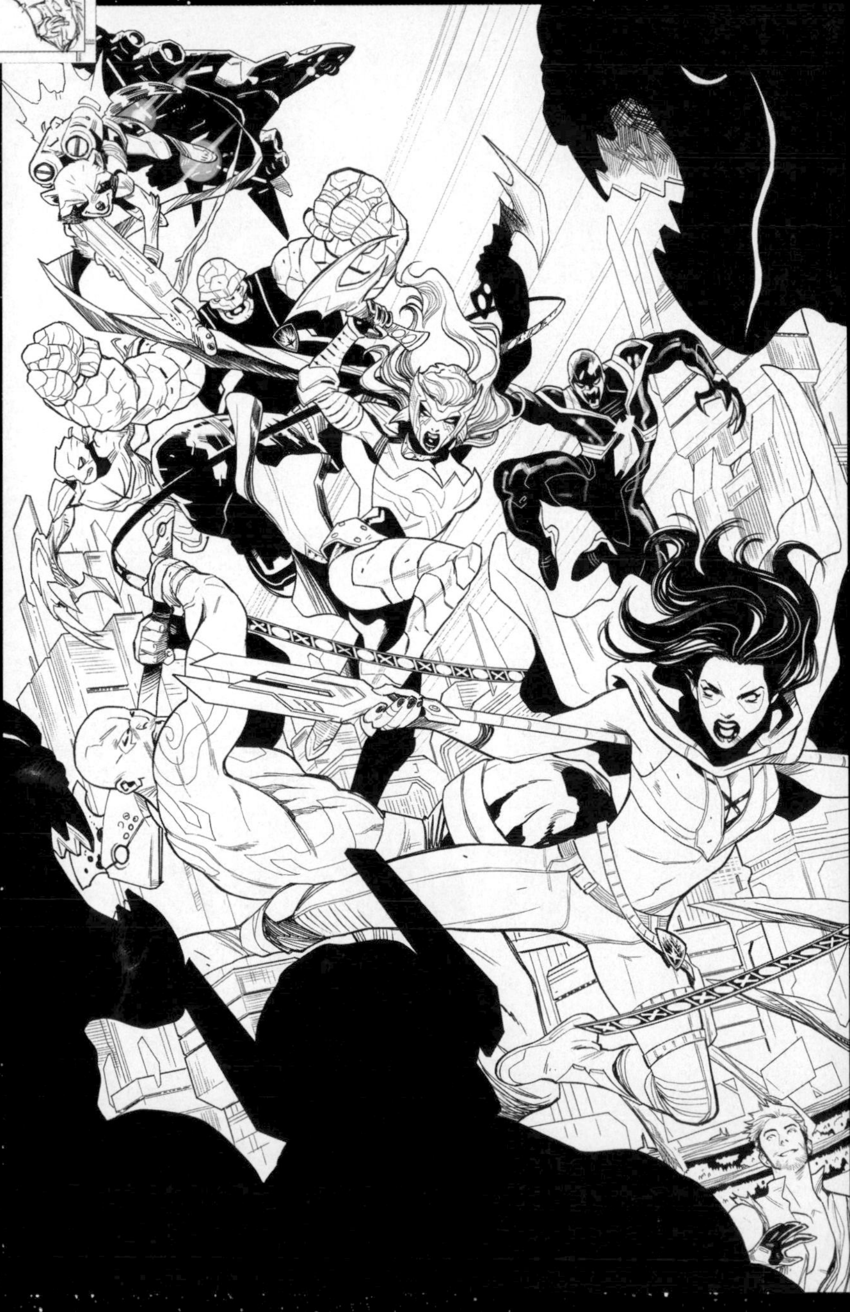

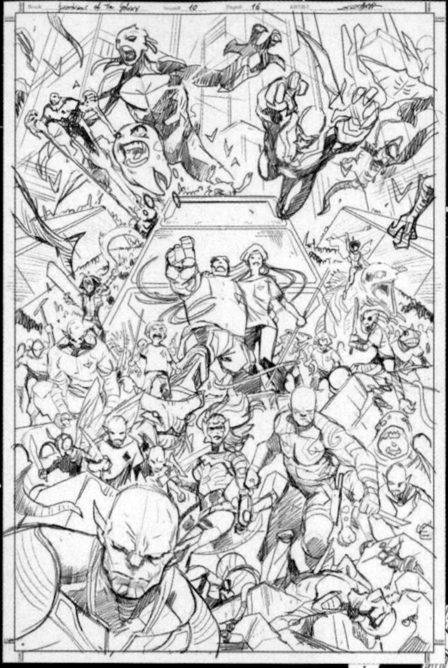

#10, PAGE 15 ART PROCESS BY
**VALERIO SCHITI**

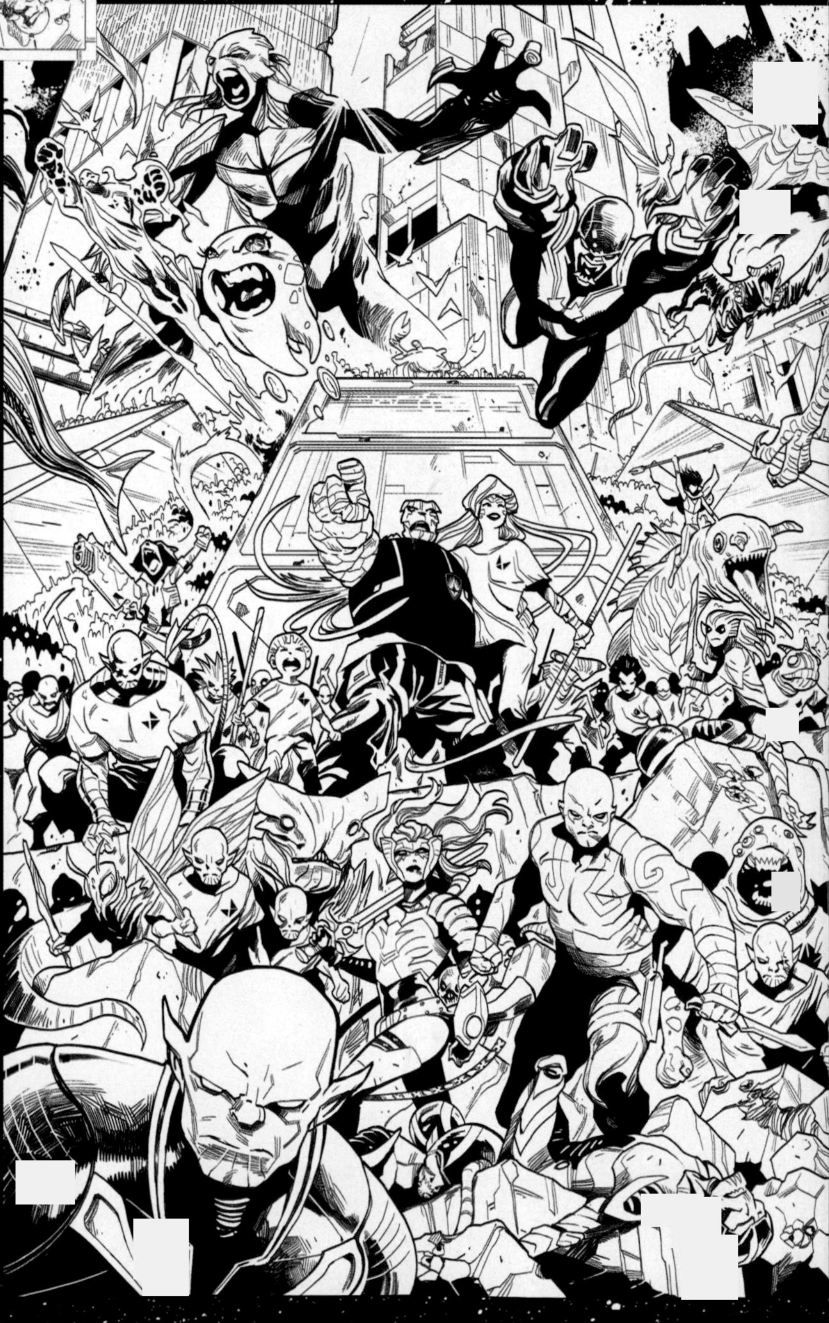

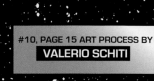

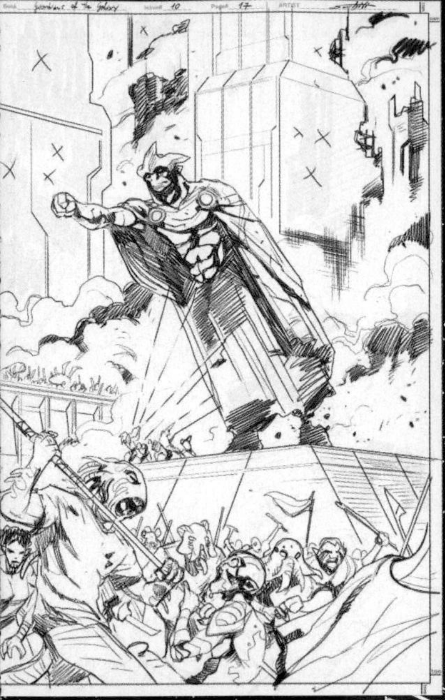

#10, PAGE 16 ART PROCESS BY

**VALERIO SCHITI**

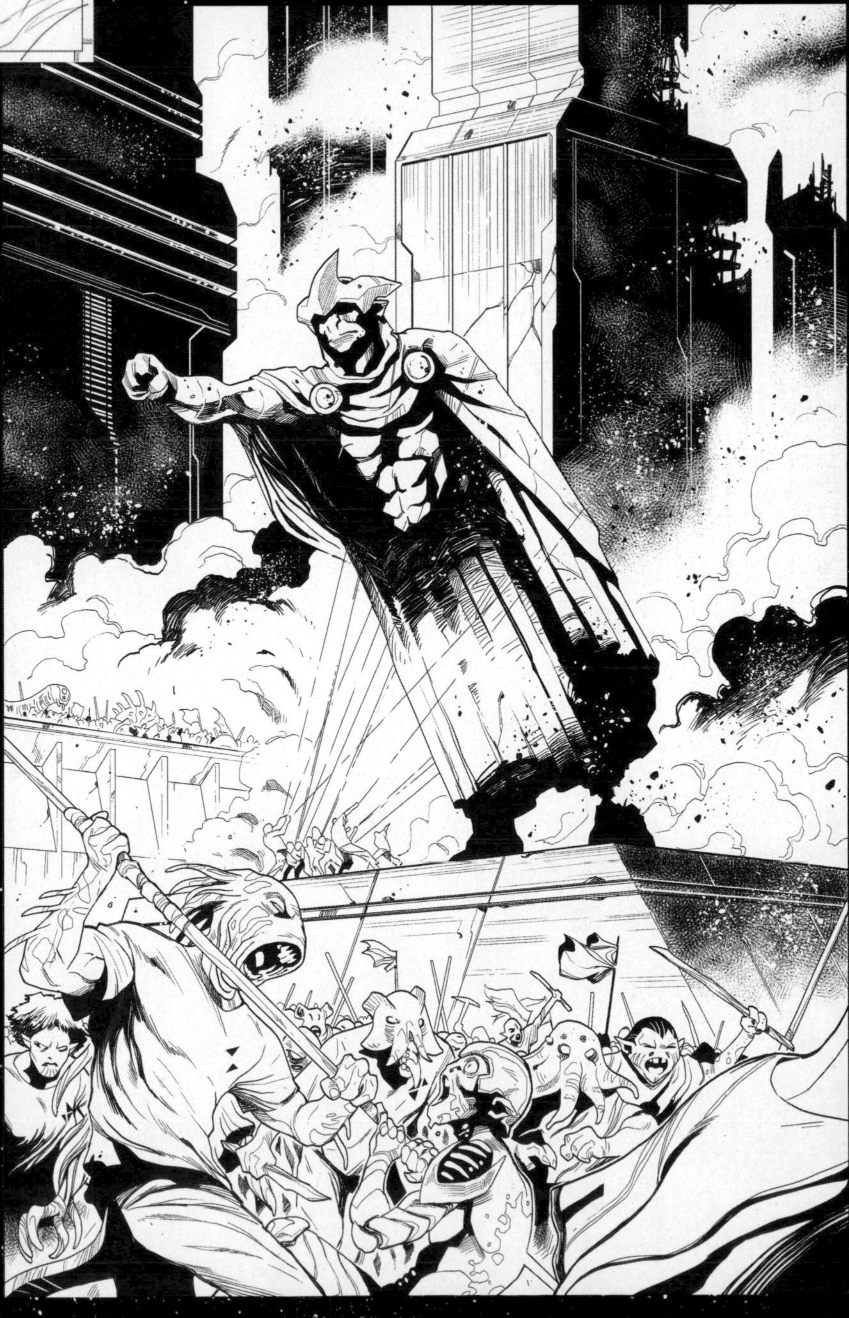